Deep Control

Deep Control

ESSAYS ON FREE WILL AND VALUE

John Martin Fischer

OXFORD
UNIVERSITY PRESS

OXFORD
UNIVERSITY PRESS

Oxford University Press, Inc., publishes works that further
Oxford University's objective of excellence
in research, scholarship, and education.

Oxford   New York
Auckland   Cape Town   Dar es Salaam   Hong Kong   Karachi
Kuala Lumpur   Madrid   Melbourne   Mexico City   Nairobi
New Delhi   Shanghai   Taipei   Toronto

With offices in
Argentina   Austria   Brazil   Chile   Czech Republic   France   Greece
Guatemala   Hungary   Italy   Japan   Poland   Portugal   Singapore
South Korea   Switzerland   Thailand   Turkey   Ukraine   Vietnam

Published by Oxford University Press, Inc.
198 Madison Avenue, New York, New York 10016

www.oup.com

Library of Congress Cataloging-in-Publication Data
Fischer, John Martin, 1952-
Deep control : essays on free will and value / John Martin Fischer.
p.   cm.
ISBN 978-0-19-974298-1 (alk. paper)
1. Free will and determinism. 2. Values. 3. Fortune. I. Title.
BJ1461F485 2011
123'.5—dc22   2010053173

1 3 5 7 9 8 6 4 2

Printed in the United States of America
on acid-free paper

CONTENTS

ACKNOWLEDGMENTS

I gave previous versions of chapters 2 ("The Frankfurt Cases: The Moral of the Stories"), 8 ("Conditional Freedom and the Normative Approach to Moral Responsibility"), 9 ("Judgment-Sensitivity and the Value of Freedom"), 10 ("Sourcehood: Playing the Cards That Are Dealt You"), 11 ("Guidance Control"), and 12 ("The Triumph of Tracing") as the Hourani Lectures on Human Values at the State University of New York at Buffalo in the fall of 2008. I thank the people at the Department of Philosophy, SUNY at Buffalo, for the opportunity to give the lectures and for their many generous and helpful comments, as well as for their warm hospitality. I am also very grateful to Patrick Todd and Garrett Pendergraft for their assistance in preparing this book for publication, and to Patrick Todd, Justin Coates, and Neal Tognazzini for insightful comments on the introductory essay.

Permission to reprint the following articles is hereby acknowledged:

"Introduction: Deep Control: The Middle Way"; the first two sections contain material that is a lightly revised version of John Martin Fischer, "Precis of *My Way: Essays on Moral Responsibility*" (Part of a book symposium on *My Way*), *Philosophy and Phenomenological Research* 80 (2010): 229–41.

"The Frankfurt Cases: The Moral of the Stories," *The Philosophical Review* 119 (2010): 315–36.

"Freedom, Foreknowledge, and Frankfurt: A Reply to Vihvelin," *Canadian Journal of Philosophy* 38 (2008): 327–42.

"The Importance of Frankfurt-Style Argument," *Philosophical Quarterly* 37 (2007): 464–71.

"Blame and Avoidability: A Reply to Otsuka" (with Neal A. Tognazzini), *Journal of Ethics* 14 (2009): 43–51.

"Indeterminism and Control: An Approach to the Problem of Luck," in Michael Freeman, ed., *Current Legal Issues: Law and Neuroscience* (Oxford: Oxford University Press, 2010), 41–59.

"The Direct Argument: You Say Goodbye, I Say Hello." in D. Cohen and N. Trakakis, eds., *Essays on Free Will and Moral Responsibility* (Newcastle upon Tyne: Cambridge Scholars Publishing, 2009): 31–44.

"Conditional Freedom and the Normative Approach to Moral Responsibility," revised and expanded version of part of "Responsibility and the Kinds of Freedom," *Journal of Ethics* 12 (2008): 203–28.

"Judgment-Sensitivity and the Value of Freedom," revised and expanded version of part of "Responsibility and the Kinds of Freedom," *Journal of Ethics* 12 (2008): 203–28.

"Sourcehood: Playing the Cards That Are Dealt You," revised version of "Playing the Cards That Are Dealt You," *Journal of Ethics* 10 (2006): 235–44; also, additional material from "My Way and Life's Highway: Replies to Steward, Smilansky, and Perry," *Journal of Ethics* 12 (2008): 167–89.

"Guidance Control," revised versions of material from "Manipulation and Guidance Control: A Reply to Long," in Joseph Keim Campbell, Michael O'Rourke, and Harry S. Sliverstein, eds., *Action, Ethics, and Responsibility* (Cambridge, MA: MIT Press, 2010): 175–86; "Reply: The Free Will Revolution," part of a book symposium on John Martin Fischer and Mark Ravizza, *Responsibility and Control: A Theory of Moral Responsibility, Philosophical Explorations* 8 (2005): 145–56; and "The Free Will Revolution (Continued)," *Journal of Ethics* 10 (2006): 315–46.

"The Triumph of Tracing" (with Neal A. Tognazzini), revised version of "The Truth About Tracing," *Nous* 43 (2009): 531–56.

Deep Control

1

Deep Control: The Middle Way

In work over the last three decades I have sought to present what I have called a "general framework for moral responsibility."[1] In this introductory essay, I shall sketch some of the leading ideas in my overall framework and draw out a few implications. I hope that this will help to situate the essays in the current volume within a larger context. I shall also highlight some of the important themes I address in this book.[2]

I. A Framework for Moral Responsibility

I.1. MOTIVATION AND THE CONCEPT OF RESPONSIBILITY

The framework I have presented for moral responsibility involves a portfolio of different ideas in a certain arrangement. I start by presenting some basic "motivating ideas"—some considerations that render my overall approach attractive. Perhaps the key idea here stems from the appeal of a certain sort of "resiliency." I believe that our fundamental status as agents—our being deeply different from mere nonhuman animals insofar as we engage in practical reasoning and are morally responsible for

---

[1] See John Martin Fischer, *The Metaphysics of Free Will: An Essay on Control* (Oxford: Blackwell Publishers, 1994); *My Way: Essays on Moral Responsibility* (New York: Oxford University Press, 2006); and *Our Stories: Essays on Life, Death, and Free Will* (New York: Oxford University Press, 2008). Also see John Martin Fischer and Mark Ravizza, *Responsibility and Control: A Theory of Moral Responsibility* (New York: Cambridge University Press, 1998) and John Martin Fischer, Robert Kane, Derk Pereboom, and Manuel Vargas, *Four Views on Free Will* (Oxford: Blackwell Publishers, 2007).

[2] The material in the first two sections of this essay is a lightly revised version of John Martin Fischer, "Precis of My Way: Essays on Moral Responsibility" (part of a book symposium on *My Way*) *Philosophy and Phenomenological Research* 80 (2010): 229–241. I am deeply thankful to Patrick Todd, Neal Tognazzini, and Justin Coates for extremely helpful comments on previous versions of this essay.

our behavior—should not depend on certain subtle ruminations of theoretical physicists. That is, I do not think that our status as genuine *agents* should hang on a thread—that it should depend on whether natural laws have associated with them (say) probabilities of 0.99 or 1.0. In my view, *that sort* of empirical difference should not *make a difference* as to our moral responsibility.

So, for example, if in the future I am convinced that the fundamental laws of nature are—or can be regimented as—(among other things) universally generalized conditionals with probabilities of 1.0 rather than similar conditionals with probabilities of 0.99, this would not issue in any inclination on my part to give up my view of myself and others as genuine agents and legitimate participants in the practices constitutive of moral responsibility. Now this is simply one consideration, and it specifies a *desideratum* of an adequate theory of moral responsibility. In my view, it counts in favor of a theory of moral responsibility—it is a reason to accept such a theory—if the theory does not conceptualize moral responsibility as hanging on a thread (in the indicated way). Of course, the proponent of such a theory must still address the difficult skeptical worries about the relationship between causal determinism, free will, and moral responsibility, as well as do some sort of philosophical cost-benefit analysis that considers all relevant factors.

Note that, insofar as I take it that it would be desirable to have an account of moral responsibility according to which our fundamental status as morally responsible agents does not "hang on a thread," it would follow that we should not give up our views of ourselves as morally responsible and deeply different from nonhuman animals (in the relevant ways) if we are convinced (in the future) that the fundamental laws of nature have irreducible *indeterminacies* associated with them. Suppose, for example, that we discover that these laws are or can be conceptualized as (among other things) universally quantified conditionals with 0.99 probabilities. In my view, this in itself should not issue in any inclination to discard or revise our views of ourselves and others as genuine agents and subject to moral responsibility. Again, I am simply articulating what I take to be a *desideratum* of an adequate theory of moral responsibility—that it be suitably resilient to certain sorts of empirical discoveries.[3] A proponent of such a theory still needs to address the difficult skeptical worries about the relationship between causal indeterminism and *control* (and moral responsibility).

A second element in the overall framework for moral responsibility consists in an articulation of the "concept" of moral responsibility. I accept some sort of distinction between the concept and its conditions of application; I, of course, recognize that the legitimacy of this sort of distinction has been called into question. And yet

---

[3] In sketching the "resiliency desideratum" in this introductory essay, I have simply tried to lay out my view. This is perhaps not the appropriate venue to address difficulties and objections—of which there are (lamentably) many. Indeed, I am grateful to Helen Steward, Kevin Timpe, Randolph Clarke, Dan Speak, Chris Franklin, Michael Nelson, and Patrick Todd for discussions of these issues in their written work and also in many probing conversations. I hope further to explore these issues in future work.

I continue to think that there is *some* reasonable way (or ways) of making the relevant kind of distinction, even if it is not straightforwardly a matter of distinguishing "analytic" from "synthetic" truths, or matters of meaning from empirical matters. I simply presuppose that there is some tolerably clear way of distinguishing (roughly speaking) the concept of moral responsibility from the conditions in which moral responsibility actually obtains (or, in a slightly different vocabulary, the *concept* of moral responsibility from various *conceptions* of moral responsibility).

As I said before, my overall framework for moral responsibility is a suite of ideas in a certain arrangement. Part of this structured portfolio is a set of options in regard to the concept of moral responsibility; but I do not take a firm stand on these options. That is, I chart out different ways of articulating our inchoate concept of moral responsibility, but I do not argue that one (rather than the others) is the correct specification. I am not even sure that there is one unique specification. Rather, I focus most of my attention on specifying the conditions of application of the concept of moral responsibility, and I contend that accepting these conditions is completely *compatible* with accepting any of the specific options with respect to the *concept* of moral responsibility.

To be a bit more specific about the concept of moral responsibility, perhaps the most salient view might be called the "Strawsonian" view, following the classic presentation by Peter Strawson in "Freedom and Resentment."[4] In this view, being morally responsible is a matter of being an appropriate target of a set of distinctive attitudes Strawson dubbed the "reactive attitudes," such as gratitude, love, respect, hatred, and resentment. In the Strawsonian approach, moral responsibility also involves being appropriate participants in activities, such as moral praise and blame and punishment, which presuppose the application of the relevant attitudes. It was important to Strawson that the "appropriateness" of the attitudes does not depend on the target agent's meeting some "theoretical condition," such as possessing the freedom to do otherwise (or, as I interpret him, *any* sort of freedom); additionally, it does not depend (for Strawson) on the world's meeting certain specific conditions, such as that causal determinism is false (or, for that matter, true).

Another account of the concept of moral responsibility is associated with the metaphor of a "moral ledger." On the moral ledger view, we are morally responsible insofar as we are apt targets of specifically *moral* judgments. In this view, we are deeply different from nonhuman animals in that we can have *moral* properties—we can act rightly or wrongly, we can be good or bad, courageous or cowardly, and so forth. In yet another view, we are morally responsible insofar as we can legitimately be asked to provide *explanations* or *accounts* of our behavior. As I said, I do not know whether there is a *single* correct specification of our shared concept of moral responsibility. It is plausible to me that "moral responsibility" is what Wittgenstein called a "family-resemblance" term or what we might call a "syndrome." In any case,

---

[4] *Proceedings of the British Academy* 48 (1962): 1–25.

I contend that my account of the conditions in which moral responsibility obtains is compatible with *any* of the plausible attempts to specify the concept.

I.2. CONTROL AND THE CONDITIONS FOR MORAL RESPONSIBILITY

I accept the traditional view (stemming perhaps from Aristotle's discussion of voluntariness) that moral responsibility involves a *freedom* or *control* component and an *epistemic* component. But whereas I agree that moral responsibility requires control, I distinguish two kinds of control: guidance and regulative control. The two kinds of control can be pried apart analytically through the use of certain thought-experiments (the "Frankfurt-style examples," to which I return shortly). One kind of control involves access to alternative possibilities (freedom to choose and do otherwise); I call this "regulative control." The other kind of control does not require such access. It is a distinctive kind of control that does not involve freedom to choose or do otherwise; I call this "guidance control." My claim is that guidance control is the freedom-relevant or control component of moral responsibility. Thus, an agent can legitimately be held morally responsible for his behavior, even though he lacks regulative control (or freedom to choose and do otherwise). The freedom-relevant condition is combined with an "epistemic" condition to get a full theory of moral responsibility.

To develop these notions of control (and their relationship), let us consider the following cases.[5] Suppose that I am driving my car. It is functioning well, and I wish to make a right turn. (We assume that the gas pedal is working properly and that I am depressing it to give the car gas.) As a result of my intention to turn right, I signal, turn the steering wheel, and carefully guide the car to the right. Further, I here assume that I was able to form the intention not to turn the car to the right but to turn the car to the left instead. In this ordinary case, I guide the car to the right, but I could have guided it to the left. I control the car, and also I have a certain sort of control *over* the car's movements. Insofar as I actually guide the car in a certain way, I shall say that I have "guidance control." Further, insofar as I have the power to guide the car in a different way, I shall say that I have "regulative control." (Of course, here we are not making any "special assumptions," such as that causal determinism obtains or God exists and foreknows our future behavior.)[6]

Consider, now, a second case. Here I again guide my car in the normal way to the right. The car's steering apparatus *works properly* when I steer the car to the right (as does the gas pedal). But unknown to me, the car's steering apparatus is broken in such a way that, if I were to try to turn it in some other direction, the car would veer off to the right in precisely the way it actually goes to the right. Since

---

[5] I take these cases from Fischer, *My Way*: 39.

[6] For discussions of the relationship between God's omniscience and human freedom, see John Martin Fischer, ed., *God, Foreknowledge, and Freedom* (Stanford: Stanford University Press, 1989); and Fischer, *The Metaphysics of Free Will*: 111–130.

I actually do not try to do anything but turn to the right, the apparatus functions normally, and the car's movements are precisely as they would have been if there had been no problem with the steering apparatus. Indeed, my guidance of the car to the right is precisely the same in this case and the first car case.

Here, as in the first car case, it appears that I control the movement of the car in the sense of guiding it in a certain way to the right. I do not simply cause it to go to the right (say, as a result of sneezing or having an epileptic seizure or involuntary spasm). Thus, I exhibit guidance control of the car. (I control the car and I have control *of* the car, but I do not have control *over* the car's movements; the different prepositions typically indicate the different kinds of control.) Generally, we assume that guidance control and regulative control go together. But this case (which has some of the salient structural features of a Frankfurt-type case) helps to show that they can at least in principle pull apart: one can have guidance control without regulative control.

The second car case should elicit the intuition that we do not need regulative control (genuine access to alternative possibilities) in order to have the kind of control involved in moral responsibility. The second car case is rather like John Locke's famous example of a man who is in a room that, unknown to him, is locked; the man thinks about whether to leave the room, but decides to stay in the room for his own reasons. The fact that the door is locked plays no role in the man's practical reasoning. Locke says that the man stays in the room voluntarily, although he could not have left the room. Similarly, it seems that I exhibit guidance control of the car, although I could not have caused the car to go to the left.

But in Locke's case the man *did* have various options available to him. After all, he could have decided to open the door, he could have tried to open it, and so forth; and similarly, in the second car example I could have decided to steer the car to the left, I could have tried to do so, and so forth. Some philosophers might then insist that it is *in virtue of the existence of these alternative possibilities* that the agent is morally responsible. And it must be conceded that we have not yet produced an example in which an agent is intuitively thought to be morally responsible and yet has *no* alternative possibilities (*no* regulative control).

This is precisely the point at which Harry Frankfurt offers a remedy for the gap in the original cases.[7] In Frankfurt's examples, a "counterfactual intervener" stands by ready to intervene in the relevant agent's brain processes, if he shows even an inclination to choose to do otherwise. Although Frankfurt was rather vague about exactly how the counterfactual intervener can succeed in expunging all access to alternative possibilities, Frankfurt's followers have filled in the template in various ways. Here is my favorite version of a Frankfurt case:[8]

---

[7] Harry Frankfurt, "Alternate Possibilities and Moral Responsibility," *Journal of Philosophy* 66 (1969): 829–839.

[8] For such an example, see John Martin Fischer, "Responsibility and Control," *Journal of Philosophy* 79 (1982): 24–40.

Because Black dares to hope that the Democrats finally have a good chance of winning the White House, the benevolent but elderly neurosurgeon, Black, has come out of retirement to participate in yet another philosophical example. (After all, what would these thought-experiments be without the venerable *eminence grise*—or should it be *noir*?) He has secretly inserted a chip in Jones's brain which enables Black to monitor and control Jones's activities. Black can exercise this control through a sophisticated computer that he has programmed so that, among other things, it monitors Jones's voting behavior. If Jones were to show any inclination to vote for McCain (or, let us say, anyone other than Obama), then the computer, through the chip in Jones's brain, would intervene to assure that he actually decides to vote for Obama and does so vote. But if Jones decides on his own to vote for Obama (as Black, the old progressive, would prefer), the computer does nothing but continue to monitor—without affecting—the goings-on in Jones's head.

Now suppose that Jones decides to vote for Obama on his own, just as he would have if Black had not inserted the chip in his head. It seems, upon first thinking about this case, that Jones can be held morally responsible for this choice and act of voting for Obama, although he could not have chosen otherwise and he could not have done otherwise.[9]

Over the years I have offered a sustained argument that the Frankfurt examples provide a strong plausibility argument for the conclusion that moral responsibility does not require genuine metaphysical access to alternative possibilities (regulative control). The leading idea in my argument is that any proponent of the regulative control requirement should say that the alternative possibilities in question must be *robust* and not *mere flickers of freedom*. That is, if the basis of moral responsibility is access to at least one alternative possibility, the alternative possibility in question cannot be *any old sort of possibility* of something different happening; such an alternative possibility might be a mere flicker of freedom and thus too thin a reed to support the superstructure of moral responsibility.

The situation here is precisely like the problem faced by proponents of indeterministic accounts of moral responsibility; how can the mere addition of a certain sort of alternative possibility—say an event the happening or not-happening of which is entirely arbitrary or accidental, from the agent's point of view—render it true that the agent has the control associated with moral responsibility, given that the agent lacks such control in the absence of *any* alternative possibilities? (I return to this question below.) In previous work, I have asked the proponent of regulative control a similar question: "Given (for the sake of discussion) that an agent without *any* alternative possibilities cannot be deemed morally

---

[9] Whew! Black was right. I began writing this paper before the elections of 2008; obviously, the specifics of the case are now out of date, but what matters is the structure of the example.

responsible, how can the mere addition of an *exiguous* alternative possibility in the Frankfurt cases—say an event the happening or not-happening of which is entirely arbitrary or accidental from the agent's point of view—render it true that the agent has the control associated with moral responsibility?" Note that the worry behind this question is exactly why the prominent libertarian philosopher Robert Kane has essentially agreed with me on this point, positing the "dual voluntariness" requirement for moral responsibility.

My claim, then, is that versions of the Frankfurt cases can be given in which it is very plausible to say that the agent in question is morally responsible for his behavior, and yet he has no access to the *relevant sort* of alternative possibility—a sufficiently robust alternative possibility. In addition to presenting a systematic defense of the contention that the Frankfurt cases show moral responsibility not to require regulative control, I have pointed out that the rejection of the requirement of regulative control does not depend on the Frankfurt cases. There are various other routes to the same conclusion, including the Strawsonian contention that our ordinary responsibility practices do not presuppose the requirement of regulative control.[10] Also, Daniel Dennett has presented various arguments against the requirement of regulative control.[11] I believe that the fact that there are various different routes to the same conclusion helps to establish the plausibility of the conclusion; if one finds thought-experiments such as the Frankfurt cases unattractive, or if one finds the Frankfurt cases unconvincing, there are still good reasons to accept that moral responsibility does not require regulative control.

So my preliminary conclusion is that *if* causal determinism rules out moral responsibility, this is *not* in virtue of its eliminating regulative control (if it does indeed eliminate regulative control). This is an important point; I believe it is the "moral of the Frankfurt stories," no matter how they are told and retold. Further, if this point is correct, it allows us to sidestep the traditional debates about the relationship between such doctrines as God's omniscience and causal determinism, on the one hand, and "freedom to do otherwise" or regulative control, on the other. That is, we can sidestep these debates if we are simply interested in moral responsibility. Insofar as these traditional debates have issued in what I have called Dialectical Stalemates—black holes in Dialectical Spacetime—avoiding them may open the possibility of real philosophical progress.

This having been said, I have never suggested that the *mere fact* that regulative control is not required for moral responsibility would allow us to conclude *straightaway* that causal determinism is compatible with moral responsibility. Indeed, in my 1982 paper, "Responsibility and Control," I emphasized that causal determinism

---

[10] For a version of this sort of strategy, see R. Jay Wallace, *Responsibility and the Moral Sentiments* (Cambridge, MA: Harvard University Press, 1994).

[11] Daniel Dennett, *Elbow Room* (Cambridge, MA: MIT Press, 1984); and *Freedom Evolves* (New York: Viking, 2003). For a discussion, see John Martin Fischer, "Dennett on the Basic Argument," (part of a book symposium on Daniel Dennett, *Freedom Evolves*) *Metaphilosophy* 36 (2005): 427–435.

might rule out moral responsibility *directly* (and not in virtue of ruling out alternative possibilities). I thus identified what has come to be called "Source Incompatibilism," and I pointed out that it must be taken seriously. I concluded that theorists of moral responsibility should adopt a laserlike focus on the *actual sequence* that issues in any particular choice or behavior and should, in particular, consider whether causal determination in the actual sequence crowds out moral responsibility.

In subsequent work, I identified and evaluated a number of different factors that might be invoked to explain why causal determination rules out moral responsibility directly (i.e., in virtue of their presence in the actual sequence, and *not* in virtue of ruling out alternative possibilities). I concluded that none of these factors provides a good reason to suppose that causal determination *in itself and apart from ruling out alternative possibilities* is incompatible with moral responsibility. I believe that when one shifts from consideration of the relationship between causal determination and regulative control to a focus on actual-sequence features of causally deterministic processes, the philosophical terrain becomes significantly more hospitable to compatibilism.

Given that I do not think that causal determinism rules out moral responsibility by threatening regulative control, and I also do not think that there are other good reasons to suppose that causal determinism rules out moral responsibility, I present an account of moral responsibility that is compatible with causal determinism. More precisely, I present an account of "guidance control," the freedom-relevant condition necessary and sufficient for moral responsibility (in my view).

An insight from the Frankfurt cases helps to shape the account of guidance control: moral responsibility is a matter of the history of an action (or behavior)—of how the actual sequence unfolds—rather than the genuine availability of alternative possibilities.[12] In this view, alternative scenarios or non-actual possible worlds might be relevant to moral responsibility in virtue of helping to specify or analyze modal or dispositional properties of the actual sequence, but not in virtue of indicating or providing an analysis of *access* to alternative possibilities.

Note that, in a Frankfurt-type case, the actual sequence proceeds "in the normal way" or via the "normal" process of practical reasoning. In contrast, in the alternative scenario (which never actually gets triggered and thus never becomes part of the actual sequence of events in our world), there is (say) direct electronic stimulation of the brain—intuitively, a different way or a different kind of mechanism. (By "mechanism" I simply mean, roughly speaking, "process"—I do not

---

[12] Of course, it might be that the availability of alternative possibilities is in some sense "part of the actual sequence"; I am indebted to both Carl Ginet and Patrick Todd for this point. My contention in the text relies on the intuitive notion that we can separate "actual-sequence" from "alternative-sequence" facts, but this might be too quick. In any case, my view is that moral responsibility attributions should not depend on the actual-sequence facts leaving it open that the agent in question has alternative possibilities. For a very interesting recent discussion of the contention that moral responsibility supervenes on the actual sequence, see: Carolina Sartorio, "Actuality and Responsibility," *Mind*, (forthcoming).

mean to reify anything.) I assume that we have intuitions at least about clear cases of "same mechanism," and "different mechanism." The actually operating mechanism (in a Frankfurt-type case)—ordinary human practical reasoning, unimpaired by direct stimulation by neurosurgeons, and so forth—is in a salient and natural sense "responsive to reasons." That is, holding fixed that mechanism (the kind of process that actually unfolds), the agent would presumably choose and act differently in a range of scenarios in which he or she is presented with sufficient reasons to do so.

This suggests the rudiments of an account of guidance control of action.[13] In this account, we hold fixed the kind of mechanism that actually issues in the choice and action, and we see whether the agent responds suitably to reasons (some of which are moral reasons). My account presupposes that the agent can recognize reasons, and, in particular, recognize certain reasons as moral reasons. The account distinguishes between reasons-recognition (the ability to recognize the reasons that exist) and reasons-reactivity (choice in accordance with reasons that are recognized as good and sufficient), and it makes different demands on reasons-recognition and reasons-reactivity. The sort of reasons-responsiveness linked to moral responsibility, in my view, is "moderate reasons-responsiveness."

But one could exhibit the right sort of reasons-responsiveness as a result (say) of clandestine, unconsented-to electronic stimulation of the brain (or hypnosis, brainwashing, etc.). So moderate reasons-responsiveness of the actual-sequence mechanism is necessary but insufficient for the control linked to moral responsibility. I contend that there are two elements of guidance control: reasons-sensitivity of the appropriate sort and mechanism-ownership. That is, the mechanism that issues in the behavior must (in an appropriate sense) be the *agent's own* mechanism. (When one is secretly manipulated through clandestine mind control as in *The Manchurian Candidate*, one's practical reasoning is not *one's own*.)

I have argued for a "subjective" approach to mechanism-ownership. In this approach, a mechanism becomes one's own in virtue of one having certain beliefs about one's own agency and its effects in the world, that is, in virtue of *seeing oneself in a certain way*. (Of course, it is *not* simply a matter of saying certain things— one actually has to have the relevant constellation of beliefs.) In my view, an individual becomes morally responsible in part at least by taking responsibility; he makes his mechanism his own by taking responsibility for acting from that kind of mechanism. In a sense, then, one acquires control by *taking control*. When I act on *my own* suitably reasons-responsive mechanism, I do it *my way*.[14]

---

[13] Again, I borrow from the introduction to *My Way*: 17–19.

[14] In the Philippines, there is a lamentably high incidence of what has come to be called "*My Way* killings." This is the phenomenon described in the following excerpt from an article in *The New York Times*:

After a day of barbering, Rodolfo Gregorio went to his neighborhood karaoke bar still smelling of talcum powder. Putting aside his glass of Red Horse Extra Strong beer, he grasped a microphone with a habitué's self-assuredness and briefly stilled the room with the Platters' "My Prayer."

I ended my 1982 paper, "Responsibility and Control," by saying that we must "decode the information in the actual sequence" leading to behavior for which the agent can legitimately be held morally responsible and ascertain whether it is compatible with causal determination. The account of guidance control—with the two chief ingredients, moderate reasons-responsiveness and mechanism ownership—are the "secrets" revealed by close scrutiny of the actual sequence, and I have argued that they are entirely compatible with causal determination. (As I point out below, they are also entirely compatible with causal indeterminism; thus, in my approach, moral responsibility does *not* hang on a thread.)

Further, I have shown how we can build a *comprehensive* account of guidance control from an account of guidance control of *actions*. That is, we can develop an account of guidance control of omissions, consequence-particulars, consequence-universals, and perhaps even emotions and character traits by invoking certain basic ingredients contained in the account of guidance control of actions. I argue that it is a point in favor of my account of moral responsibility that it can give a comprehensive account that builds on simple, basic ingredients. Additionally, I contend that this comprehensive account systematizes our intuitive judgments

---

Next, he belted out crowd-pleasers by Tom Jones and Engelbert Humperdinck. But Mr. Gregorio, 63, a witness to countless fistfights and occasional stabbings erupting from disputes over karaoke singing, did not dare choose one beloved classic: Frank Sinatra's version of "My Way."

"I used to like 'My Way,' but after all the trouble, I stopped singing it," he said. "You can get killed."

The authorities do not know exactly how many people have been killed warbling "My Way" in karaoke bars over the years in the Philippines, or how many fatal fights it has fueled. But the news media have recorded at least half a dozen victims in the past decade and includes them in a subcategory of crime dubbed the "My Way Killings."

The killings have produced urban legends about the song and left Filipinos groping for answers. Are the killings the natural by-product of the country's culture of violence, drinking, and machismo? Or is there something inherently sinister in the song?

Whatever the reason, many karaoke bars have removed the song from their playbooks. And the country's many Sinatra lovers, like Mr. Gregorio here in this city in the southernmost Philippines, are practicing self-censorship out of perceived self-preservation.

"The trouble with 'My Way,' " said Mr. Gregorio, "is that everyone knows it and everyone has an opinion."

Others, noting that other equally popular tunes have not provoked killings, point to the song itself. The lyrics, written by Paul Anka for Mr. Sinatra as an unapologetic summing up of his career, are about a tough guy who "when there was doubt," simply "ate it up and spit it out." Butch Albarracin, the owner of Center for Pop, a Manila-based singing school that has propelled the careers of many famous singers, was partial to what he called the "existential explanation."

" 'I did it my way'—it's so arrogant," Mr. Albarracin said. "The lyrics evoke feelings of pride and arrogance in the singer, as if you're somebody when you're really nobody. It covers up your failures. That's why it leads to fights." ("Sinatra Song Often Strikes Deadly Chord," *The New York Times* [New York Edition], February 6, 2010: A6.)

There are additional curmudgeonly animadversions on *My Way* in Sarah Vowell's amusing essay, "Ixnay on the *My Way*," in Sarah Vowell, *Take the Cannoli* (New York: Simon & Schuster, 2000): 159–166. And the author of an entry on the "EGR Weblog," (http://www.rageboy.com/2003_05_25_bloggerarchive. html), accessed April 17, 2006, compares the lyrics of "My Way" to the definition of "narcissistic personality disorder." Here is a brief quotation from the (lengthy) diatribe:

about a wide range of examples involving moral responsibility. It thus helps us to achieve a philosophical homeostasis, or, in John Rawls's famous term, a reflective equilibrium.[15]

I.3. THE VALUE OF ACTING FREELY

In addition to presenting the motivation for the account of guidance control and the specifics of the account, I have sought to articulate the nature of the *value* we place on exhibiting guidance control (and thus acting so that we can legitimately be held morally responsible). In my essay, "Responsibility and Self-Expression," I claimed that the value of acting so as to be morally responsible is the value of a certain sort of

---

I did it my way, the guy says. Your sleek self-confident blue-eyed boy, and underneath, an arrogant urbane brutality. Swingin. Cool. As cold as they come. Where's the love in Sinatra's love songs, I'm wondering... I wonder how he treated his women in Vegas. Like a gentleman, no doubt. Like one-a the guys. Like Luciano and Giancana. Smooth operators all. Made in the shade.

Regrets? Not me. F— you, Frank. ("Have It Your Way: DSM IV Meets Sid Vicious," May 27, 2003)

For a thoughtful and rather gentler development of the worry that a "My Way"-inspired approach to moral responsibility might be too atomistic or even narcissistic, see Angela Smith, "Making a Difference, Making a Statement, and Making a Conversation," (part of a book symposium on John Martin Fischer, *My Way: Essays on Moral Responsibility*) *Philosophical Books* 47 (2006): 213–221; I reply in John Martin Fischer, "A Reply to Pereboom, Zimmerman, and Smith," *Philosophical Books* 47 (2006): 235–244.

It is indisputable that moral responsibility is importantly a "social" notion. But it is perhaps a delicate issue how exactly to capture this point in one's conceptualization of moral responsibility. It should suffice to note that I have adopted as a working hypothesis a "Strawsonian" interpretation of the concept of moral responsibility, i.e., being morally responsible is understood as being an apt target for the reactive attitudes. And, as Gary Watson and others have pointed out, this way of understanding moral responsibility is essentially *communicative*: Gary Watson, "Responsibility and the Limits of Evil: Variations on a Strawsonian Theme," in Ferdinand David Schoeman, ed., *Responsibility, Character and the Emotions* (New York: Cambridge University Press, 1987): 256–286. Insofar as moral responsibility is modeled on a conversation, and assuming that one will not always simply talk to oneself, moral responsibility is construed as a social phenomenon.

[15] For further reflections on various features of my account of guidance control (and thus the freedom-relevant component of moral responsibility), see John Martin Fischer, "The Free Will Revolution," (part of a book symposium on John Martin Fischer and Mark Ravizza, *Responsibility and Control: A Theory of Moral Responsibility*) *Philosophical Explorations* 8 (2005): 145–156; and "The Free Will Revolution (Continued)," (part of a special issue on the work [pertaining to moral responsibility] of John Martin Fischer) *Journal of Ethics* 10 (2006): 315–345; and "*My Way* and Life's Highway: Replies to Steward, Smilansky, and Perry," *Journal of Ethics* 12 (2008): 167–189.

There are certain features of my account of guidance control that a disconcerting cohort of (otherwise!) thoughtful philosophers have found rather less than irresistible, especially the subjective element and the contention that "reactivity is all of a piece." In the trio of articles above, I argue (among other things) that (if need be) I could adjust my account so as to do without these contentious features while maintaining all of my major claims: that moral responsibility does not require regulative control, that causal determination is compatible with moral responsibility, that moral responsibility is an essentially historical notion, and so forth. Although I, of course, think that much can be said for the various particularly contentious elements of the account of guidance control, it is perhaps helpful to note that

artistic self-expression.[16] I have gone on to argue that in acting freely, we transform our lives in such a way that the chronicles of our lives become genuine *stories* or *narratives*. That is, I argue that acting freely is the ingredient which, when added to others, makes it the case that our lives admit of distinctively *narrative* explanation and have irreducibly narrative dimensions of evaluation. Thus acting freely—exhibiting the signature freedom-relevant control, guidance control—makes us the authors of our narratives. As such, we are artists, and I contend that the value of acting freely is thus the value of artistic self-expression. When we act freely, we do not necessarily make a difference—but we do make a statement. That is, in acting freely, we are writing a sentence in the books of our lives, or a bit less metaphorically, we are doing something that corresponds to a sentence in the stories of our lives.[17]

We are thus artists in fashioning our lives. But it does not follow that we ought to treat aesthetic reasons as hegemonic in our practical reasoning. Nor does it follow from the fact that our free activity is a species of artistic self-expression that the *value* we place on such activity is primarily or exclusively aesthetic. To infer in this way from the essence of the activity to the nature of the value would be to commit what I have called "the aesthetic fallacy."[18]

There is then an important discordance between the essential nature of our free activity (aesthetic) and the typical or primary sort of value we place on it (prudential or ethical, broadly speaking). I suggest that we can better understand the ways in which our lives are meaningful by conceptualizing free activity as at the "intersection" of the aesthetic and practical realms. I contend that we care especially about this particular *route* to moral and prudential evaluation—a route that is aesthetic in nature. And we care especially about aesthetic activities whose products are centrally evaluated along prudential and ethical dimensions.[19]

---

they are not essential to an adequate account of guidance control that achieves the main results at which I aim; thus, it will not be sufficient for many critics to attach what they might perceive to be easier targets (the low-hanging fruit, as it were).

[16] "Responsibility and Self-Expression," *The Journal of Ethics* 3 (1999): 277–297; reprinted in Fischer, *My Way*: 106–123.

[17] John Martin Fischer, "Free Will, Death, and Immortality: The Role of Narrative," *Philosophical Papers* (Special Issue: Meaning in Life) 34 (2005): 379–404; reprinted in Fischer, *Our Stories*: 145–164.

[18] John Martin Fischer, "Stories and the Meaning of Life," *Philosophic Exchange* 39 (2008–09): 2–16; reprinted in Fischer, *Our Stories*: 165–177.

[19] Susan Wolf has argued that meaningfulness in life occurs at the intersection between the subjective and objective realms; that is, for Wolf meaningfulness arises from the intersection between the subjectively attractive and the objectively worthwhile: Susan Wolf. *Meaning in Life and Why It Matters* (Princeton, NJ: Princeton University Press, 2010.)

Something—such as counting blades of grass—might be compelling to someone, but it is not objectively worthwhile, and thus it cannot give rise to meaningfulness. Similarly, no matter how objectively worthwhile a certain goal is, it cannot give meaningfulness to one's life if one is indifferent to it.

If one combines Wolf's point with mine, one gets to the idea that meaningfulness in life arises from a certain intersection of intersections. That is, meaningfulness occurs in contexts in which there is a linkage between subjective engagement and objective worth, as well as a linkage between the aesthetic and the moral/prudential realms. It is plausible that meaningfulness emerges from a certain kind of complexity, and thus it is not too far-fetched to suppose that meaningfulness distinctively emerges from this specific intersection of intersections, what I might dub *the nexus of meaningfulness*.

II. Some Features and Implications of My Overall Approach to Moral Responsibility

As I stated earlier, I believe that our status as morally responsible agents should not "hang on a thread"; specifically, neither the discovery that the laws of nature have associated with them probabilities of 1.0 nor the discovery that they have associated with them probabilities of 0.99 should incline us to give up our views of ourselves as deeply different from other creatures insofar as we can engage in practical reasoning and be morally responsible. Much of my work has focused on the deterministic side of the equation, so to speak. But note that my account of guidance control is entirely compatible with the *falsity* (as well as the truth) of causal determinism. Indeed, Carl Ginet has kindly suggested that an indeterminist should accept the core of my account of the responsibility-conferring kind of control (in my view, guidance control) and simply add a condition specifying that causal determinism must be false.[20] My account then is compatible with causal indeterminism.

It is, as I have emphasized, a considerable advantage of my approach that it renders agency and moral responsibility *resilient* to certain (although not all) empirical discoveries. Indeed, I consider it an important desideratum of an adequate account of moral responsibility that it does not *depend* on any contentious doctrine. So, for example, if one's account of moral responsibility *depended* on (say) the existence of irreducible agent-causation or the falsity of "reductionism" (of a certain sort) in metaphysics or the falsity of materialism about the mind, this would be a strike against the account. Similarly, if one's theory of moral responsibility depended on a particular view about *reasons*—their ontological status or their "logic" or even their specific content—this would count against the theory.

Although I cannot argue for these claims here, I contend that my accounts of guidance control (and moral responsibility) are compatible with a wide range of plausible views about these contentious empirical and philosophical matters. For example, my account of guidance control certainly does not presuppose that there

---

But perhaps the deepest, most compelling sort of meaning involves a kind of unity in diversity. Nozick called this sort of meaning, "the value of organic unity": Robert Nozick, *Philosophical Explanations* (Cambridge, MA: Harvard University Press, 1981): 415–422. This kind of meaning requires not just the presence of disparate elements, but their unification in a distinctive way. Perhaps one can think of our narratives—our stories—as precisely this unifying element (or, at least, as *providing* this element). After all, as Velleman and others have emphasized, narrative understanding involves some sort of unification—an "aha" moment that brings everything together in a certain characteristic way. Perhaps we can think of our stories as what unifies the diverse elements in the nexus of meaning. More specifically, perhaps our lives can have a distinctive kind of meaning—corresponding to Nozick's notion of the value of organic unity—in virtue of the unification provided by our stories—a unification of diverse elements. Put metaphorically, our stories are (or provide) elements that mold and structure the "space" in the nexus of meaningfulness: the place where subjective and objective value intersects, and where we arrive at a product that is typically evaluated morally and prudentially via a distinctively aesthetic path.

[20] Carl Ginet, "Working with Fischer and Ravizza's Account of Moral Responsibility," *Journal of Ethics* 10 (2006): 229–253.

is irreducible, indeterministic agent-causation; it thus does not depend, for its acceptance, on some sort of defense of this highly contentious doctrine. On the other hand, I believe that the core of the account is compatible with the existence of irreducible, indeterministic agent-causation. As with Ginet's suggestion, there would perhaps need to be certain adjustments or clarifications; but there is nothing in the core ideas of the account that requires either the truth or falsity of claims about agent-causation. I would contend that the situation is similar with respect to the other contentious doctrines mentioned above. It is then a big advantage of my account that it is *significantly resilient*; it can be "nested" within total packages with a wide range of particular views about the nature of the mind, normativity, and the world. In contrast, a libertarian's philosophical views—and perhaps his life— would be turned upside down if in the future scientists were to discover that causal determinism is true. At least I can sleep well at night. (Or, perhaps better: my recurrent insomnia is at least not caused by the fact that crucial and central features of my philosophical views hang by a thread!)

I have always attempted to take incompatibilism seriously.[21] In particular, I believe that the strongest argument for a compatibilist conclusion stems from granting the incompatibilist as much as possible. Approaches that simply reject out of hand the most plausible parts of incompatibilism—such as the Consequence Argument or worries about manipulation—are not appealing to me.[22] After all, the Consequence Argument employs ingredients—such as the fixity of the past and natural laws—that are deeply ingrained in our commonsense ways of understanding the world and our agency, and it has been around—in one form or another, including versions that pertain to the prior truth values of propositions or God's omniscience—for millennia.

My approach is to credit—and, indeed, to seek to accommodate—the extremely plausible kernel of incompatibilism: that causal determinism rules out regulative control (freedom to do otherwise). Additionally, I take seriously the possibility that our mental states can be manipulatively induced; thus, I seek to provide an *explanation* of the difference between such manipulation and *mere* causal determination. Whereas many compatibilists either ignore or simply don't take seriously the Consequence Argument or the possibility of manipulative induction of mental states, I seek to capture what is true and important about these worries.

My "Semicompatibilism" is thus an attempt to capture what is most appealing in various leading approaches to free will and moral responsibility. Semicompatibilism is the view that causal determinism is compatible with moral responsibility, quite apart from whether causal determinism rules out regulative control. (Semicompatibilism is officially agnostic about whether causal determinism does

---

[21] Although, as Patrick Todd has reminded me, not seriously enough for many of my libertarian friends!

[22] The term, "Consequence Argument," is due to Peter Van Inwagen, *An Essay on Free Will* (Oxford: Clarendon Press, 1983).

indeed rule out regulative control.) Thus, a Semicompatibilist might accept the conclusion of the Consequence Argument, but still hold that causal determinism is compatible with moral responsibility. A Semicompatibilist can thus accommodate a kernel insight of the incompatibilist but also embrace the attractive features of compatibilism, most notably, the *resiliency* of our fundamental views of ourselves (with respect to certain abstract scientific theories). Of course, a Semicompatibilist *need not* accept the conclusion of the Consequence Argument. It is no part of the essence of Semicompatibilism that causal determinism is incompatible with regulative control; rather, the fundamental idea is that moral responsibility depends on how the actual sequence unfolds, not on whether the agent has access to alternative possibilities. Semicompatibilism is, as I have emphasized, an "actual-sequence" model of moral responsibility.

III. The Plan of the Book

III.1. PART ONE: FRANKFURT CASES AND THE PRINCIPLE OF ALTERNATIVE POSSIBILITIES

Although there are various plausible ways of attempting to defend an actual-sequence model of moral responsibility, I focus considerable attention on the Frankfurt cases. In the first set of essays in the book, I seek to defend Frankfurt's conclusion that the examples give a strong argument against the Principle of Alternative Possibilities (PAP), according to which moral responsibility requires regulative control or access to alternative possibilities. ("The Frankfurt Cases: The Moral of the Stories," "Freedom, Foreknowledge, and Frankfurt," "The Importance of Frankfurt-Style Argument," and "Blame and Avoidability.") In the various essays I attempt to address a range of interesting objections to the notion that the Frankfurt cases do indeed call PAP into question.

Perhaps the most salient and influential objection to the "anti-PAP-ist" analysis of the Frankfurt cases is the "Dilemma Defense."[23] Here is the argument: Return to the version of the Frankfurt examples I presented earlier, and note, first, that I was not explicit about whether causal determinism holds in the scenario. So let us first assume that causal determinism does not obtain; specifically, assume that indeterminism obtains (at the relevant point, whatever that is taken to be) in the sequence that leads to the choice and action. Now how can Black's device help

---

[23] See, especially, Robert Kane, *Free Will and Values* (Albany: State University of New York Press, 1985), and *The Significance of Free Will* (New York: Oxford University Press, 1996), 142–145; David Widerker, "Libertarianism and Frankfurt's Attack on the Principle of Alternative Possibilities," *Philosophical Review* 104 (1995): 247–261; Carl Ginet, "In Defense of the Principle of Alternative Possibilities: Why I Don't Find Frankfurt's Argument Convincing," *Philosophical Perspectives* 10 (1996): 403–417; Keith Wyma, "Moral Responsibility and Leeway for Action," *American Philosophical Quarterly* 34 (1997): 57–70; and Stewart Goetz, "Frankfurt-Style Counterexamples and Begging the Question," *Midwest Studies in Philosophy* 29 (2005): 83–105.

Black to know that Jones will choose to vote on his own for Obama (and indeed vote for Obama on his own)? It would seem that, given indeterminism in the right place, all the evidence Black could muster about Jones prior to his decision would leave it open that Jones at least begin to decide to vote for McCain. Of course, at that point Jones's brain would be zapped, but it would be *too late* to prevent Jones's having had access to an alternative possibility, exiguous as it might be. After all, whether a flicker of freedom is robust is not a matter of size, but of voluntariness or "oomph."

Suppose, specifically that Jones decides "on his own" at *t2* to vote for Obama; and imagine that Jones involuntarily exhibits some sign, such as (appropriately enough) a furrowed left brow, at an earlier time *t1*. When Jones furrows his left brow at *t1* in this sort of way, he typically chooses at *t2* to vote for the Democrat. The problem for Black is that, although this may in general be a reliable "prior sign," given indeterminism, it is possible that Jones began to decide to vote for McCain, even though he exhibited the relevant sign—the furrowed left brow—at *t1*. Under the assumption of causal indeterminism (of the right sort), it seems that there is no way for Black to expunge all (relevant) alternative possibilities; thus we do not yet have a counterexample to PAP. That is, we do not yet have a case in which an individual is morally responsible for something, although he has no alternative possibilities. According to certain philosophers—and, of course, this is one of the very questions at issue in this dialectical context—it is the very existence of the possibility of beginning to choose to vote for McCain that renders Jones morally responsible for his actual choice and action.

Now assume that causal determinism obtains in the example. On this horn of the dilemma, the skeptic about the anti-PAP-ist conclusion will insist that we cannot now baldly state that Jones is morally responsible for his choice to vote for Obama and his act of voting for Obama. After all, it is precisely the issue under debate whether causal determinism would rule out such moral responsibility; it would be question-begging to assume that causal determinism is true in the example (quite independently of the presence of Black's device) and also to hold that it is uncontroversial that Jones is morally responsible for his choice and action. Thus, again, we do not yet have a case in which we are entitled to say that an individual is morally responsible for something and yet he has no alternative possibilities.

The Dilemma Defense is a deep and challenging objection to the contention that Frankfurt cases provide a dialectical route (although perhaps not the only one) to an actual-sequence model of moral responsibility. In "The Frankfurt Cases: The Moral of the Stories," I provide a template for a strategy of response to the Dilemma Defense. This strategy depends heavily on two crucial insights. First, as I emphasized previously, it is important to note that the mere presence of *any old alternative possibility* is not sufficient to ground moral responsibility attributions. That is, a proponent of alternative possibilities for moral responsibility must concede that *mere* flickers of freedom are too exiguous to support the superstructure of moral responsibility practices; moral responsibility requires at least *robust* alternative possibilities.

The second crucial insight is nicely articulated by Frankfurt:

> The fact that a person could not have avoided doing something is a sufficient condition of his having done it. But, as some of my examples show, this fact may play no role whatever in the explanation of why he did it. It may not figure at all among the circumstances that actually brought it about that he did what he did, so that his action is to be accounted for on another basis entirely… Now if someone had no alternative to performing a certain action but did not perform it because he was unable to do otherwise, then he would have performed exactly the same action even if he *could* have done otherwise. The circumstances that made it impossible for him to do otherwise could have been subtracted from the situation without affecting what happened or why it happened in any way. Whatever it was that actually led the person to do what he did, or that made him do it, would have led him to do it or made him do it even if it had been possible for him to do something else instead… When a fact is in this way irrelevant to the problem of accounting for a person's action it seems quite gratuitous to assign it any weight in the assessment of his moral responsibility.[24]

Frankfurt's "Quite Gratuitous Point" implies that Black's presence and device are irrelevant to Jones's moral responsibility.

Not only do these two insights—the irrelevance of mere flickers of freedom and the irrelevance of the mere presence of Black—provide the basis for a promising reply to the Dilemma Defense, but I argue in "Indeterminism and Control" that these very ingredients can also be invoked to provide a reply to the notorious "Luck Problem" for indeterministic approaches to moral responsibility. Thus, I argue that a plausible strategy of response to one of the central worries about the relationship between causal determinism and moral responsibility is importantly similar to such a strategy of response to one of the central worries about the relationship between causal indeterminism and moral responsibility. Indeed, I contend that the challenges from causal determinism and indeterminism are structurally parallel at a deep level; thus, it should not be surprising that the responses to these worries should exhibit a striking structural similarity.

Once one sees that moral responsibility is fundamentally a matter of how the actual sequence unfolds, one can reply to both the challenges from causal determinism and indeterminism in a similar way: both replies rely heavily on scenarios that posit *counterfactual interveners*. In the reply to the challenge from determinism, *untriggered ensurers* such as Black play a crucial role; in the reply to the

---

[24] Frankfurt, "Alternate Possibilities and Moral Responsibility," 836–837.

challenge from indeterminism, *untriggered preemptors* (such as the "Random Machine" I introduce in "Indeterminism and Control") play the parallel role. In both cases the replies depend importantly on untriggered or counterfactual interventions. That is, the parallel replies depend on the key insight that it would indeed be "quite gratuitous" to assign any weight (in attributions of moral responsibility) to merely counterfactual interventions.

III.2. PART TWO: DEEP CONTROL: A MIDDLE PATH

In the second part of the book I develop and defend an account of guidance control, which in various ways represents a moderate position along a spectrum of views about moral responsibility. ("The Direct Argument: You Say Goodbye, I Say Hello," "Conditional Freedom and the Normative Approach to Moral Responsibility," "Judgment-Sensitivity and the Value of Freedom," "Sourcehood: Playing the Cards That Are Dealt You," "Guidance Control," and "The Triumph of Tracing.") At the risk of oversimplification, it might be useful to invoke the famous Buddhist notion of a "Middle Way" or "Middle Path." After receiving enlightenment under the bodhi tree, the Buddha delivered his first sermon in the Deer Park at Benares. In this sermon he renounced two untenable extremes—of excessive sensual indulgence, on the one hand, and self-abnegation, on the other. Famously, in this sermon he endorsed a Middle Way—a path of moderation. The Buddha purportedly understood the meaning of the Middle Way when he sat by a river and heard a lute player in a passing boat. The Buddha noted that the lute string must be tuned neither too tight nor too loose in order to produce a beautiful sound.[25]

Deep control is a middle path between two untenable extreme positions: "superficial control" and "total control." It is plausible that our freedom is the power to add to the given past, holding fixed the laws of nature; that is, we must be able to conceptualize our actions as extensions of a line that represents the actual past. (This is, in my view, the essential insight of the Consequence Argument.) In "connecting the dots," we engage in a distinctive sort of self-expression. In the first group of essays in this volume, I argue that we do not need genuine access to alternative possibilities in order to be morally responsible. Thus, the line need not branch off at crucial points (where the branches represent metaphysical possibilities available to us). In the rest of the collection I argue that deep control—a kind of "middle way" between what I take to be two extreme and implausible positions—is the freedom condition on moral responsibility. In so arguing, I contend that *total control* is too much to ask—it is a form of "metaphysical megalomania." ("Sourcehood: Playing the Cards that Are Dealt You.") So we do not "trace back" all the way to the beginning of the line (or even further) in seeking the relevant kind of freedom or control.

---

[25] There are various interpretations in Buddhism of the central notion of the "Middle Way." For our purposes, I simply picked one.

Additionally, I contend that various kinds of "superficial control"—such as several versions of "conditional freedom" and "judgment-sensitivity"—are too shallow; they don't trace back *far enough* along the line. ("Conditional Freedom and the Normative Approach to Moral Responsibility," and "Judgment-Sensitivity and the Value of Freedom.") Further, standard hierarchical identification theories (such as that of Harry Frankfurt) and nonhierarchical "mesh theories" (such as the approach suggested by Gary Watson in his classic early work) are similarly problematic. The envisaged mesh or harmony of designated mental elements could be produced by responsibility-undermining manipulative induction, and thus these approaches are not sufficiently historical. Finally, I argue that "guidance control," understood as including both a historicist "taking responsibility" component and a "tracing requirement," is precisely the deep control necessary and sufficient for moral responsibility. Guidance control, as Goldilocks would have it, is *just right*. ("Guidance Control" and "The Triumph of Tracing.") It is perhaps worth noting that the Buddha described the Middle Way not only as the path of "wisdom," but also of "liberation" or *freedom*.

I have emphasized the importance of a *historical* approach to moral responsibility, contending that it matters to moral responsibility attributions how we got to be the way we are. Such attributions do not supervene on current time-slice properties. But it is also important to see that certain approaches to moral responsibility require us to trace back excessively far into the past; this is, as I have argued, a form of overreaching or "metaphysical megalomania." ("Sourcehood: Playing the Cards that Are Dealt You.") Galen Strawson and Robert Kane both—in different ways—put forward exceedingly stringent sourcehood requirements. Although I am inclined to agree that an agent must be the source of his behavior, in order to be morally responsible for it, I do not conclude from this intuitive point that such an agent must be the "ultimate source," in a sense that requires causal indeterminism (or certainly a sense that requires a kind of impossible self-creation). I believe that our moral responsibility requires that we play the cards that are dealt us (in a certain way—a way that crucially involves guidance control); but surely this does not require that we deal ourselves the cards, or that we own the factory that made the cards (as well as all of the inputs into the manufacturing process), and so forth.

Of course, if causal determinism is true, then how we play the cards we are dealt is "settled" in advance, and, if the incompatibilist is correct, it is not "up to us" how we play the hand we are dealt. But it is no part of my invocation of the analogy of card games and the associated metaphor of playing the cards that are dealt us that it is up to us how we play the cards or that we have the freedom to play the cards differently from how we actually play them.[26] Rather, the point is that, even

---

[26] It is perhaps a natural thought that, although moral responsibility does not require that we deal ourselves the cards, it does require that it be open to us how we play them. I am indebted to Patrick Todd for pressing me on this point.

in a causally deterministic world, we can play the cards in our hand freely—we can exhibit the signature sort of control in virtue of which we can legitimately be held morally responsible. So the picture is *not* that even though nature and nurture deal us certain cards that must be treated as fixed inputs into our practical reasoning, from there on out we have leeway, or freedom to play the hand however we want. It may or may not be true that such leeway is compatible with causal determinism, but my invocation of the metaphor does *not* require or presuppose the possibility of such freedom in a causally deterministic world. All that's presupposed is that its being determined that I play the cards as I do need not get in the way of my doing so freely. Causal determination need not crowd out guidance control, and thus I can still play my hand *my way*, even in a deterministic world.

It is perhaps interesting that the two leading metaphors here, "the buck stops here" and "playing the cards that are dealt you" derive from card games. A buck is a marker and is often used in poker to indicate who is in charge of dealing the hand. Indeed, President Harry S. Truman was an avid poker player, and perhaps the famous sign on his desk "The Buck Stops Here" appealed to him for this reason. Robert Kane invokes the notion that the buck stops here to defend an indeterministic interpretation of ultimate sourcehood. But, taking seriously the roots of the metaphor, I would insist that the indeterministic interpretation is a gratuitous add-on. After all, if the marker points to you, it shows that you are "responsible" for dealing the cards in the sense that you are in charge of it. Again, this does not in any way suggest that you have made up the rules of the game, that you own the plant that manufactured the cards, or any such thing. The metaphor, "The buck stops here," does not suggest an indeterministic requirement on sourcehood; it is more a matter of who is in charge of a certain task than a matter of the etiology of the distribution of tasks. When the marker points to a player, that player must deal the cards—he must ensure that everyone gets the right number of cards, and so forth. This is a matter of *authority*, not history.

Alternatively, perhaps it is a matter of *explanation*.[27] When the buck stops here, the proper explanation of the phenomenon in question *ineliminably* involves me. So, if we are seeking to explain why everyone got the correct number of cards, the explanation involves the dealer. Insofar as the buck stops at the dealer, it is the dealer who is invoked in the explanation of the distribution of cards. This in itself does not entail anything about the (entire) causal history of the events in question; an intermediate event in a deterministic causal sequence can play the appropriate explanatory role, given certain explanatory contexts. As with the point about authority before, it seems to me to be a gratuitously strong interpretation of the buck-stopping metaphor to import anything about etiology, and, in particular, an indeterministic requirement.

---

[27] I am indebted here to Justin Coates. Also, for an excellent recent discussion of the context-relativity of explanation, and its relationship to issues about moral responsibility, see Gunnar Björnsson and Karl Persson, "The Explanatory Component of Moral Responsibility," *Nous* (forthcoming).

As I wrote above, the Buddha recognized, in the Deer Park at Benares, that a lute string must be tuned just right—not too loose, and not too tight. A virtue of my middle way approach to tracing back along the agency line is that it can help to illuminate the scenarios posited by "Initial Design Arguments." For example, consider the Initial Design hypothesis presented by Alfred Mele:

> Diana [a goddess with special powers] creates a zygote Z in Mary. She combines Z's atoms as she does because she wants a certain event E to occur thirty years later. From her knowledge of the state of the universe just prior to her creating Z and the laws of nature of her deterministic universe, she deduces that a zygote with precisely Z's constitution located in Mary will develop into an ideally self-controlled agent who, in thirty years, will judge, on the basis of rational deliberation, that it is best to A and will A on the basis of that judgment, thereby bringing about E. If this agent, Ernie, has any unsheddable values at the time, they play no role in motivating his A-ing. Thirty years later, Ernie is a mentally healthy, ideally self-controlled person who regularly exercises his powers of self-control and has no relevant compelled or coercively produced attitudes. Furthermore, his beliefs are conducive to informed deliberation about all matters that concern him, and he is a reliable deliberator. So he satisfies a version of my proposed compatibilist sufficient conditions for having freely A-d.[28]

Mele proposes this thought-experiment as a challenge for compatibilists, because all plausible compatibilist-friendly conditions (including guidance control) are met by Ernie, and yet some might judge that he is not morally responsible insofar as he is merely living out the detailed plans of Diana.

I concede that this captures a legitimate worry of many thoughtful people, but upon reflection, I simply do not see how it can matter for Ernie's moral responsibility what Diana's intentions and plans were some thirty years prior to the time of the relevant behavior—and, indeed, before Ernie was even born! Insofar as Ernie exhibits guidance control, what difference does it make whether the sequence was set in motion by Diana thirty years ago, or by a single parent through artificial insemination, or by a couple having voluntary intercourse? To trace back to a time prior to Ernie's birth is to go back too far. Whereas we need a genuinely historical approach to moral responsibility, to trace back along the sequence to a point prior to Ernie's birth is surely too extreme. The path of wisdom here is the Middle Way.[29]

---

[28] Alfred Mele, *Free Will and Luck* (New York: Oxford University Press, 2006): 188.

[29] I discuss Initial Design Arguments, such as the Zygote Argument, in greater detail in John Martin Fischer, "The Zygote Argument Remixed," *Analysis* 71 (2011): 267–272. My discussion in the text (and even in the forthcoming article) leaves various interesting nuances untouched; I am indebted to Patrick Todd for many illuminating conversations on these topics. He has developed his critique of my approach to the Zygote Argument in Patrick Todd, "Defending (A Modified Version Of) the Zygote Argument: Reply to Fischer," (unpublished manuscript, University of California, Riverside, Department of Philosophy).

In defending my account of moral responsibility, I also offer a discussion of so-called normative approaches to moral responsibility. Much has been made of a putative distinction between "metaphysical" and "normative" approaches to specifying the conditions for moral responsibility. I make a preliminary attempt to identify the core features of "normative" approaches, discuss the various different versions of such approaches, and subject them to critical scrutiny. I contend that the distinction between "metaphysical" and "normative" approaches to the conditions for moral responsibility is not so easy to characterize as some might have supposed, and the implications of certain plausible characterizations of the distinction might be surprising.[30] ("Conditional Freedom and the Normative Approach to Moral Responsibility.")

IV. A New Paradigm: The Pilgrimage

The traditional and perhaps still "standard" view of our agency is that we *make a difference* by selecting from a suite of genuinely open possibilities. A metaphor that corresponds to this idea is the "garden of forking paths." According to the standard view, the future is a garden of forking paths, and we make a difference in the world by selecting one of the paths. In his story, "The Garden of Forking Paths," the Argentine fabulist, Borges, describes a fictional labyrinth or garden in soaring terms:

> Under the trees of England I meditated on this lost and perhaps mythical labyrinth. I imagined it untouched and perfect on the secret summit of some mountain; I imagined it drowned under rice paddies or beneath the sea; I imagined it infinite, made not only of eight-sided pavilions and of twisting paths but also of rivers, provinces and kingdom. I thought of a maze of mazes, of a sinuous, ever growing maze which could take in both past and future and would somehow involve the stars.[31]

But I have argued that, even if the future is not a garden of forking paths (in the sense involving open possibilities), we can still exercise the control that grounds attributions of moral responsibility. We can display guidance control, even in the absence of regulative control, and guidance control is all the freedom required for moral responsibility. In controlling our behavior in this way, we transform our lives into stories, strictly speaking, with an irreducible narrative dimension of value. Our agency then essentially involves *making a statement* insofar as our free

---

[30] For additional thoughts on how best to characterize the distinction between so-called metaphysical and normative approaches to moral responsibility, see John Martin Fischer, "Reply to Pamela Hieronymi, Making a Difference," in "Replies," *Social Theory and Practice* (special issue: Fischer's Way and Our Stories) 37 (2011): 143–181.

[31] Jorge Luis Borges, "The Garden of Forking Paths," in his *Fictions* (London: Calder and Boyars): 81–92.

activity corresponds to a sentence in the book of our lives. What matters at the most basic level—what we care about in acting freely—is making a statement, not making a difference.

I thus invite a change in our guiding metaphor from the garden of forking paths to the *pilgrimage*. A pilgrimage is typically a preset path from one point to another; it does not—nor need not—involve alternative pathways. Even if there are such alternative paths, the *point* of a pilgrimage is to travel from a preset starting point to a preset terminus, and thus the existence of such byways is irrelevant. Despite the fact that the pilgrimage route is laid out in advance, the pilgrims can achieve great personal growth and transformation; indeed, such a pilgrimage can be one of the most meaningful experiences in one's life.

Consider, for example, the pilgrimage route (a part of which is depicted on the cover of this book) from Lu Puy, in south-central France, to Santiago de Compostela, in northwestern Spain. This pilgrimage was laid out in the medieval *Pilgrim's Guide*.[32] Although the route is, as it were, "preset," the pilgrim may well experience remarkable spiritual growth and transformation. I claim that the beauty and meaningfulness of the experience does not in any way derive from selection from available paths; rather, it is a matter of how one walks along a predetermined route. Indeed, in the twelfth-century *Pilgrim's Guide*, the author employs rhetoric reminiscent of Borges in describing a part of the pilgrimage route as it reaches the peak of the Pyrenees:

> Its height is so great that it seems to reach all the way to the heavens—to the person ascending it, it seems that he himself is able to touch the heavens with his own hand.[33]

I grant that even though the "route" of a pilgrimage is typically set out in advance, there will nevertheless remain many "options" as to how one takes the route—whether one starts a day early or late, hikes more or less each day, stops here or there for the night, and so forth. There will also presumably be various options as to one's "mind-set." For example, does one focus on one's sore feet or on higher things? And so forth. If all of these alternatives are ruled out, then it is unclear just how far we can get with the metaphor of a pilgrimage. After all, it might be the case that our intuition that one can have a meaningful experience on a preset path might depend implicitly on the existence of such alternative possibilities.[34]

Of course, the metaphor of a pilgrimage is—like all metaphors—merely suggestive, and I do not have a knockdown argument that alternative possibilities need

---

[32] In *The Pilgrim's Guide to Santiago de Compostela: A Gazetteer*, ed. and trans. Annie Shaver-Crandell and Paula Gerson, with the assistance of Alison Stones (London: Harvey Miller, 1995). I am deeply indebted in this section to the excellent work by my colleague at the University of California, Riverside, in Art History, Conrad Rudolph, *Pilgrimage to the End of the World: The Road to Santiago de Compostela* (Chicago and London: The University of Chicago Press, 2004).

[33] As quoted in Rudolph, *Pilgrimage to the End of the World*: 65.

[34] I am grateful to Patrick Todd for bringing up these points.

not matter to the experience of a pilgrimage. I would contend, however, that the dialectical situation here is analogous to the situation with respect to the "mere flickers of freedom" that emerge in even the most sophisticated Frankfurt-style cases. Recall that, although I concede that it is extremely difficult to deracinate such alternatives, they do not play the required role in the argument of the proponent of the Principle of Alternative Possibilities insofar as they are *mere* flickers of freedom (and not sufficiently robust to ground ascriptions of moral responsibility).[35] I contend that the same point is reinscribed with respect to the relationship between alternative possibilities and the potential meaningfulness of a pilgrimage.

To explain. Consider the joy pilgrims typically experience when they reach their destination—say the great cathedral at Santiago de Compostela. I do not find it plausible that the joy is in any way linked to the existence of alternative possibilities along the pilgrimage route. It would be most implausible to attribute the joy to a judgment that one chose not to take a shortcut along the way (where such a path was genuinely available), or that one made a wise or prudent choice in footwear (where other choices were available), or that one started out at a suitable time each day (where alternatives were available). The joy in reaching the destination is not a matter of wise or prudent selection from among genuine possibilities.[36] The joy and sense of accomplishment (and even extraordinary transformation) would

---

[35] Michael McKenna pursues a similar strategy for defending the anti-Pap-ist interpretation of the Frankfurt cases. He presents a case in which Betty is deliberating about cheating on her taxes, and the sole alternative possibility open to her is just heading home and roasting a chicken. McKenna points out that the mere existence of such a possibility cannot plausibly ground Betty's moral responsibility; the alternative possibility in question, although not a mere flicker of freedom (because it would be fully voluntary), is entirely irrelevant to Betty's moral responsibility. How could simply adding the possibility that Betty roast a chicken transform her from not being morally responsible to being morally responsible? The existence of certain alternative possibilities—mere flickers of freedom and also normatively irrelevant alternatives—cannot ground moral responsibility attributions. See Michael McKenna, "Robustness, Control, and the Demand for Morally Significant Alternatives," in David Widerker and Michael McKenna, eds., *Moral Responsibility and Alternative Possibilities: Essays on the Importance of Alternative Possibilities* (Aldershot, UK: Ashgate, 2003): 201–217.

[36] The following is an excerpt from a news item from the International Islamic News Agency (accessed online on November 17, 2010):

> MINA (Saudi Arabia), Dhul Qadah 2/Oct.10 (IINA)-Hundreds of thousands of Muslim pilgrims will ride a new railway metro transport system for the first time when they converge on the Saudi holy city of Makkah next month, according to the local media. The Gulf Kingdom, where millions of Muslims from around the world gather every year for their annual hajj (pilgrimage) season, has just completed the first stage of a train that will eventually transport nearly two million people. Officials said around 170,000 pilgrims would be able to use the Chinese-built metro during this hajj season, which is expected to start in mid November. (http://www.iina.me/english/news.php?go=fullnews&newsid=840)

Given the choice between taking the last stage of the hajj by foot or train, a given Islamic pilgrim might choose to take the train (and thereby avoid congestion and its attendant distractions and even dangers). But surely the joy and intense feelings of completion on reaching the holy destination stem from reaching the destination itself, and not even in part from pride in making a prudent choice about alternative routes at the end.

in no way be diminished if the pilgrim were told at Santiago de Compostela, "By the way, although you believed that a shortcut was available, it was actually blocked off, and you would have had to return to the main route, if you had started along the alternative path."

Think also of mountain treks—say treks in the Cordilleras Blanca in Peru or to the top of Mount Everest or K2.[37] These great mountain treks may have no shortcuts, no alternative paths, and only certain specified places to stay for the night.[38] But the fact that the treks are "laid out in advance" in these ways surely is irrelevant to the meaningfulness that many hikers experience on the treks. Although it is difficult to prove this point, I would contend that an analogous point applies even to alternative possibilities with respect to one's "mind-set" and attentiveness. As I stated above, what matters is *how* one takes the path, not on whether one *selects* from among genuinely available options. Although talk of "how" one walks down a path might suggest a reemergence of alternative possibilities, I would maintain that the significance of the pilgrimage should be conceptualized more "directly" in terms of how the actual sequence unfolds. After all, a pilgrim might take a certain route rather than another, not knowing that the other route is blocked off and unavailable; and he or she might naturally adopt a set of attitudes toward the pilgrimage without any thought of adopting another mind-set.

It might be objected that at least the pilgrim has *chosen* to take the pilgrimage; perhaps the meaningfulness of the pilgrimage stems from its being up to the pilgrim whether to take the pilgrimage in the first place. Plausibly, the meaningfulness of various religious and spiritual practices does indeed stem from the free choices of the individuals in question. But note first that it is contentious here whether the pilgrim's freely choosing to take the pilgrimage indeed requires that

---

We could drive the point home as follows. Suppose, to begin, there is just one preset hajj route, with no alternative possibilities, including the new Chinese-built train at the end. If the pilgrims cannot gain in the meaningfulness of their lives by taking such a preset route with no alternative possibilities, how could merely adding the possibility of taking a train at the end confer any incremental meaningfulness? One might as well imagine that, instead of the option of a railway at the end, the pilgrim could instead stop the journey and roast a (halaal) chicken! But the possibility of stopping and roasting a halaal chicken surely does not add meaningfulness; a choice to continue to the destination, in light of such alternatives, is no more meaningful than taking the ancient pilgrimage in the traditional manner.

[37] For a guidebook to the Cordillera Blancas in Peru, see Jim Bartle. *Trails of the Cordillera Blancas and Huayhuash of Peru.* The book is self-published (Jim Bartle, June 1982: ISBN-10: 0933982100; ISBN-13: 978-09339982109). Jim, an old friend of mine, is one of the leading experts on the mountain routes of Peru.

[38] Consider also the "Nose" at El Capitan in Yosemite, arguably the most famous rock-climbing venue in the world. There is only one route up to the very top of El Capitan, although there are multiple routes up to the final ascent. The topological map of the route spells out exactly what you are supposed to do at each stage (e.g., climb X feet, stop, climb X feet, stop, move left into a different crack, stop, etc.). And yet this is the most famous route in the world, over 3,000 ft. People who accomplish this climb are proud simply of doing the climb—there are no alternative ways of doing it, and the pride is in having made the climb, not having done it in a certain way rather than another. I am indebted to Alan Moore for this example.

he or she could have done otherwise. Further, it seems to me that even someone forced against his will to begin a pilgrimage may well find it meaningful and transformative. As before, there is a danger of tracing back too far along the sequence in search of freedom; there are many contexts in life in which one simply finds oneself thrown into a situation, and one makes the best of it: we play the cards that are dealt us. Even someone kidnapped and forced to undertake a pilgrimage might find it deeply meaningful. Many of us have found ourselves in similar situations over the course of our lives—required to undertake a project by our parents, friends, spouse, or children. The lack of alternative possibilities, or even coercive initial circumstances, need not etiolate the potential for meaningfulness, transformation, and deep value.

The extraordinary possibilities for growth and transformation along the preset route of the pilgrimage are described beautifully by Conrad Rudolph:

> You are told the route, but it's all the same: it's all new, it's all strange, it's all foreign, it's all a sea of strangeness and foreignness... [The pilgrimage] forces the susceptible person to enter into one of the most fundamental elements of human existence...the simple recognition that history is part of existence, whether cultural or individual, that there is a past as well as a present, that the past has very much to do with the present, and that the past belongs to those who belong to the present... From the medieval point of view, the pilgrimage was not just the physical arrival at a holy place but the experience of progressing toward that destination, an experience that was as much a part of the phenomenon as was the holy place itself. From the modern point of view of the "curious" pilgrim, the pilgrimage is an intensely internal experience in an intensely physical context in which the journey, more than the destination, is the goal.
>
> But it's also something more than that. People instinctively want something to believe in, whether they believe in anything much or not. From the medieval perspective, the pilgrimage was undertaken for the very specific reason that the great physical hardships of pain, hunger, thirst, exposure to the elements, and general loss of comfort and of all that's familiar are conducive to inducing a mental state eminently suited for the spiritual exercise that the pilgrimage fundamentally was and can still be—to a certain extent, the adoption of monastic spiritual practices in the non-monastic medium of the visitation of a holy site: this was the purpose of such a long and grueling journey. For the modern pilgrim, the "curious" pilgrim, the vast epic quality of the pilgrimage still instills at the very least much of the sensation of a journey with a deeper purpose, but with this difference: that the undertaking is spiritual not in the sense of being religious but in the sense of having to do with the spirit.[39]

---

[39] Rudolph, *Pilgrimage to the End of the World*: 36–39.

My point is not just the somewhat well-worn insight that what matters is the journey, rather than the destination; I contend further that the journey can be deeply meaningful, even in the absence of alternative possibilities and forking paths. After all, the path from Le Puy to Santiago de Compostela is laid out in advance. And even if we do indeed sometimes have alternative possibilities, it is not *in virtue of* the presence of forking paths that our pilgrimage down the road of life can be full of meaning—of beauty, friendship, love, frustration, tragedy, and even great triumph. As I said at the very end of *The Metaphysics of Free Will*:

> The future may—or may not—contain more than one genuinely open path: I do not know. It is quite natural to think of the future as open, but it may turn out that the various paths I picture in my mind are mere tantalizing chimeras. Employing a slightly different metaphor, there is just one line extending from the present into the past, and the future may indeed be symmetric—there may be just one line extending into the future. But even so—even if there is just one available path into the future—I may be held accountable for *how I walk down this path*. I can be blamed for taking the path of cruelty, negligence, or cowardice. And I can be praised for walking with sensitivity, attentiveness, and courage. Even if I somehow discovered there is but one path into the future, I would still care deeply how I walk down this path. I would aspire to walk with grace and dignity. I would want to have a sense of humor. Most of all, I would want to do it my way.[40]

---

[40] Fischer, *The Metaphysics of Free Will*: 216.

PART ONE

An Actual-Sequence Approach to Moral Responsibility

2

The Frankfurt Cases: The Moral of the Stories

I. Keeping up with the Joneses (and Black)

Harry Frankfurt's article, "Alternate Possibilities and Moral Responsibility," triggered a huge literature discussing whether Frankfurt presents a case (or perhaps a template for a case) in which an individual is morally responsible for behavior that he or she could not have avoided.[1] In his seminal article (which in a sense goes back to an example originally presented by John Locke in *An Essay Concerning Human Understanding*), Frankfurt seeks to impugn the Principle of Alternate Possibilities (PAP).

PAP: An agent is morally responsible for performing a given act *A* only if he or she could have done otherwise.

I have benefited from giving a previous version of this essay as the first in a series of lectures delivered at the State University of New York at Buffalo in fall 2008: The Hourani Lectures in Human Values. I am grateful to the Department of Philosophy for the opportunity to give these lectures, and I thank David Hershenov, David Braun, and John Kearns for comments on the first lecture. Also, I have delivered previous versions at Syracuse University, Cornell University, and the University of Colorado, Boulder. At Cornell, my commentator was Sean Stapleton, who gave me very helpful comments. I have learned much about these issues from presenting some of the material in this essay to two graduate seminars; I am grateful to the participants in the seminar at UCLA (winter 2006) and UC Riverside (spring 2007). The following have also given me extremely helpful comments on previous versions: Neal Tognazzini, Mark Heller, Robert Van Gulick, Carl Ginet, Derk Pereboom, Bernard Berofsky, Michael McKenna, Ishtiyaque Haji, and two anonymous readers for the *Philosophical Review*.

[1] Harry Frankfurt, "Alternate Possibilities and Moral Responsibility," *Journal of Philosophy* 66 (1969): 829–839. For some of the debates, see David Widerker and Michael McKenna, *Moral Responsibility and Alternative Possibilities: Essays on the Importance of Alternative Possibilities* (Aldershot, UK: Ashgate, 2003). For a recent contribution to the literature, see Neil Levy, "Counterfactual Intervention and Agents' Capacities," *Journal of Philosophy* 105 (2008): 223–239.

Here is a somewhat updated version of the sort of example Frankfurt presented:[2]

> Because he dares to hope that the Democrats finally have a good chance of winning the White House, the benevolent but elderly neurosurgeon, Black, has come out of retirement to participate in yet another philosophical example. (After all, what would these thought-experiments be without the venerable éminence grise—or should it be *noir*?) He has secretly inserted a chip in Jones's brain that enables Black to monitor and control Jones's activities. Black can exercise this control through a sophisticated computer that he has programmed so that, among other things, it monitors Jones's voting behavior. If Jones were to show any inclination to vote for McCain (or, let us say, anyone other than Obama), then the computer, through the chip in Jones's brain, would intervene to assure that he actually decides to vote for Obama and does so vote. But if Jones decides on his own to vote for Obama (as Black, the old progressive, would prefer), the computer does nothing but continue to monitor—without affecting—the goings-on in Jones's head.
>
> Now suppose that Jones decides to vote for Obama on his own, just as he would have if Black had not inserted the chip in his head. It seems, upon first thinking about this case, that Jones can be held morally responsible for his choice and act of voting for Obama, although he could not have chosen otherwise and he could not have done otherwise.[3]

This sort of case—a Frankfurt-style case—appears to threaten PAP. Although PAP has traditionally been accepted by both compatibilists and incompatibilists about causal determinism and moral responsibility, the denial of PAP potentially opens up an interesting new route to compatibilism about causal determinism and moral responsibility; that is, one might contend that causal determinism is perfectly compatible with moral responsibility, quite apart from the issue of whether causal determinism entails that no agent has "genuine metaphysical access to alternative possibilities." That is, a denial of PAP would seem to allow a compatibilist about causal determinism and moral responsibility to *sidestep* the contentious and evidently intractable debates about the relationship between causal determinism and "freedom to do otherwise" (or real access to alternative possibilities). Insofar as causal determinism's threat to alternative possibilities is, if not decisive, at least significant, Frankfurt's suggestion that we reject PAP would appear to help us make philosophical progress. More precisely, it would seem to allow us to avoid

---

[2] For such an example, see John Martin Fischer, "Responsibility and Control," *Journal of Philosophy* 79 (1982): 24–40.

[3] Whew! Black was right. I began writing this essay before the elections of 2008; obviously, the specifics of the case are now out of date, but what matters is the structure of the example.

getting entangled in dialectical stalemates and to reconfigure the debate in terms of whether causal determination *directly* rules out moral responsibility, that is, whether causal determination in itself and apart from considerations pertaining to alternative possibilities rules out moral responsibility. Here the ground has shifted from the traditional debates about causal determinism and alternative possibilities, and arguably it has shifted to more compatibilist-friendly terrain.[4]

Whereas some philosophers have been persuaded by Frankfurt that we should reject PAP, many have not been convinced by the arguments of Frankfurt or the proponents of Frankfurt-style compatibilism. Some skeptics reject the contention that Frankfurt has provided cases (or templates of cases) in which an individual is morally responsible for something and in which he or she could not have prevented *that very thing*; thus, these philosophers insist that we are not forced by the Frankfurt-style cases to give up PAP. Other skeptics about Frankfurt-style argumentation are willing to jettison PAP, but they insist that causal determinism rules out moral responsibility for *some reason other than eliminating alternative possibilities*. Of course, both sides of the debate here will agree that Frankfurt cases, even if they show PAP false, do not in themselves and without further argumentation establish the compatibility of causal determinism and moral responsibility.[5] But whereas "Frankfurt-style compatibilists" contend that there is no other consideration in virtue of which we should conclude that causal determination rules out moral responsibility, the skeptics will insist that there is precisely such a reason; for some, causal determination is inconsistent with an individual's being the "source" of his behavior in the way required for moral responsibility.[6]

As I said before, there is a huge literature surrounding the Frankfurt cases and their philosophical implications. In many ways the situation is similar to the literature that was triggered by Edmund Gettier's famous article, "Is Justified True Belief Knowledge?"[7] Here, I do not propose to give a comprehensive overview of the literature discussing the Frankfurt cases; nor do I aspire to go into much of the literature at all. Rather, what I hope to do is to focus on an important subset of the issues with an eye to crystallizing a crucial insight of the Frankfurt cases—the moral of the stories. Yes, the literature is large, intricate, and complicated; I can understand why Harry Frankfurt once complained to me that the literature surrounding his examples was "a young person's sport." As I become less qualified to

---

[4] For a more detailed explanation of this compatibilist strategy, and a (limited) defense of the contention that the new terrain is more compatibilist-friendly, see John Martin Fischer, "Frankfurt-Style Compatibilism," in *Contours of Agency: Essays on Themes from Harry Frankfurt*, ed. Sarah Buss and Lee Overton (Cambridge, MA: MIT Press, 2002), 1–26; reprinted in *Free Will*, 2nd ed., ed. Gary Watson (Oxford: Oxford University Press, 2003), 190–211; and John Martin Fischer, *My Way: Essays on Moral Responsibility* (New York: Oxford University Press, 2006), 124–143.

[5] For an early articulation of this point, see Fischer, "Responsibility and Control."

[6] For a development of Source Incompatibilism, see Derk Pereboom, *Living without Free Will* (New York: Cambridge University Press, 2001).

[7] Edmund Gettier, "Is Justified True Belief Knowledge?" *Analysis* 23 (1963): 121–123.

participate in such sports, I seek to find the simple, powerful lesson of the litera-ture—abstracting away from the details.

Without further ado and at the risk of spoiling the drama, here is what I take to be the basic insight of the Frankfurt cases: if causal determinism rules out moral responsibility, it is not in virtue of eliminating alternative possibilities. At the most basic level, it is that simple! I do not suppose that the Frankfurt cases provide a decisive or knockdown argument for the basic insight; rather, they provide part of a strong plausibility argument for it. Nor, as above, do I suppose that the cases—or the associated argument—in themselves establish the compat-ibility of causal determinism and moral responsibility; rather, they arguably help us to reconfigure the argumentation in a way that will be advantageous to the compatibilist.

So I claim that the moral of the Frankfurt stories is this: if causal determinism rules out moral responsibility, it is not in virtue of eliminating alternative possi-bilities. But whereas this is a rather simple point, it is highly contentious whether it is indeed a lesson we can learn from the Frankfurt cases. In my view, the most important challenge to my contention that this is the moral of the Frankfurt stories comes from an argument called "The Dilemma Defense." Philosophers such as Robert Kane, David Widerker, Carl Ginet, Keith Wyma, Stewart Goetz, Derk Pereboom, and David Palmer have vigorously explored the Dilemma Defense (although not all of these philosophers end up endorsing it).[8] In this essay I propose to present a reply to the Dilemma Defense and thereby protect what I have identi-fied as the simple, basic lesson of the Frankfurt cases.

II. The Dilemma Defense

The Dilemma Defense is one of the most potent tools in the arsenal of the first group of skeptics about Frankfurt-style argumentation: those who deny that Frankfurt cases successfully impugn PAP. Here is the argument. Note, first, that

---

[8] Robert Kane, *Free Will and Values* (Albany: State University of New York Press, 1985), and *The Significance of Free Will* (New York: Oxford University Press, 1996), 142–145; David Widerker, "Libertarianism and Frankfurt's Attack on the Principle of Alternative Possibilities," *Philosophical Review* 104 (1995): 247–261; Carl Ginet, "In Defense of the Principle of Alternative Possibilities: Why I Don't Find Frankfurt's Argument Convincing," *Philosophical Perspectives* 10 (1996): 403–417; Keith Wyma, "Moral Responsibility and Leeway for Action," *American Philosophical Quarterly* 34 (1997): 57–70; Stewart Goetz, "Frankfurt-Style Counterexamples and Begging the Question," *Midwest Studies in Philosophy* 29 (2005): 83–105; Derk Pereboom, "Reasons-Responsiveness, Alternative Possibilities, and Manipulation Arguments against Compatibilism: Reflections on John Martin Fischer's *My Way*," *Philosophical Books* 47 (2006): 198–212, and "Defending Hard Determinism Again," in *Essays on Free Will and Moral Responsibility*, ed. Nick Trakakis and Daniel Cohen (Newcastle-upon-Tyne: Cambridge Scholars Press, 2008), 1–33; and David Palmer, "New Distinctions, Some Troubles: A Reply to Haji and McKenna," *Journal of Philosophy* 102 (2005): 474–482. I have also benefited from unpublished work on these topics by David Palmer and David Goldman.

often the Frankfurt stories are told without an explicit assumption about whether causal determinism holds. So let us be explicit about this matter and first assume that causal determinism does not obtain; more specifically, assume that indeterminism obtains (at the relevant point, whatever that is taken to be) in the sequence that leads to the choice and action. Now how can Black's device help Black to know that Jones will choose to vote on his own for Obama (and indeed vote for Obama on his own)? It would seem that, given indeterminism in the right place, all the evidence Black could muster about Jones prior to his decision would leave it open that Jones at least begins to decide to vote for McCain. Of course, at that point Jones's brain would be zapped, but it would be *too late* to prevent Jones's having had access to an alternative possibility, exiguous as it might be.

Let us be even more explicit, and let us suppose that Jones decides "on his own" at t2 to vote for Obama; and imagine that Jones involuntarily exhibits some sign, such as (appropriately enough) a furrowed left brow, at an earlier time t1. When Jones furrows his left brow at t1 in this sort of way, he typically chooses at t2 to vote for the Democrat. The problem for Black is that, although this may in general be a reliable "prior sign," given indeterminism, it is possible that Jones begins to decide to vote for McCain, even though he exhibited the relevant sign—the furrowed left brow—at t1. Under the assumption of causal indeterminism (of the right sort), it seems that there is no way for Black to expunge all (relevant) alternative possibilities; thus we do not yet have a counterexample to PAP. That is, we do not yet have a case in which an individual is morally responsible for something, although he or she has no alternative possibilities. Arguably, it is the very existence of the possibility of beginning to choose to vote for McCain that renders Jones morally responsible for his actual choice and action.

Now assume that causal determinism obtains in the example. On this horn of the dilemma, the Frankfurt skeptic will insist that we cannot now baldly state that Jones is morally responsible for his choice to vote for Obama and his act of voting for Obama. After all, it is precisely the issue under debate whether causal determinism would rule out such moral responsibility; it would be question-begging to assume that causal determinism is true in the example (quite independently of the presence of Black's device) and also to hold that it is uncontroversial that Jones is morally responsible for his choice and action. Thus, again, we do not yet have a case in which we are entitled to say that an individual is morally responsible for something and yet has no alternative possibilities.

Stewart Goetz has presented an additional objection to the views of some of the proponents of Frankfurt-style compatibilism, on the deterministic horn.[9] Goetz assumes that causal determinism eliminates genuine metaphysical access to alternative possibilities. Now suppose that there is a deterministic relationship

---

[9] Goetz, "Frankfurt-Style Counterexamples and Begging the Question."

between the state of the universe at t1 and Jones's choice at t2 to vote for Obama. It follows—without any invocation of Black and his device—that Jones is unable (at t2 or just prior to t2) to choose to vote for a Republican (and to vote for a Republican). Goetz's point is that what really renders it true (on the deterministic horn) that Jones is unable to choose otherwise at t2 is the prior state of the universe at t1 combined with the laws of nature; the elderly and admittedly somewhat benighted neurosurgeon Black and his fancy device are quite beside the point. Goetz puts the point as follows:

> [The Frankfurt-style example] creates the appearance that it is Black's device, which is in the alternative sequence of events, that makes it the case that Jones is not free to choose otherwise. This appearance is *illusory* because without the obtaining of causal determinism in the actual sequence of events, the device cannot prevent Jones from making an alternative choice, and with causal determinism in the actual sequence of events it is not the device that prevents Jones from making an alternative choice. In short, if Jones is not free to choose otherwise, it is because of the occurrence of causal determinism in the actual sequence of events and not because of Black's device in the alternative sequence.[10]

Put in terms of Goetz's point, the Dilemma Defense is as follows. Either causal determinism is true (in the appropriate place) in the Frankfurt cases or it is not. If causal determinism obtains, then Black and his device "drop out"—they play no role in rendering it true that Jones is unable to do otherwise. And, given this, the putative irrelevance of Black and his device to Jones's moral responsibility is neither here nor there; it would *not* show that the fact that Jones is unable to do otherwise is irrelevant to Jones's moral responsibility.[11] And if causal determinism is false, then Black and his device are impotent—they cannot prevent Jones from at least beginning to choose to vote for McCain. Goetz suggests that it is as if Frankfurt has brought us into a "house of mirrors"; we are distracted by the intriguing philosophical machinery, and we are tricked into thinking that (on either horn) Black plays the crucial role of eliminating alternative possibilities. When the deception is revealed, it can be seen that Black and his device do *not* play this role at all.

---

[10] Ibid., 85.

[11] Although I have sympathy with Zagzebski's point, the following passage seems to be grist for Goetz's mill: "My real reaction to F[rankfurt] cases does not depend upon their being literal counterexamples to PAP. The beauty of these thought experiments is that they force us to confront what it is in a situation in virtue of which we judge the agent responsible. What we see in a[n] F[rankfurt] situation, I believe, is that we *don't care* what Black's mechanism is capable of doing because it doesn't actually do anything at all. And since the lack of alternate possibilities is tied to what the mechanism is capable of doing rather than to what it actually does, we see that we don't care whether or not the agent has alternate possibilities." Linda Zagzebski, "Does Libertarian Freedom Require Alternate Possibilities?" *Philosophical Perspectives* 14 (2000): 242–243.

III. Reply to the Dilemma Defense: The Indeterministic Horn

In this essay I wish to focus on the deterministic horn, but I will say a few words about the indeterministic horn. Previously I have argued that it is not enough for the critic of the Frankfurt cases to point to some residual alternative possibility; rather, the alternative possibility must be sufficiently *robust* to ground plausibly attributions of moral responsibility.[12] Robert Kane, who is a libertarian, agrees with me about this point; he has emphasized what he takes to be the "plurality" conditions on moral responsibility.[13] After all, it is a well-known challenge for libertarians that the *mere possibility of something different occurring* is not sufficient for the presence of the *kind of alternative possibility* involved in moral responsibility. The insufficiency of nonrobust alternative possibilities in the context of the Frankfurt examples is then a special case of the larger problem of "luck" and its relationship to control.

Various philosophers have sought to present explicitly indeterministic versions of the Frankfurt cases in which the agent has no *robust* alternative possibilities. Of particular interest to me is a class of "Buffer Zone" Frankfurt cases presented by such philosophers as David Hunt and Derk Pereboom.[14] In these cases, it is imagined that there is some *necessary condition* for the agent (say Jones) to choose to do otherwise—a necessary condition the satisfaction of which does not in itself seem enough to ground moral responsibility. Perhaps it is necessary for Jones to choose otherwise that he have a certain thought by a certain time—the thought (say) that Republicans are better at protecting national security and the fat paycheck to which Jones (although not a neurosurgeon) has become accustomed. We suppose that having this (no doubt pathetically misguided) thought (by a certain time) is both necessary for Jones to choose otherwise and not in itself causally sufficient (even together with the natural laws) for such a choice; further, it just seems that merely having the thought (perhaps not even voluntarily) is not sufficiently robust to ground an attribution of moral responsibility. Black's device can be set up so that it is triggered by the mere having of the relevant sort of thought, and it can thus prevent Jones's access to a *robust* alternative possibility.[15]

---

[12] Fischer, "Responsibility and Control."

[13] Kane, *The Significance of Free Will*, esp. 109–111; Kane defends what he calls the "plurality" condition on control that is relevant to moral responsibility. This is the same basic point as the point I have insisted upon—that *if* one adopts a model of moral responsibility that requires alternative possibilities, the alternative possibilities in question must be robust. (Kane affirms the antecedent as well as the conditional.)

[14] Pereboom, *Living without Free Will*, esp. 18–28; and David Hunt, "Moral Responsibility and Unavoidable Action," *Philosophical Studies* 97 (2000): 195–227, and "Moral Responsibility and Buffered Alternatives," *Midwest Studies in Philosophy* 29 (2005): 126–145.

[15] The distinctive feature of a Buffer Case is not merely the presence of a necessary condition for doing otherwise. Rather, this type of case features a necessary condition for doing otherwise *the absence of which at any specific time will not be a sufficient condition for the agent performing the action he or she does.* In Pereboom's "Tax Evasion," the necessary condition for not deciding to evade taxes, that is, the

In the Buffer Zone versions of the Frankfurt cases, it is as though a "no-man's land" is established between the border of Country A and Country B. To get from Country A to Country B, it is necessary that one enter the no-man's land, but if one does, one can still avoid or be prevented from entering Country B. The no-man's land is a kind of buffer zone. Such examples, although contentious, have some promise of providing explicitly indeterministic versions of the Frankfurt cases in which an agent lacks the *relevant kind of alternative possibility* and yet is morally responsible.

I certainly recognize that I have only sketched the indeterministic cases, and I have only scratched the surface of an adequate analysis. But for my purposes here, I simply want to motivate the idea that the jury is still out with respect to the indeterministic horn of the Dilemma Defense. I wish to emphasize that it is not enough to point out that if indeterminism obtains, there will always be *some sort of residual alternative possibility*; the alternative possibility must be of the right sort—it must be sufficiently robust to ground attributions of moral responsibility. Arguably, explicitly indeterministic versions of the Frankfurt cases can be developed in which it is highly plausible that the agent is morally responsible and yet lacks access to robust alternative possibilities. Intuitively, the lack of access to robust alternative possibilities in these cases is *irrelevant* to the agent's status as morally responsible.

IV. Reply to the Dilemma Defense: The Deterministic Horn

Return to what I have articulated as the kernel insight of the Frankfurt cases: if causal determinism rules out moral responsibility, it is not in virtue of eliminating alternative possibilities. In previous work I suggested a "two-step" reply to the Frankfurt skeptics, on the deterministic horn.[16] That is, supposing that we explicitly assume that causal determinism obtains in the cases, it is important first to note that I do *not* propose that we precipitously conclude, from mere reflection on the cases, that (say) Jones is morally responsible for his choice and action. Rather, the initial conclusion is that if he is not morally responsible, it is not because he lacks appropriate alternative possibilities. *This initial conclusion does not beg the question against the incompatibilist.* Further, a Frankfurt-style compatibilist will go on to consider various *other* reasons why causal determinism might be alleged to rule out moral responsibility. If such a theorist concludes that, since there are

---

specified level of attentiveness to the moral reasons, is the right sort of necessary condition since its absence at any specific time is not a sufficient condition for Joe's deciding to evade taxes. Rather, its absence at any specific time is compatible with both Joe's deciding to evade taxes and with his not deciding to evade taxes. Pereboom, *Living without Free Will*, 18–28.

[16] John Martin Fischer, "Recent Work on Moral Responsibility," *Ethics* 110 (1999): 93–139; and "Frankfurt-Style Compatibilism."

no *other* reasons that constitute good and sufficient reasons to believe that causal determinism rules out moral responsibility, causal determinism is indeed compatible with moral responsibility, this too would *not* beg the question against the incompatibilist.

But various philosophers have challenged my initial conclusion that if Jones is not morally responsible, this is not because he has no (sufficiently robust) alternative possibility.[17] My basis for this conclusion was that Black's role in the example both rendered it true that Jones could not choose (and do) otherwise and also seemed to me to be *irrelevant* to Jones's moral responsibility. These philosophers have pointed out that Black and his device *in themselves* do *not* render it true that Jones could not have chosen or done otherwise. Rather, it is only with the additional assumption of causal determinism that one can eliminate alternative possibilities. But now Goetz's point becomes pressing: if causal determinism *already* rules out access to alternative possibilities, Black "drops out," and his role becomes nugatory. Thus, the intuition that might be elicited by the Frankfurt cases to the effect that Black is *irrelevant* to Jones's moral responsibility is seen to be quite beside the point. Since Black alone, by himself, is *not* a factor that renders it true that Jones cannot choose and do otherwise, we do not yet have an argument that Jones's inability to choose and do otherwise is irrelevant to his moral responsibility.

To bring out the force of the objection to my previous attempt to defend Frankfurt-style compatibilism, given the deterministic horn, note that I contended that in the Frankfurt cases there are *two* analytically separable factors that render it true that the relevant agent (Jones) lacks genuine metaphysical access to alternative possibilities: Black (and his device), on the one hand, and causal determination, on the other.[18] Then I presented the following sort of argument:

1. Assume that causal determinism obtains and that the Frankfurt case of Jones and Black unfolds as above.
2. Black's presence (and device) and dispositions in themselves and apart from the assumption of causal determinism rule out Jones's access to alternative possibilities. (Causal determinism in itself and apart from Black also rules out alternative possibilities, but this will not be pertinent here.)
3. Black's presence (and device) and dispositions in themselves are irrelevant to moral responsibility.
Thus, from 2 and 3:
4. Lack of alternative possibilities is in itself irrelevant to moral responsibility.
Thus:

[17] For a sampling, see the proponents of the Dilemma Defense referred to in n. 8.
[18] Fischer, "Free Will and Moral Responsibility," in *Oxford Handbook of Ethical Theory*, ed. David Copp (New York: Oxford University Press, 2006), 321–354; reprinted in Fischer, *My Way*, 182–216.

5. If causal determinism rules out moral responsibility, it is not in virtue of eliminating access to alternative possibilities.

The objection is that Black's presence (and device) and dispositions in themselves and apart from the assumption of causal determinism do *not* eliminate alternative possibilities. As above, it is *only* with the assumption of a causally deterministic relationship between the state of the universe at t1 and Jones's choice at t2 that the possibility of Jones at least *beginning* to choose to vote for McCain is eliminated. Thus, premise 2 is false, and the argument is unsound.

IV.1. THE AGNOSTIC ASSUMPTION

I accept the criticism, but I wish to present a refined articulation of the basic insight I have been seeking to capture. I still think that one can defend Frankfurt-style compatibilism, on the deterministic horn, and that the defense will be similar to the defense I articulated above; but it will be subtly different in a way that both better captures the basic insight and also avoids the criticisms I have sketched. A key point is that we begin by assuming causal determinism, but we *take no stand* about whether causal determinism eliminates genuine metaphysical access to alternative possibilities. That is, we remain officially *agnostic* about the relationship between causal determinism and freedom to choose and do otherwise. This agnosticism is congenial to me, as it is officially built into my doctrine of Semicompatibilism. Semicompatibilism, after all, is simply the claim that causal determinism is compatible with moral responsibility, quite apart from whether causal determinism eliminates access to alternative possibilities. Thus, agnosticism about the relationship between causal determinism and alternative possibilities is part of the official doctrine of Semicompatibilism, although I myself am inclined to accept (as an additional view) that causal determinism eliminates access to alternative possibilities. At the very least, we should be able to seriously entertain the hypothesis of agnosticism and begin our newly formulated defense of Frankfurt-style compatibilism with it.

So we assume causal determinism obtains and that the case of Jones and Black unfolds as above, and we make *no* assumption about the relationship between causal determinism and access to alternative possibilities. Black checks and sees the "prior sign" at t1 that is associated with a subsequent vote for the Democrat— say, the furrowed *left* brow. Given that Black knows that causal determinism obtains, he can now relax, as it were; under these circumstances, Black knows that Jones in fact will subsequently choose to vote for Obama and carry out that choice. It is *also* true, given Black's device and dispositions, that if Jones were to show the sign at t1 associated with voting for a Republican at t2 (appropriately enough, the furrowed *right* brow), Black's device would swing into action and stimulate Jones's brain so as to ensure that he chooses at t2 to vote for Obama and does so vote at t3. I claim that this additional fact, when added to the assumption of causal determinism and the fact that Black can thus be sure that Jones's showing the prior sign at t1 will in fact be followed by his choosing accordingly at t2, renders it true that Jones cannot at t2 choose to vote for McCain (or subsequently vote for McCain). These two facts *together* make it the case that Jones cannot at t2 choose to vote for McCain or carry out such a choice.

Note that in the case as analyzed I do not claim that Jones cannot at t1 involuntarily exhibit a different sign—the sign associated with his subsequently voting for a Republican. After all, we are *not* at this point in the argument assuming that causal determinism expunges alternative possibilities. But the possibility of exhibiting a different sign is a mere flicker of freedom and obviously not sufficiently robust to ground attributions of moral responsibility. We can see, then, that the deterministic example works in a similar way as the indeterministic examples: they are all cases in which the relevant agent lacks access to *robust* alternative possibilities (even if they in fact have access to mere flickers of freedom).

Note also that it is a crucial feature of the case, as I am presenting it, that it is a necessary condition of Jones's choosing at t2 to vote for McCain (and so voting at t3) that he have (say) furrowed his right brow by t1. That is, the necessary-condition-specifying conditional, "If Jones were to choose at t2 to vote for McCain, he would have (say) furrowed his right brow by t1," must be true in the example. Given that my interpretation of the example assumes that this sort of conditional must be true, this raises the question of whether my example is simply a "special case" of the Buffer Zone strategy (discussed previously); and, given this, one might wonder why I need to assume causal determinism at all.[19]

I agree that my strategy here is similar to the Buffer Zone versions of the cases and that its plausibility comes from a similar source. That is, it seems that in the example I have presented, it is a necessary condition of not voting for Obama that Jones raise his right eyebrow in advance. So, in order not to vote for Obama after raising his left eyebrow at t1, Jones would have to have raised his right eyebrow first, whereupon Black would intervene. In this interpretation, it seems clear that Jones is unable at t2 not to vote for Obama, and it also might appear as if we do not need to assume causal determinism.

I do not have any objection to this construal of the case. It is not at all clear that the example *must* be construed deterministically. All I wish to show here is that a Frankfurt case that *is* clearly deterministic can be successful. There are various reasons why I believe that it is helpful to have an explicitly causally deterministic version of the Frankfurt cases (and the associated reply to the deterministic horn of the Dilemma Defense). First, various philosophers (I am not one of them) hold that moral responsibility *requires* causal determinism; they contend that we would not have the sort of control associated with moral responsibility in the absence of causal determination of our choices and actions.

---

[19] Here I am indebted to Derk Pereboom.

Additionally, it may well be the case that the relevant necessary-condition-specifying conditionals are easier to defend in the context of causal determination; in the absence of causal determination, many philosophers would resist the claim that it can be a necessary condition of an agent's performing a certain action that (for example) he or she have had a certain thought in the past. These philosophers—and presumably including Sartre—would deny that the agent cannot begin to choose to perform the relevant action at the subsequent time, despite not having shown the appropriate sign at the previous time; they would insist that an agent's freedom cannot be constrained in this way. So, for instance, these philosophers would say that if indeterminism obtains (in the relevant place), it would have to be possible for Jones not to vote for Obama after raising his left eyebrow at t1 *without* raising his right eyebrow first. It is hard to *prove* that this contention is false. Thus, although I am in considerable sympathy with the Buffer Zone strategy, it may well be useful to have available a reply to the deterministic horn of the Dilemma Defense.[20]

So the situation is as follows. The assumption of causal determinism cannot *in itself* be taken (in this dialectical context) to entail that Jones cannot at t2 choose otherwise. It is only after the addition of Black and his device and dispositions that it follows that Jones cannot at t2 choose otherwise. So Black and the associated machinery are not supernumerary or a dangling and redundant distraction; Black (unlike many people these days) is not unemployed. Of course, Black and his device and dispositions may not be enough to rule out alternative possibilities without the assumption of causal determinism; but I do not see any objection to conceding this fact and yet providing a defense of Frankfurt-style compatibilism, regimented as follows:

1. Assume that causal determinism obtains and that the Frankfurt case of Jones and Black unfolds as above.
2. At this point in the argument, causal determinism is not assumed in itself to rule out access to alternative possibilities. (Neither is it to be supposed here that Black's presence, device, and dispositions in themselves rule out such access.)
3. Causal determinism plus Black's presence, device, and dispositions rule out Jones's freedom at t2 to choose otherwise.
4. If Jones is not morally responsible for choosing at t2 to vote for Obama at t3, it is not in virtue of the *mere* fact that he was not free at t2 to choose otherwise.

---

[20] Note that if my overall template offered in this essay for a reply to the Dilemma Defense is satisfactory, then I will have shown that an example that features determinism in the actual sequence can sidestep Goetz's criticism to the effect that Black "drops out." Nothing that Pereboom or Hunt say about the Buffer Zone cases can explain why this is so. (I thank Derk Pereboom for this generous point.)

Thus:

5. If causal determinism rules out Jones's moral responsibility for his choice at t2, it is *not* in virtue of its eliminating alternative possibilities (if in fact it does eliminate alternative possibilities).[21]

The generalized conclusion is precisely what I have identified as the moral of the Frankfurt stories: if causal determinism rules out moral responsibility, it is not in virtue of eliminating alternative possibilities. We have derived this conclusion by invoking a Frankfurt case that assumes causal determinism; but since it explicitly does *not* presuppose that causal determinism rules out alternative possibilities, there is a distinctive and substantive role for Black to play. In my previous defense of Frankfurt-style compatibilism (given the deterministic horn of the Dilemma), I had supposed that both causal determinism and Black were in themselves sufficient to rule out alternative possibilities; here I have supposed (for the sake of the argument) that neither can be assumed in itself to be sufficient, but that they work in combination to expunge alternative possibilities.

I wish to say a few more words about premise 3 and also the transition from 3 to 4. Begin with 3. Why exactly do I say that causal determinism plus Black rules out alternative possibilities, when I am not here supposing that mere causal determinism does not? Well, it is supposed to work as follows. Black knows that, given that Jones has exhibited the Democratic sign at t1, he need not intervene at all since Jones is going to vote for the Democrat. But, given our assumptions, Jones *can* exhibit the Republican sign at t1. But Black will be there monitoring the situation, and if he were to see the Republican sign at t1, then he would immediately zap Jones's brain and thereby prevent Jones from choosing to vote for McCain at t2 (or voting for McCain at t3). Without Black, there is nothing in the example that rules out Jones's power to choose and do otherwise; but with Black (together with causal determinism), we get the result that Jones cannot choose at t2 to vote for McCain (and cannot so vote at t3). (Without the assumption of causal determinism, as I pointed out, even if Jones shows the Democratic sign at t1, Jones might still begin to choose to vote for McCain at t2.)[22]

---

[21] Note that certain philosophers hold that if the prior sign (say Jones's furrowing his left eyebrow at t1) *causally determines* his choice at t2, then he cannot be morally responsible for it. Of course, this is precisely what is at issue, and so it is not available at this point in the development of the dialectic. Further, it is important to see that the conclusion of the argument (5) is completely compatible with the contention in question. (5) does not state that causal determination does not rule out moral responsibility; rather, it makes a *conditional* claim. This shows that, if one were to contend that the prior sign's causally determining the subsequent choice rules out moral responsibility for that choice, this would be no objection to my argument here; at this point in the dialectic, I have no horse in that race.

[22] Now it might seem that my argument would work equally well if it is simply true at t1 that Jones will choose to vote for McCain at t2 (and Jones knows this), and thus that the assumption of causal determinism is not really necessary. (I am grateful to Neal Tognazzini for this point.) Perhaps this is so, but it is essentially contentious whether it could be true at t1 that Jones would choose at t2 to vote for McCain unless causal determinism were true. That is, it is unclear that "Jones will choose at t2 to vote

How exactly do I get from premise 3 to 4? I want to hold the following three claims:

A. Black's device together with causal determinism rule out Jones's ability to do otherwise, even though I am not supposing (at this stage of the argument) that either would do so on its own.
B. Black's device and dispositions are irrelevant to Jones's moral responsibility.
C. The fact that Black's device and dispositions in a causally deterministic context rule out Jones's freedom to choose and do otherwise is irrelevant to Jones's moral responsibility.

Claim C underwrites the transition from premise 3 to 4. But whereas it is relatively clear that I can assert A and B without begging the question against the incompatibilist, can I legitimately hold C without begging the question against the incompatibilist?[23] Although Black and his device are clearly irrelevant to Jones's moral responsibility, causal determinism cannot be taken to be irrelevant to Jones's moral responsibility. (After all, causal determinism might rule out moral responsibility *directly*, quite apart from considerations pertaining to alternative possibilities.) But given that causal determinism is not clearly irrelevant, it seems questionable to claim that something for which causal determinism is in part responsible—namely, Jones's lack of alternatives—is irrelevant to Jones's moral responsibility. That is, since causal determinism is needed in order to deracinate alternative possibilities, then it might seem that I cannot claim that lack of alternative possibilities is irrelevant to moral responsibility without implicitly claiming that causal determinism is irrelevant. And this is not dialectically kosher.

But there is nothing inappropriate in the move from 3 to 4—nothing, as far as I can see, that violates the dietary laws of philosophical arguments. (That is not to say that the conclusion will be digestible, or even palatable, to the Frankfurt skeptics—but that's a different issue entirely.) In order to see more clearly that there is nothing inappropriate in the move from 3 to 4 via Claim C, consider the following analogy. Suppose that one needs two medicines, M1 and M2, to cure Disease D. Each medicine is necessary for the cure, and together they are sufficient. Suppose, further, that the combination of M1 and M2 produces two distinct effects: an increase in Substance S in the blood and an independent increase in the body temperature. Additionally, it turns out that M1 and M2 are each necessary for the increase in body temperature (as well as the cure). Imagine, further, that it is

---

for McCain" can be true at t1 without a truthmaker that obtains at t1; and it is unclear that such a truthmaker could exist at t1 unless causal determinism were true. Here there are interesting questions (beyond the scope of this essay) about the relationship between the doctrines of eternalism and presentism in philosophy of time and the Frankfurt examples.

[23] I am indebted to Neal Tognazzini for this question.

the increase in Substance S that leads to the cure of D; the increase in body temperature is causally inefficacious in curing the disease.

It seems that this structure of claims is entirely coherent. Further, it seems to me that it is analogous to the situation with respect to causal determinism, moral responsibility, and alternative possibilities in the Frankfurt case we have discussed. That is, M2 is necessary for the increase in body temperature, but the fact that M1 and M2 together cause an increase in body temperature is *irrelevant* to the cure of the disease, even though M2 (together with M1) is clearly relevant to the cure of the disease. Similarly, the fact that causal determinism together with Black rule out alternative possibilities is *irrelevant* to Jones's moral responsibility, even though causal determinism may well be relevant to Jones's moral responsibility. (E.g., it may be that causal determination *also* issues in lack of "sourcehood," in a sense relevant to moral responsibility.) Thus, I can maintain Claim C, and the transition from 3 to 4 need not implicitly beg the question against the incompatibilist.

In this section I have adopted the assumption of agnosticism about the relationship between causal determinism and access to alternative possibilities, and I have essentially considered two options, one on which the assumption of causal determinism is *not* required and one on which it is. (More carefully, although I have in this section taken it as a working hypothesis that causal determinism is true in the case under discussion, I have also paused to consider whether the case could be construed indeterministically.) I have argued that on *either* option, the case is successful. Here I have not contended that we *must* adopt the deterministic option, only that we *can*. My primary aim in this section has been to show that there is no dialectical impropriety in construing the case deterministically.

IV.2. RELAXATION OF THE ASSUMPTION OF AGNOSTICISM

Thus far I have insisted on agnosticism, but I shall now relax this assumption. Although some philosophers believe that the assumption (or even a compatibilist assumption here) is *essential* to the defense of Frankfurt-style compatibilism (on the deterministic horn), I contend that a similar defense can be mounted, even with the strong assumption that causal determinism eliminates access to alternative possibilities.[24] So we make all the same assumptions as above, but this time we also assume that causal determinism is incompatible with genuine metaphysical access

---

[24] Here I disagree with Haji and McKenna: Ishtiyaque Haji and Michael McKenna, "Dialectical Delicacies in the Debate about Freedom and Alternative Possibilities," *Journal of Philosophy* 101 (2004): 299–314, and "Defending Frankfurt's Argument in Deterministic Contexts: A Reply to Palmer," *Journal of Philosophy* 103 (2006): 363–372. Although I have considerable sympathy for their views, and I have learned much from their work on these topics, my position is even bolder than theirs. Of course, if necessary, one could fall back on a more conservative approach, such as that of Haji and McKenna, according to which the Frankfurt examples would target only a certain audience—the uncommitted voters, as it were.

to alternative possibilities. I claim that *exactly the same core argument* as employed above can be given, even in the context of the incompatibilist assumption. In fact, nothing in the argument *uses* or *exploits* the assumption that causal determinism is incompatible with alternative possibilities; thus, the argument can proceed in *exactly the same way* as above. That is, one first notes that Black can, as it were, relax when he sees that Jones has exhibited at t1 the sign associated with Jones's voting Democratic. Also, we know that if Jones were to show the sign associated with subsequent Republican voting, Black's device would zap his brain, thus ensuring a Democratic vote. These facts make it the case that Jones cannot at t2 choose otherwise; we have not invoked the incompatibilist assumption.

But now Goetz might press his point, saying that causal determinism "already" rules out alternative possibilities; thus there is no dialectical space for Black to play a role in eliminating alternative possibilities. But I frankly cannot see why it makes a difference to relax the assumption of agnosticism and move to an incompatibilistic assumption about the relationship between causal determinism and access to alternative possibilities. And it is not at all clear that the mere fact that a prior state of the universe (together with the laws of nature) explains why Jones cannot at t2 choose otherwise entails that *no other fact* can play this sort of explanatory role.[25] Why does the explanation in terms of causal determination "crowd out" all other explanations, including the explanation in which Black plays a crucial role?

Let's say that materialism about mental states is true, and, further, that causal determinism obtains. So there presumably exists an explanation of an agent's choices and behavior entirely in terms of physical states and laws of nature. Why does it follow—without all sorts of additional considerations and perhaps fancy philosophical footwork—that we cannot also have a perfectly good explanation of the agent's choices and behavior in terms of his desires, beliefs, and intentions? Why is it *just obvious* that the existence of the one sort of explanation crowds out the other? Why, more specifically, is it *just obvious* that a prior state of the universe (together with the laws of nature) explaining why Jones cannot at t2 choose otherwise leaves no room for *any other explanation* of Jones's inability—such as the presence of Black, his device, and his dispositions (in a causally deterministic context)?[26]

It has become a kind of conventional wisdom that the Frankfurt cases that feature determinism in the actual sequence cannot be used on an "audience" of committed incompatibilists about causal determinism and genuine access to alternative possibilities. But my argument shows that this is a gratuitous

---

[25] For this point, see Haji and McKenna, "Defending Frankfurt's Argument in Deterministic Contexts"; I have also benefited from reading unpublished material by Michael McKenna.

[26] For a classic development of the notion that the belief-desire explanation and the "deterministic" explanation are compatible, see Daniel C. Dennett, "Mechanism and Responsibility," in *Essays on Freedom of Action*, ed. Ted Honderich (Boston: Routledge and Kegan Paul, 1973), 157–184. Dennett has argued persuasively that we can explain the behavior of the same creature (or object) either mechanistically or teleologically; the explanations are entirely compatible.

concession.[27] The argument I employed above to defend Frankfurt-style compatibilism, given the deterministic horn, can be employed without any changes within the context of an incompatibilistic assumption. As far as I can see, the argument proceeds in exactly the same way. Further, the contention that since causal determination rules out alternative possibilities, there can be no *other* factor that eliminates alternative possibilities (or the invocation of which explains the lack of alternative possibilities) is, at best, highly controversial.

V. Widerker's Critique

It might be illuminating to apply the analysis of the previous section to David Widerker's influential version of the Dilemma Defense. Widerker lays out the following thesis:

> (IRR): There may be circumstances in which a person performs some action which although they make it impossible for him to avoid performing that action, they in no way bring it about that he performs it.[28]

He then contends that Frankfurt's case against PAP "depends crucially on his ability to convince us of the plausibility of IRR."[29] Widerker goes on to argue that Frankfurt and his followers have been unable to provide a scenario in virtue of which IRR would be true. Widerker presents his own (rather ghoulish) version of a Frankfurt case, in which

> (1) If Jones is blushing at t1, then, provided no one intervenes, Jones will decide at t2 to kill Smith

plays an important part. For Widerker, (1) specifies the prior sign of Jones's actual decision. Now Widerker says:

> My strategy, then, of resisting Frankfurt's argument for IRR is to put before Frankfurt the following dilemma: Either the truth of (1) is grounded in some fact that is causally sufficient (in the circumstances) for Jones's decision at t2 to kill Smith, or it is not. If it is, then the situation described by Frankfurt is not an IRR situation, since the factor that makes it impossible for Jones to

---

[27] Thus, Haji and McKenna are incorrect in their restriction of the appropriate target audience. In more recent work, Haji has presented a Frankfurt case that features causal determinism in the actual sequence: Ishtiyaque Haji, *Incompatibilism's Allure* (Peterborough, Ontario: Broadview Press, 2009), 63–76.

[28] Widerker, "Libertarianism and Frankfurt's Attack on the Principle of Alternative Possibilities," 248.

[29] Ibid., 248–249; for a similar thesis, see David Widerker and Michael McKenna, "Introduction," in Widerker and McKenna, *Moral Responsibility and Alternative Possibilities*, 1–16; and David Widerker, "A Defense of Frankfurt-Friendly Libertarianism," *Philosophical Explorations* 12 (2009): 87–108.

avoid his decision to kill Smith *does* bring about that decision. On the other hand, if the truth of (1) is not thus grounded, it is hard to see how Jones's decision is unavoidable.[30]

In an interesting footnote to this passage, Widerker says, "Frankfurt seems to concede that to ensure that Jones's decision to kill Smith is unavoidable, the decision has to be caused by an earlier state of Jones's. This is puzzling given that he undertakes to establish a thesis such as IRR."[31]

But I would reply that Frankfurt need not seek to establish IRR, and, more important, he would not accept Widerker's contention that IRR is crucial to his (Frankfurt's) case against PAP. This is because IRR would rule out any causally deterministic version of the Frankfurt cases (given that "bring about" is understood deterministically, which is Widerker's intended interpretation here). Given the analysis I offered in the previous section, it should be clear that it is not appropriate to rule out *ex ante* a causally deterministic version of the Frankfurt cases.

How might Widerker defend his claim that IRR is required for the case against PAP? Of course, it is not decisive what Frankfurt himself has suggested or even said; the question is about the logic of the situation. And given the analysis of the previous section, Widerker cannot simply say that any causally deterministic version of the cases would be question-begging. As I argued above, there may be cases in which some package of factors deterministically brings about a choice, but where it is intuitively plausible that its ruling out the freedom to make a different choice is *irrelevant* to the agent's moral responsibility. This is all that is required to get the case against PAP going. It is *not* necessary here to assume or presuppose that the factor's bringing about the choice deterministically is irrelevant to the agent's moral responsibility, and thus such a scenario need not beg the question against an incompatibilist.

Thus Widerker is not entitled to his contention that defending IRR is crucial to the case against PAP, and it becomes less puzzling as to why Frankfurt suggested that in order to ensure that (say) Jones's decision to kill Smith is unavoidable, it would have had to be (deterministically) caused by an earlier state of Jones's. In any case, to force proponents of the Frankfurt cases as providing counterexamples to PAP to defend IRR is to put them in a Procrustean Bed.

VI. Conclusion: The Death of the Dilemma Defense

The literature surrounding the Frankfurt cases is voluminous and somewhat daunting. But despite the complicated nature of much of the discussion, the cases

---

[30] Widerker, "Libertarianism and Frankfurt's Attack on the Principle of Alternative Possibilities," 251.
[31] Ibid., 251, n. 8.

strike a chord. They continue to compel and fascinate in part because they exhibit a distinctive structure that helps us to see a set of simple, powerful points. When we consider examples with this signature structure (involving preemptive over-determination), an initial reaction is that there are cases in which the agent's lack of access to a certain sort of alternative possibility appears to be irrelevant to his or her status as morally responsible for the relevant behavior. If this is correct, then PAP appears to be false. Building on this initial reaction, we can rather naturally and straightforwardly be brought to the view that if causal determinism (or, for that matter, God's omniscience) rules out moral responsibility, it is *not* in virtue of eliminating alternative possibilities. This insight can be an important part of a defense of compatibilism about causal determinism (or, say, God's omniscience) and moral responsibility.

Upon reflection, many philosophers have resisted accepting even the initial reaction to the cases. One of the most powerful bases for their skepticism is the Dilemma Defense. Indeed, a large cohort of philosophers appears to think that the Dilemma Defense, in some form or other, is a decisive argument against Frankfurt-style compatibilism (or, more precisely, the first step in such compatibilism—the rejection of PAP). I have here sought to defend Frankfurt-style compatibilism against the Dilemma Defense.

A key part of my strategy is to emphasize that even a true believer in PAP should accept that the alternative possibilities in question must be *robust*. That is, it is *not* enough to protect PAP to identify *any old alternative possibility*. The possibilities must have the features in virtue of which their existence can plausibly ground attributions of moral responsibility; they must be *robust*. This key insight drives the most promising indeterministic versions of the Frankfurt cases, and it also drives my strategy for developing deterministic versions of the cases. I have argued here that we can give deterministic versions of the Frankfurt cases that do *not* beg the question against incompatibilists and that give a distinctive and substantive role to Black (the "counterfactual intervener").

Thinking about the Frankfurt examples may sometimes issue in a kind of philosophical vertigo (as can consideration of the complicated examples inspired by Gettier), but this is not a necessary implication of the cases. Rather than stepping into a house of mirrors, employing Frankfurt cases is more like using a magnifying glass that can assist us in prying apart features that are conflated by the unaided philosophical eye. A careful evaluation of the cases can help us to see even more clearly the simple lesson that moral responsibility is a matter of *how I walk down the path of life*, rather than selection from among a suite of available options. In taking the path that extends into the future, I may exhibit the kind of control that is the basis of moral responsibility, even if I lack genuine access to other paths. And in displaying this signature sort of control, I can do it *my way*, even in a causally deterministic world.

Given the history of debates about the Frankfurt cases, it would be naive in the extreme to suppose that this will be the "last word" on the examples, or that everyone will agree with my "coroner's report" on the status of the Dilemma Defense. Nevertheless, and especially in light of the widespread acceptance of the strategy of the Dilemma Defense, I believe that it is important to lay out the template for a reply to this strategy. I thus unfurl my banner and proclaim, "Mission Accomplished!"

3

Freedom, Foreknowledge, and Frankfurt: A Reply to Vihvelin

I. Introduction

In a fascinating and challenging article, Kadri Vihvelin presents a spirited and vigorous critique of the strategy of defending compatibilism about causal determinism and moral responsibility that employs (in part, at least) the "Frankfurt-examples."[1] Here is her presentation of such an example:

> ...Jones...chooses to perform, and succeeds in performing, some action X. Tell the story so that it is vividly clear that Jones is morally responsible for doing X. If you are a libertarian, you may specify that Jones is an indeterministic agent who can choose otherwise, given the actual past and the laws. If you are a compatibilist, you may fill in the details so that Jones does X in a way that satisfies your favorite account of the counterfactual or dispositional facts that make it true that Jones could have done otherwise in the sense you think relevant to responsibility. Now, add to your story the following facts: there is standing in the wings another agent, Black. Black is interested in what Jones does. In particular, he wants Jones to do X and, moreover, Black has it in his power to prevent Jones from doing anything other than X.
>
> The addition of Black to the story means that Jones could not have done other than X. But, Frankfurt argued, Jones is still responsible for doing X. After all, though Black could have intervened, he didn't. He didn't have to. Jones chose to do X and did X without any interference from Black. So the addition of Black to our story doesn't remove or in any way diminish Jones's responsibility for doing X.
>
> Such is the recipe for telling a Frankfurt story.[2]

---

[1] Kadri Vihvelin, "Freedom, Foreknowledge, and the Principle of Alternate Possibilities," *Canadian Journal of Philosophy* 8 (2000): 1–24.
[2] "Freedom, Foreknowledge, and the Principle of Alternate Possibilities," 4.

Vihvelin is a vigorous critic of the Frankfurt stories.[3] Vihvelin's claims are vehement, and her argument intriguing. In light of these facts and also because I believe the issues are important, I wish to explore and critically evaluate her argument.[4] I shall begin by laying out the skeletal structure of the argument, after which I shall offer some critical ruminations.

II. Vihvelin's Critique of Frankfurt-Style Compatibilism

The Frankfurt examples purport to show that an agent can be morally responsible for his actions (and even choices), even if he could not have done otherwise.[5] The examples actually go back (in some form or another) to John Locke, who argued that a man could voluntarily stay in a room, even though, unbeknownst to the man, the door to the room is locked.[6] The examples have been highly contentious, and their analysis and significance have generated a huge literature.[7] Some of us have agreed with Frankfurt's claim that moral responsibility does not require alternative possibilities, and additionally we have suggested that this fact can help in an overall argument (an argument that employs other ingredients as well) for

---

[3] Among other strongly critical statements, Vihvelin says:

> If Frankfurt's aim was to convince libertarians that even if determinism renders us unable to do otherwise, it does not undermine responsibility, he has failed. If his aim was to make it easier to defend compatibilism, he has failed. And if his aim was to bypass questions about the truth-conditions of "can do otherwise" claims, he has also failed, for the debate that has arisen in the wake of his original thought experiment is now mired deep in the very metaphysical questions he sought to avoid.

> It is my view that this literature is a philosophical dead end. Although I am a compatibilist, I think that Frankfurt's strategy for defending compatibilism is a bad one. If we begin with the commonsense view that someone is morally responsible only if she could have done otherwise, then Frankfurt stories will not and *should not* change our minds. If we are persuaded by Frankfurt, it is because we have been taken in by a bad argument ("Freedom, Foreknowledge, and the Principle of Alternate Possibilities," 2–3).

[4] In a recent post on the blog, "The Garden of Forking Paths," (http:gfp.typepad.com), Terrance Tomkow states:

> It seems to me that Kadri Vihvelin (USC) demonstrated some time ago (CJP 2000) that Frankfurt's arguments turn on a modal fallacy. No matter how you tell these stories, Frankfurt Style Cases simply fail to describe agents who "cannot do otherwise."
> If that's so then FSC cases have nothing to tell us about free will and the whole of the debate about FSCs has been a snare and a delusion.
> To my knowledge no one has answered Vihvelin's arguments. So my question is: does anyone have an answer to Vihvelin or does the Frankfurt literature just keep stumbling forward out of inertia?

[5] Harry G. Frankfurt, "Alternative Possibilities and Moral Responsibility," *Journal of Philosophy* 66 (1969): 829–839.

[6] John Locke, *An Essay Concerning Human Understanding*, bk. 2, chap.21, sec. 10.

[7] For some of this literature, see John Martin Fischer, "Some Recent Work on Moral Responsibility," *Ethics* 111 (1999): 99–137; and David Widerker and Michael McKenna, eds., *Moral Responsibility and Alternative Possibilities: Essays on the Importance of Alternative Possibilities* (Aldershot, U.K.: Ashgate 2003), 235–250.

the compatibility of causal determinism and moral responsibility.[8] My contention has been that, even though the arguments fall short of being decisive, there are strong plausibility arguments for the conclusion that the Frankfurt examples show that moral responsibility does not require alternative possibilities. Further, I have contended that the elements of the *direct* arguments for the incompatibility of causal determination and moral responsibility are considerably weaker than the ingredients of the arguments for the incompatibility of causal determinism and genuine metaphysical access to alternative possibilities (and thus the *indirect* arguments for the incompatibility of causal determinism and moral responsibility).[9]

Vihvelin believes that all of the participants in the debates about the Frankfurt examples have failed to see some fundamental distinctions and logical problems. She highlights this view as follows:

> I think we should have avoided this mess. Things went wrong from the start. No one should ever have been persuaded by Frankfurt's argument.[10]

Vihvelin begins her diagnosis of the errors of those of us who have invoked the Frankfurt examples by drawing a distinction between "two ways of getting someone to do what you want":

> Suppose you want to ensure that someone does whatever you want him to do, but, like Black, prefer to avoid showing your hand unnecessarily. There are two different methods you might employ…I will call these "the method of conditional intervention" and "the method of counterfactual intervention."
>
> What makes someone a *conditional intervener* is the fact that his intervention is causally triggered by the beginnings of any action (overt or mental) contrary to the intervener's plan. If the subject begins to try or begins to do any undesired action, the intervener will prevent him from succeeding.
>
> …What makes someone a *counterfactual intervener* is the fact that his intervention is causally triggered, *not* by the subject's trying or beginning to act contrary to the intervener's plan, but by some *earlier* event that is a reliable indicator of the fact that the subject will, in the absence of intervention, choose or act contrary to the intervener's wishes. This earlier event might be a blush, twitch, or other involuntary sign that occurs just before the subject begins to make an unwanted decision…[11]

---

[8] John Martin Fischer, *The Metaphysics of Free Will: An Essay on Control* (Oxford: Blackwell Publishers 1994); "Frankfurt-Type Compatibilism," in S. Buss and L. Overton, eds., *Contours of Agency: Essays on Themes from Harry Frankfurt* (Cambridge, MA: The MIT Press 2002), 1–26, reprinted in G. Watson, ed., *Free Will: Oxford Readings in Philosophy*, 2nd ed. (Oxford: Oxford University Press 2003), 190–211; and John Martin Fischer and Mark Ravizza, *Responsibility and Control: A Theory of Moral Responsibility*.

[9] For an elaboration and discussion of the two distinct kinds of arguments (direct and indirect), see John Martin Fischer and Mark Ravizza, *Responsibility and Control: A Theory of Moral Responsibility* (New York: Cambridge University Press, 1998).

[10] "Freedom, Foreknowledge, and the Principle of Alternate Possibilities," 8.

[11] "Freedom, Foreknowledge, and the Principle of Alternate Possibilities," 9.

Vihvelin goes on to state that this distinction has not been explicitly recognized in the literature about the Frankfurt examples, and that understanding it is "the key to understanding both the seductive charm of Frankfurt stories and why they ulti-mately fail."[12] Here her position is that mere conditional intervention cannot show that moral responsibility does not require *any* alternative possibilities (including freedom to choose otherwise), whereas counterfactual intervention can be seen to be problematic (logically defective). That is, it cannot "in principle" work to show that moral responsibility does not require any alternative possibilities.[13]

Vihvelin's strategy for arguing that counterfactual intervention "cannot in principle work" involves telling a certain story, evaluating it, and then claiming that Frankfurt stories are in the relevant ways parallel. It will be helpful to have Vihvelin's presentation in some detail:

> In my story you and I make a bet on the outcome of the toss of a coin. I bet heads—I always bet heads; you bet tails. It comes up heads. I win. You pay up. The question is: Did I win fairly? Well, of course it depends on whether it was a fair coin and a fair toss. Let's stipulate that it was. That is, let's stipulate that there was nothing about the physics of the coin or its toss that made it more likely that the coin would come up heads rather than tails. The odds were 50/50 that this toss would come up heads, and in the course of the toss no outside forces intervened to change those odds.[14]

Now Vihvelin adds that she has a "confederate" named Black who can somehow or other (it is not known how) always predict the coin toss correctly. She goes on as follows:

> Thanks to his unusual predictive powers, Black also has the ability to act ahead of time in a way that ensures that the coin will come up the way he wants it to. Here's how he does it. Black makes his predictions in the morning; we never toss the coin until evening. This leaves Black with plenty of time to fix either the coin or its environment, if need be, in a way that nomologically guarantees that the coin will come up the way that he wants. But Black also prefers not to show his hand unless he has to. If he predicts that the coin will come up the way he wants, then he does nothing. Either way, his job is done by noon. By the time we toss the coin, Black has retired for the day. You may imagine him far away, or fast asleep.
>
> Finally, let's stipulate that Black is a friend of mine. He wants me to win. If he had predicted that without his intervention this particular coin toss would have come up tails, he would have fixed things so that it would have been nomologically necessary on this toss that the coin would come up heads.

---

[12] "Freedom, Foreknowledge, and the Principle of Alternate Possibilities," 11.

[13] "Freedom, Foreknowledge, and the Principle of Alternate Possibilities," 11.

[14] "Freedom, Foreknowledge, and the Principle of Alternate Possibilities," 14–15.

But as a matter of fact, on that last toss, Black didn't intervene. He predicted (somehow) that the coin was going to come up heads, so he did nothing.[15]

Vihvelin maintains that, even in the scenario as elaborated in this way, she has won "fair and square." Her view is that, although it is true that the coin *will* never (given Black's powers) come up tails, nevertheless, given that Black does not intervene, the coin *could have* come up tails. She says that the "complicated truth" about any given coin toss, under the circumstances described in the story, as filled in above, is:

> EITHER the coin comes up heads even though it could have come up tails OR the coin comes up heads and could not have come up tails.[16]

Vihvelin goes on to say:

> It follows from this that the coin *will* never come up tails, not that it *can't*. On some tosses the coin can [come] up tails as easily as it can come up heads. But, thanks to the peculiar setup, it so happens that the coin *can* come up tails only on those occasions that it actually comes up heads.[17]

Vihvelin's view, in short, is that the game is not rigged, when Black does not intervene, although it is rigged, when he does.

Finally, Vihvelin asserts that her story is parallel in relevant aspects to the Frankfurt stories. She says that both the libertarian and the compatibilist must say that the counterfactual intervener in a Frankfurt story does not rob the agent of the ability to choose otherwise.[18]

Vihvelin ends her article by suggesting that those of us who contend that an agent such as Jones is morally responsible but cannot choose or do otherwise are guilty of a logical blunder:

> More austerely, the point is this. The inference from:
>   (P and Possibly not-P) or (P and Necessarily P)
> To
>   Necessarily P
> is fallacious. To suppose otherwise is to permit the inference from:
>   P
> To
>   Necessarily P
> And this is the logic of the fatalist.[19]

---

[15] "Freedom, Foreknowledge, and the Principle of Alternate Possibilities," 15–16.

[16] "Freedom, Foreknowledge, and the Principle of Alternate Possibilities," 18.

[17] "Freedom, Foreknowledge, and the Principle of Alternate Possibilities," 18.

[18] "Freedom, Foreknowledge, and the Principle of Alternate Possibilities," 22–23. Vihvelin goes on to assert that a "complicated truth"—parallel to the complicated truth about her story—obtains here.

[19] "Freedom, Foreknowledge, and the Principle of Alternate Possibilities," 23.

III. Reply to Vihvelin

I wish to commend Vihvelin for her subtle, probing, and suggestive critique. It will be helpful to analyze Vihvelin's critique carefully. Before delving into her "story," I wish to express my agreement with Vihvelin that there is indeed an important distinction between "purely conditional interveners" and "counterfactual interveners." Further, I agree that a purely conditional intervener cannot be invoked to show (without further argumentation) that moral responsibility does not require *any* alternative possibilities. Vihvelin and I are in agreement that the focus should be on counterfactual interveners, rather than purely conditional interveners.

Turn back to Vihvelin's story. Note, again, the way she describes her Black. Among other things, she says, "Black is able, somehow, to predict how any given coin toss will turn out if he does not intervene and his predictions are *always* right, no matter how fair the coin and its environment."[20] It is unclear what the italics add to "always," but they clearly play some rhetorical role at least. Perhaps the italics help to suggest that Black somehow has *knowledge* of the future, although Vihvelin backs off from such a suggestion in footnote 23.[21] For my purposes, I could grant that somehow or other Black has genuine knowledge of the future; nothing in my reply to Vihvelin depends on whether Black has knowledge (as opposed to belief with a high degree of justification or confidence).

Suppose that Black does indeed know in advance how the coin will come up later in the day. He then "retires for the day," well before the coin is flipped. My claim is that, given that Black has indeed retired for the day—he is "asleep or far away"—the following counterfactual is true (at the relevant time—just prior to the coin toss): if the coin were about to come up tails, Black would not be able to intervene and thus the coin would in fact come up tails. Given the setup of the situation, even assuming Black's knowledge in the morning, if the coin were about to turn up tails, it would do so; under this scenario, although Black actually knows how the future will come up, he would not have known (in the alternative sequence). That is, he would have had a false belief in the scenario in which the coin turns up tails. (Again, nothing depends on supposing Black actually has knowledge—we could equally well suppose that he simply has confident belief, a belief that would have turned out false in the alternative sequence.)

My diagnosis of the flaw in Vihvelin's argument is that she posits that her story is parallel to Frankfurt stories, but it is in fact crucially different: the relevant counterfactuals are *not* true in her story, whereas they *are* true in the Frankfurt examples. In virtue of this lack of parallelism in the counterfactuals, the modal facts in Vihvelin's story and the Frankfurt examples are crucially different. That is, whereas it is not true in Vihvelin's story that the coin could not have turned up

---

[20] "Freedom, Foreknowledge, and the Principle of Alternate Possibilities," 15.
[21] "Freedom, Foreknowledge, and the Principle of Alternate Possibilities," 15.

tails, it seems to me that in the Frankfurt examples the relevant agent lacks the power to choose and do otherwise.

Note that Vihvelin has not supposed that Black is somehow essentially infallible; that is, Black is not alleged to be such that he has as part of his "essence" that he has all and only true beliefs.[22] Under such an assumption, it would arguably be the case that the relevant counterfactual would be true; that is, it would be true that if the coin were about to come up tails, then Black would have known this and would have taken precautions to ensure that it would not have succeeded in coming up tails. But whereas the assumption of Black's essential infallibility would arguably underwrite the truth of the sorts of counterfactuals that are true in the Frankfurt cases, Vihvelin does not make such an assumption. Further, this assumption would render it completely contentious that the coin could have come up tails, as all of the intractable debates about the relationship between essential foreknowledge and "possibility" would be engaged.[23]

I wish to elaborate here. It is generally conceded that there is a crucial difference between mere human foreknowledge and (say) divine foreknowledge. If some human being genuinely knows a contingent proposition about the future, then it follows that the proposition will turn out to be true; this is because knowledge implies truth of the proposition known. But it is widely recognized that it does *not* follow from the fact that some human being knows a contingent proposition about the future that the proposition is *necessarily* true (in the relevant sort of necessity), or that the events described or contained in the proposition *must* take place (in the relevant sense of "must"). Although the *conditional* "If S knows that *p*, then *p* is true" is necessary, this necessity does not attach to the consequent of the conditional, even given the truth of the antecedent. (This of course reflects the well-known distinction between the "necessity of the consequence" and the "necessity of the consequent.")

So even if we assume that in Vihvelin's story Black is able to predict a later coin toss in such a way as genuinely to know how the coin will come up, it does not follow merely from this fact that later the coin cannot come up differently. If the coin flip had come up differently, then Black would have had a false belief—he would not have known something he actually did know. In contrast, if an essentially omniscient agent—say God—knows how a later coin toss will turn out, then the only way it could have come up differently would be if the past had been different from what it actually was; that is, the only way it could have come up differently would be if God had had a different belief in the past. But since the past is in relevant ways "fixed" and "over-and-done-with," it is not clear that, given the assumption of God's essential omniscience, the coin *could* have come up

---

[22] For discussions of the assumption of essential infallibility, see John Martin Fischer, ed., *God, Foreknowledge, and Freedom* (Stanford: Stanford University Press 1989).

[23] John Martin Fischer, ed., *God, Foreknowledge, and Freedom* and John Martin Fischer, "Recent Work on God and Freedom," *American Philosophical Quarterly* 29 (1992): 91–109.

differently. (This is obviously an analogue of the problem of the apparent incompatibility of God's foreknowledge and human freedom, in the sense that requires "freedom to do otherwise.")

The key point is that nothing in Vihvelin's story (as she tells the story—and without an assumption of Black's essential omniscience) plausibly rules it out that, although Black knows how the coin toss will come out, the coin can come up on a different side. Presumably Black could still ensure that the coin come up heads, if he were to stay on the scene and monitor the situation. But, according to Vihvelin, he does *not* do this: "he retires for the day," and is thus not in a position to ensure that the coin comes up heads. A babysitter might well be in a position to ensure that a young child stay in his room by standing outside the door and monitoring the situation; if the child were to try to come out the door, the babysitter can stop him from doing so. But if the babysitter decides to watch television in another part of the house, or just goes home (every parent's nightmare—or one of them!), then the babysitter is obviously no longer in a position to prevent the child from leaving the room.

In summary, the problem then with Vihvelin's argument is that it posits that her stories are parallel to the Frankfurt stories, but they differ with regard to the crucial counterfactuals. In the coin case, if the coin were about to come up tails, it would—Black's prediction would have been false, and he wouldn't be there to stop it. In the Frankfurt case, if Jones were about to refrain, he would not, because Black is there to intervene. I claim that, in virtue of the truth of the relevant counterfactuals in the Frankfurt cases, the agent in those cases lacks the freedom to choose or do otherwise. So even if it is granted that the coin could come up tails in Vihvelin's story, this would not show anything about the Frankfurt cases. And if Vihvelin were to strengthen her assumption about Black, making him essentially omniscient, then she could not safely claim that the coin could have come up tails! Thus she couldn't argue from a parallel with her story to her desired conclusion about the Frankfurt cases.

It should now be evident that I would clearly *not* argue in the fatalistic way suggested at the end of Vihvelin's paper. That is, I would not begin with:

(P and Possibly not-P) or (P and Necessarily P).

Rather, the analysis I favor would characterize the Frankfurt cases in terms of the second disjunct (together with the suggestion that the way in which the "necessity" in question is achieved is compatible with moral responsibility in the actual sequence).

IV. The Logic of the Frankfurt-Style Argument (Continued)

Not only does Vihvelin contend that a proponent of certain views about the Frankfurt cases (according to which the agent is morally responsible but does not have genuine access to alternative possibilities) is implicitly relying on problematic fatalistic modes of reasoning, but she also claims that reliance on the sorts of counterfactuals to which I have pointed above is similarly logically suspect. Vihvelin finds such reasoning in a paper I wrote with Paul Hoffman:

> If he were about to refrain (in the absence of intervention by an external agent or factor) the triggering event would already have occurred. [If the triggering event had already occurred, Black would have intervened and forced Jones to act, in which case Jones would not have been able to refrain.] If Jones were about to refrain, he would be rendered unable to refrain.[24]

But Vihvelin rejects this form of argumentation, saying:

> ...this...relies on a form of counterfactual reasoning which is generally considered invalid: hypothetical syllogism. An example: "If I jumped off this bridge, I would have arranged to be wearing a parachute. If I were wearing a parachute, I would not be killed. So if I jumped off this bridge, I would not be killed."[25]

I reply that no proponent of the conclusion—based on consideration of the Frankfurt examples—that moral responsibility does not require alternative possibilities of whom I am aware has ever proceeded by supposing that he or she could construct an argument that employs *solely* the form of reasoning identified by Vihvelin. In particular, I have never thought that one could simply argue for my favored conclusions about the Frankfurt examples by employing the form of reasoning (hypothetical syllogism involving counterfactuals), on the supposition that this is a formally valid way of reasoning. Rather, my point is that the conclusion in question follows from the relevant premises *together with other facts*. These facts about the examples are precisely the sort that help to license an inference to the relevant conclusion, even though the inference form in question is not *formally valid*.

To explain this point, consider David Lewis's remarks in his classic discussion of these matters:

> For a direct counterexample to transitivity [and presumably hypothetical syllogism], consider this argument:

[24] The passage is from John Martin Fischer and Paul Hoffman, "Alternative Possibilities: A Reply to Lamb," *Journal of Philosophy* 90 (1993): 517–527. It is quoted by Vihvelin on p. 20 (n. 30) of "Freedom, Foreknowledge, and the Principle of Alternate Possibilities."

[25] "Freedom, Foreknowledge, and the Principle of Alternate Possibilities," 20. Vihvelin here refers to various discussions of the alleged "fallacy" in question: P. J. Downing, "Subjunctive Conditionals, Time Order, and Causation," *Proceedings of the Aristotelian Society* 59 (1958–59): 125–140; David Lewis, *Counterfactuals* (Cambridge, MA: Harvard University Press 1973), 31–36; and Jonathan Bennett, "Counterfactuals and Temporal Direction," *Philosophical Review* 93 (1984): 57–91.

If Otto had gone to the party, then Anna would have gone.

If Anna had gone, then Waldo would have gone.

Therefore: If Otto had gone, then Waldo would have gone.

The fact is that Otto is Waldo's successful rival for Anna's affections. Waldo still tags around after Anna, but never runs the risk of meeting Otto. Otto was locked up at the time of the party, so that his going to it is a far-fetched supposition; but Anna almost did go. Then the premises are true and the conclusion false. Or take this counterexample, from Stalnaker:

If J. Edgar Hoover had been born a Russian, then he would have been a communist.

If he had been a Communist, he would have been a traitor.

Therefore: If he had been born a Russian, he would have been a traitor.

In general, transitivity [and presumably hypothetical syllogism] fails ... [when] the antecedent of the first premise [is] more far-fetched than the antecedent of the second, which is the consequent of the first. Then the closest worlds where the first antecedent holds are different from—and may differ in character from—the closest worlds where the second antecedent holds.[26]

Lewis goes on to characterize further the situations in which the relevant form of inference fails, and how to strengthen the premises to avoid a failure of inference.[27]

On the approach to counterfactual conditionals defended by Lewis (and Stalnaker), a counterfactual such as "If P had been the case, then Q would have been the case" is true (roughly speaking) just in case Q is true in the possible world or worlds in which P is true that is (or are) "closest" to the actual world (is—or are—the "most similar to" or "involve the least large departure from" the actual world). What is crucial for my discussion here is that transitivity and hypothetical syllogism fail in cases with a specific structure: as Lewis puts it, the antecedent of the first premise must be more far-fetched than the antecedent of the second, which is the consequent of the first. This issues in the possibility that the possible worlds relevant to the truth of the first premise are *different from* the possible worlds relevant to the truth of the second premise. This sort of "world-hopping" is the semantic basis for the possibility of the failure of the relevant forms of inference: the various premises are "sending us to different possible worlds."

Of course, it is important to ask whether anything like this is happening in the Frankfurt-examples and in my (or others') arguments that employ these examples. It seems clear to me that nothing like the structure identified by Lewis is present in

---

[26] David Lewis, *Counterfactuals*, 32–33.

[27] David Lewis, *Counterfactuals*, 33–36.

the Frankfurt stories or my (or anyone's) analysis of them. As stated above, Vihvelin's way of regimenting the argument is as follows:

> If [the relevant agent] were about to refrain (in the absence of intervention by an external agent or factor), the triggering event would already have occurred.
> If the triggering event had already occurred, Black would have intervened and forced Jones to act, in which case Jones would not have been able to refrain.
> Therefore: If Jones were about to refrain, he would be rendered unable to refrain.

As far as I can see, there is no problematic "world-hopping" in this example or the argument that accompanies it (as regimented just above). There is just one world (or set of worlds) to which the premises send us—it is not the case that the antecedent of the first premise is more far-fetched than the antecedent of the second (which is the consequent of the first). Indeed, the story is supposed to be a coherent story about one possible scenario. Hence, it would seem that the premises imply the conclusion, given the facts about the example, even if transitivity and hypothetical syllogism are formally invalid for counterfactual conditionals.[28]

Because the issues are somewhat delicate, I wish to seek to explain my view a bit more fully. Note, again, the sort of "world-hopping" that is taking place in Stalnaker's example discussed earlier:

> If J. Edgar Hoover had been born a Russian, then he would have been a communist.
> If he had been a Communist, he would have been a traitor.
> Therefore: If he had been born a Russian, he would have been a traitor.

The first premise is true in virtue of a possible world in which Hoover is a Russian; but the second premise is true in virtue of a world in which Hoover is not a Russian. In going from the first to the second premise, we have hopped from one world (or set of worlds) to another. Therefore, there is no guarantee that there is a possible world in virtue of which the conclusion is true.

---

[28] For a similar point about a different argument, see John Martin Fischer, "A New Compatibilism," *Philosophical Topics* 24 (1998): 49–66; reprinted in Laura Waddell Ekstrom, ed., *Essays on the Metaphysics of Freedom* (Boulder, CO: Westview Press 2001), 38–56. Here I respond to a criticism that a version of an argument for the incompatibility of causal determinism and freedom to do otherwise I sketched is "formally invalid." I contend that the argument is valid, given its form *and the content of the premises*. For further discussion and defense, see John M. Fischer and Mark Ravizza, "When the Will Is Free," *Philosophical Perspectives* 6 (1992): 423–452, reprinted in Timothy O'Connor, ed., *Agents, Causes, and Events* (Oxford: Oxford University Press 1995), 239–269; and John Martin Fischer and Mark Ravizza, "Free Will and the Modal Principle," *Philosophical Studies* 83 (1996): 213–230. Also, see John Martin Fischer, "Critical Notice of J. Howard Sobel's *Puzzles of the Will*," *Canadian Journal of Philosophy* 31 (2001): 427–444.

The same sort of world-hopping takes place in Lewis's example:

If Otto had gone to the party, then Anna would have gone.
If Anna had gone, then Waldo would have gone.
Therefore: If Otto had gone, then Waldo would have gone.

The first premise is true in virtue of a world in which Otto has somehow escaped the locked room of the actual world; but the second premise is true in virtue of a world in which Otto is still locked up. Therefore, as above, there is no guarantee that there is a possible world in virtue of which the conclusion is true.

But now consider again the reasoning that Vihvelin supposes is behind my analysis of the Frankfurt-type case:

If [the relevant agent] were about to refrain (in the absence of intervention by an external agent or factor), the triggering event would already have occurred.
If the triggering event had already occurred, Black would have intervened and forced Jones to act, in which case Jones would not have been able to refrain.
Therefore: If Jones were about to refrain, he would be rendered unable to refrain.

Given the story of the Frankfurt-type case, I do not see any reason to suppose that a structurally similar sort of world-hopping is taking place here. As far as I can see, the Frankfurt story posits a single possible scenario in virtue of which the two premises are true. Thus, there is no reason to suppose that there is no possible world in virtue of which the conclusion is true; it is precisely the same single world in virtue of which the premises are true.

To develop the point further, consider the form of reasoning under consideration (transitivity or hypothetical syllogism for counterfactual conditionals):

If P had been the case, then Q would have been the case.
If Q had been the case, then R would have been the case.
Therefore: If P had been the case, then R would have been the case.

David Lewis points out that in all counterexamples to the form of inference in question, the "might-counterfactual," "If Q had been the case, then P might not have been the case," is true.[29] He also points out that in some of the counterexamples (and, in particular, in the Otto-Waldo case and the J. Edgar Hoover case) the "would-counterfactual," "If Q had been the case, then it would still not have been the case that P," is non-vacuously true.[30] So, for example, in Lewis's words, "If Anna had gone, Otto would still not have; if Hoover had been a Communist, he would

---

[29] David Lewis, *Counterfactuals*, 33.
[30] David Lewis, *Counterfactuals*, 33.

still not have been born a Russian."[31] Lewis goes on to explain how "adding a third premise to the inference by transitivity, we may rule out all cases where transitivity [hypothetical syllogism] fails."[32]

For my purposes here the key point is to note that in the Frankfurt stories, the characteristic structure of a counterexample to the relevant form of inference is *absent*. In order for a Frankfurt story to be a candidate for being such a counterexample, the following "might-counterfactual" would need to be true: "If the triggering event had already occurred, then it might not have been the case that [the relevant agent] was about to refrain (in the absence of intervention by an external agent or factor)." But the Frankfurt stories include the fact that the "counterfactual intervener" is a reliable predictor of the agent's future choices and behavior, and the basis for this reliability is the "prior sign" or "triggering event" (in some Frankfurt stories, at least). That is, in the Frankfurt stories it is supposed that the prior sign or triggering event would occur if and only if the agent were about to choose or do otherwise.[33] So the specific feature identified by Lewis as common to all counterexamples to the inference-form is absent from the Frankfurt cases!

The upshot of the discussion is that, if one regiments my analysis of the Frankfurt cases as suggested by Vihvelin, this regimentation lacks the characteristic structure of counterexamples to the rule of inference it employs. Additionally, I am not at all convinced that one *needs* to regiment the analysis as suggested by Vihvelin. Here are the facts in a Frankfurt case. There is a triggering event that occurs to indicate that the agent is about to refrain. The "counterfactual intervener" watches for that and even has the power and intention to intervene upon noticing the triggering event. Further, the counterfactual intervener is a completely reliable triggering-event detector and is completely reliable in carrying out his intentions. Given these facts, it just seems intuitively obvious that if the relevant individual (Jones) were about to refrain, he would be rendered unable to refrain. And thus it seems intuitively obvious that Jones is unable to do otherwise, given the facts of the case; no argument employing hypothetical syllogism or transitivity appears to be required.[34]

---

[31] David Lewis, *Counterfactuals*, 33.

[32] David Lewis, *Counterfactuals*, 33–34.

[33] There has been considerable controversy about whether the Frankfurt cases are really cases in which this sort of biconditional is true; but Vihvelin believes we can avoid getting into the details of these discussions entirely. This is important to keep in mind when evaluating Vihvelin's critique, which she supposes is more fundamental than others, and can help us to side-step the complex and voluminous literature on Frankfurt cases. To be a bit more explicit, some might call into question some version of the counterfactual, "If [the relevant agent] were about to refrain (in the absence of intervention by an external agent or factor), the triggering event would already have occurred." It might be considered contentious, within the dialectic of the debates between compatibilism and incompatibilism, whether such a counterfactual is true. But I wish to avoid such controversies here; after all, Vihvelin has provided no argument that such a counterfactual cannot be true, and her contention is that employing her critique can help us to see a deeper, more general problem with Frankfurt examples.

[34] Of course, the discussion in the text shows that the analysis can indeed be regimented in the way suggested by Vihvelin without rendering it invalid, given that it is understood in light of the comments by David Lewis about strengthening the premises.

V. Conclusion

Kadri Vihvelin has issued an important challenge to those of us who have sought to argue that Harry Frankfurt's famous examples help to show that moral responsibility does not require genuine access to alternative possibilities. She does not focus her attention on the arcane debates in the literature about sophisticated versions of the examples or their proper analysis; rather, she contends that we are all missing some basic logical facts.

I have tried to address Vihvelin's challenge here. I have pointed out that in her "story," the relevant counterfactuals—those allegedly parallel to the relevant counterfactuals in the Frankfurt stories—are not true; it is thus natural to suppose that the modal fact that (according to many of us) obtains in the Frankfurt stories does not obtain in Vihvelin's story. Although she wishes to argue from a putative parallelism between her story and the Frankfurt examples, there is a crucial asymmetry. Further, there is no basic logical fallacy in arguing, as many of us have, that the setup of the Frankfurt cases implies that, although the agent in question acts freely and is morally responsible, he lacks the relevant sort of access to alternative possibilities.[35]

---

[35] I wish to thank Neal A. Tognazzini and four anonymous referees for the *Canadian Journal of Philosophy* for their helpful comments.

4

The Importance of Frankfurt-Style Argument

I reply to the challenges to Frankfurt-style compatibilism about causal determinism and moral responsibility presented in Daniel Speak's paper "The Impertinence of Frankfurt-Style Argument." I seek to show how Speak's critiques rest on an "all-or-nothing" attitude in various ways, and I attempt to defend the importance of Frankfurt-style argumentation in defense of compatibilism.

I. Introduction

The principle of alternative possibilities PAP, or something like it, has been at the center of many of the debates about moral responsibility:

> PAP. S is morally responsible for something S has done only if S could have done otherwise.

Certain incompatibilists about causal determinism and moral responsibility invoke PAP. They contend that causal determinism rules out ability (in the relevant sense) to do otherwise; thus they conclude via PAP that causal determinism is inconsistent with moral responsibility.

Whereas some compatibilists have rejected the contention that causal determinism implies "could not have done otherwise" (in the relevant sense), others have objected to PAP. Although there are various routes to a rejection of PAP, one path involves the famous (and in some quarters notorious) "Frankfurt-style examples."[1] In these examples, there is a signature structure involving preemptive

---

[1] H. Frankfurt, "Alternate Possibilities and Moral Responsibility," *Journal of Philosophy* 66 (1969), pp. 829–839.

overdetermination; some fail-safe device exists and ensures the actual outcome (i.e., guarantees that the actual outcome will occur) without being triggered or in any way causally influencing the way the actual sequence in fact leads to the outcome in question.[2] In previous work,[3] I have claimed that the Frankfurt-style examples are indeed examples inconsistent with PAP, and thus that the argument for the incompatibility of causal determinism and moral responsibility mentioned above can be blocked.

In a fascinating and challenging recent article, Daniel Speak gives the following Frankfurt-style example:

> Imagine that Paul has insulted John. Paul's insult comes after his own normal and rational deliberation. Nothing suggests the presence of any responsibility-undermining factors at work in the action sequence. However, Frank, a third agent, has all along wanted Paul to insult John. Indeed, Frank has implanted a chip in Paul's brain that allows him to read his intentional states and make changes to them if necessary. Since Paul's intentional states were at each point consistent with his insulting John, Frank has simply continued to monitor Paul's mental content. If, however, Paul had begun to show any inclination not to insult John, then Frank would have activated the chip in such a way as to bring about an inclination in Paul to insult John.[4]

Speak grants (for the sake of the argument) that Frankfurt-style arguments show PAP to be false in so far as Paul is morally responsible for his action even though he lacked alternatives with respect to it. But he contends that they are nevertheless entirely irrelevant to the debate between the compatibilists and incompatibilists about the relationship between causal determinism and moral responsibility. That is, Speak contends that even if the examples impugn PAP, they cannot be used to defend compatibilism about causal determinism and moral responsibility. Speak concludes his article by saying (p. 95) that in the context of debates about the relationship between causal determinism and moral responsibility, "the famous examples ought simply to be ignored." Here I shall explain why Speak comes to this conclusion, and I shall seek to show how one could reasonably reject it.

---

[2] For a helpful recent discussion of whether Frankfurt-style examples require a certain sort of preemptive overdetermination, see: K. Timpe, "Trumping Frankfurt: Why the Kane-Widerker Objection Is Irrelevant," *Philosophia Christi* 5 (2003), pp. 485–499.

[3] See, e.g., J.M. Fischer, *The Metaphysics of Free Will: An Essay on Control* (Oxford: Blackwell, 1994); J.M. Fischer and M. Ravizza, *Responsibility and Control: A Theory of Moral Responsibility* (Cambridge: Cambridge University Press, 1998); J.M. Fischer, *My Way: Essays on Moral Responsibility* (Oxford: Oxford University Press, 2006).

[4] D. Speak, "The Impertinence of Frankfurt-Style Argument," *The Philosophical Quarterly* 57 (2007), pp. 76–95, at pp. 76–77.

II. SPEAK'S CRITIQUE

As I said above, Speak is willing to concede (for the sake of this discussion) that the Frankfurt-style examples do in fact show the falsity of PAP; that is, they are cases in which an agent S is morally responsible for an action, although S could not have done otherwise. Of course, this has been a matter of considerable controversy, but Speak does not wish to enter into these debates, and I shall simply follow him here. He does, however, resist the employment of Frankfurt-style examples in seeking to block a certain sort of argument for incompatibilism.

Speak's argument is subtle, but I believe it can be reconstructed roughly as follows. Frankfurt says that the agent S is morally responsible in his examples, despite the fact that he could not have done otherwise, because S would have behaved exactly as he actually behaved, even if he could have done otherwise. That is to say, what explains S's responsibility according to Frankfurt is that S is "counterfactually stable" with respect to his actual action: he would have done the same thing, even if he could have done otherwise. But Speak argues that if counterfactual stability (of this sort) is necessary for moral responsibility, then causal determinism is incompatible with moral responsibility. This follows from Speak's contention that causal determinism would rule out the requisite counterfactual stability. Thus, according to Speak, the very basis of Frankfurt's explanation of the putative responsibility of the individuals in his examples can be employed as part of an argument for the incompatibility of causal determinism and moral responsibility.

Why would causal determinism threaten counterfactual stability? A part of the argument is this. Arguably, causal determinism rules out "could have done otherwise." If so, then the counterfactual supposition that an agent could have done otherwise requires us to move to a possible world where causal determinism is false. But given that causal determinism obtains in the actual world, when we move to a possible world where causal determinism is false, it is hard to know how to evaluate the relevant counterfactual. To be more explicit, suppose an individual S in a causally deterministic world does x. S is counterfactually stable with respect to x only if it is true that if he could have done otherwise, he would still do x. But (on the supposition specified above), the "closest" possible worlds to the actual world in which the individual could have done otherwise are causally indeterministic. So in order to evaluate the counterfactual, we must ask what the individual who is actually in a causally deterministic world would do in an indeterministic world. And this question is very difficult to answer. For example, what would be the case, if some law which actually obtained never would have been a law? Given the difficulties of evaluation, it simply will not be indisputably true that S would have done x, even if he could have done otherwise. Thus it cannot be established that an agent in a causally deterministic world is counterfactually stable in the relevant way.[5]

---

[5] See also D. Nelkin, "Irrelevant Alternatives and Frankfurt Counterfactuals," *Philosophical Studies* 121 (2004), pp. 1–25.

The heart of Speak's argument is that counterfactual stability is both required for moral responsibility and incompatible with causal determinism. According to Speak, the Frankfurt-style compatibilist is thus hoist by his own petard: the very element that explains the success of the Frankfurt-style examples is an element in a potent argument for incompatibilism.

III. WHAT FRANKFURT SHOULD HAVE SAID

Frankfurt says that the individual in his examples is morally responsible for what he does because he would have done the same thing, even if he could have done otherwise (counterfactual stability). I believe that Frankfurt should not have said this. In my view, he did not need to offer counterfactual stability as an explanation of the individual's being morally responsible. As Speak notes, Frankfurt offers three different formulations:

(a) …whatever it was that actually led [him] to do what he did, or that made him do it, would have led him to do it or made him do it even if it had been possible for him to do something else instead.

(b) He didn't do it "*because* he couldn't do otherwise."

(c) The factor that made it impossible for him to do otherwise "play[s] no role whatever in the explanation of why he did it."[6]

Speak points out that Frankfurt appears to treat these three formulations as extensionally equivalent. I would contend that Frankfurt should have stuck with (b) and (c) only, and not offered (a) as well. It seems to me that (b) and (c) are (or point to) adequate explanations of the agent's moral responsibility in the Frankfurt-style examples. Perhaps Frankfurt seeks to explain the force of (b) and (c) by offering (a); but (a) is unnecessary, and (as I pointed out above) it gets him into trouble. I would say, employing Bernard Williams' famous phrase, that (a) is "one thought too many" on Frankfurt's part.[7]

So all Frankfurt really needed to say, and what he should have said, is that the moral responsibility of an individual such as Paul (in Speak's Frankfurt-style example) is not threatened by Frank insofar as Paul does what he does on his own (and without being tampered with by Frank). The point about counterfactual stability is an unnecessary accretion—one thought too many. I do not see why it might be supposed that rejecting PAP on the basis of the Frankfurt-examples requires acceptance of the requirement of counterfactual stability; rather, I am suggesting

---

[6] Speak, p. 92; the quotations are from Frankfurt, "Alternate Possibilities and Moral Responsibility."

[7] B. Williams, "Persons, Character, and Morality," repr. in his *Moral Luck* (Cambridge: Cambridge University Press, 1981), pp. 1–19.

that a proponent of this strategy should say that Paul is morally responsible insofar as he does what he does on his own and not because of tampering by an external factor or agent such as Frank.

Philosophers often assert that an agent in a Frankfurt-style example (say, Paul) is morally responsible because he did what he did "on his own." This of course can be unpacked in various different ways. Give Paul all of the features necessary for moral responsibility, including, if you like, indeterminism (of a certain sort) in the deliberative process. Paul is, in fact, just like an agent all parties would agree is morally responsible, save for one difference: Paul is in a world containing another agent (or process) stipulated to be "causally irrelevant" to any of Paul's deliberations or actions. Such a non-factor could not make a difference to Paul's being morally responsible, could it? Metaphysically, what explains Paul's moral responsibility is all of the necessary conditions that were put in earlier. Dialectically, what allows one to continue saying that Paul is morally responsible is that the would-be intervener does not do anything.

It seems to me that counterfactual stability plays no explanatory role—it is not even mentioned or (as far as I can see) implicitly invoked; rather, reliance is placed on the idea of Paul's doing what he does "on his own" (and not because of Frank's tampering). Given the availability of this sort of Frankfurt-style strategy, I believe it is clear that a Frankfurt-inspired rejection of PAP does not require counterfactual stability; I shall further argue for this position in section V when I address Speak's response to this sort of suggestion.

Of course, from the fact that it was unnecessary for Frankfurt to invoke a requirement of counterfactual stability for moral responsibility in the earlier context it does not follow that such a requirement does not exist. I do not, however, believe that counterfactual stability is a genuine requirement for moral responsibility. Interpreted as Speak interprets it, this is manifestly too stringent a requirement, since Frankfurt-type cases can be constructed in which the agent appears responsible but it is not present. Suppose some form of indeterminism in deliberation in a Frankfurt-style case.[8] Given the indeterminism, there is no counterfactual stability; such stability entails that were we to replay the relevant stretch of history, the agent would always decide as he did, and indeterminism rules this out. A requirement of counterfactual stability seems to expunge moral responsibility even apart from the special context of Frankfurt-style examples. Thus not only would I contend that a proponent of Frankfurt-style compatibilism need not invoke counterfactual stability, I would also point out that this requirement is independently implausible.

---

[8] See, as just one example, A. Mele and D. Robb, "Rescuing Frankfurt-style Cases," *Philosophical Review* 107(1998), pp. 97–112.

IV. SPEAK'S REPLIES

To his credit, Speak anticipates the view I have suggested above (according to which one does not rely on counterfactual stability), and he offers various replies. It will be useful to consider them carefully. First, he points out (p. 92) that (a) may well be necessary for (b) and (c); he wonders how one would establish (b) or (c) without invoking (a). He does however appear to acknowledge (pp. 92–93) that one could adopt some sort of non-reductionist, "causal impact" (or, presumably, "production") view of causation on which (a) could in principle be separated from (b) and (c).

His reply (pp. 92–93) is as follows:

> Frank "plays no role" in Paul's insulting behavior (or Paul does not do the insulting *because* of Frank) if no causal force is transmitted between them. Any appeal to this sort of argument, however, will not extricate the Frankfurtian compatibilist from the impertinence I have identified. This is because the truth of causal determinism would entail that the past (together with the laws) *does* transmit causal force to any future choice or action.
>
> …There is no plausible way of extending the implications of Frankfurt-style cases into the context of determinism so as to provide any real resistance to the standard incompatibilist argument. With respect to the compatibility debate, then, the famous cases are an irrelevant distraction.

Speak also considers (pp. 93–94) a related objection that has it that the Frankfurt-style examples provide a useful first step in the defense of compatibilism, even if they are not themselves decisive components of such a defense:

> The eirenic reply to this point would be to accept it, admit that my initial claims are somewhat rhetorically inflated, but emphasize the constraints that my argument has placed on a completely satisfying Frankfurtian compatibilism. I am tempted by this reply. But I shall resist the temptation. This is because I think it would unjustifiably concede too much to the compatibilist. The guiding insight of my approach has been that (PAP) must be false *in the right way* for the compatibilist to get leverage. More specifically, (PAP) must be false in a way that can be exploited under determinism. The Frankfurtian way is not, I have argued, of the right sort in this respect.

V. THE IMPORTANCE OF FRANKFURT-STYLE ARGUMENT

I believe that the response to Speak's two replies here stems from a certain way of understanding the dialectic strategy of Frankfurt-style compatibilism.[9] The key is

---

[9] I seek to explain this sort of strategy in "Frankfurt-Style Compatibilism" and "Free Will and Moral Responsibility," both of which are reprinted in *My Way*.

not to think of the strategy as proceeding in a precipitous way; it is not a one-step argument, but involves at least two important steps or stages. The first step is that the examples show that PAP is false, so moral responsibility does not require alternative possibilities. Thus causal determinism cannot be thought to rule out moral responsibility *simply* in virtue of eliminating access to alternative possibilities. Of course, if causal determinism obtains, then alternative possibilities are ruled out *in a certain way* (i.e., via a causally deterministic actual sequence). The second step of the argument is this: if causal determinism does not rule out responsibility by eliminating access to alternative possibilities, why exactly would it be thought to rule out moral responsibility by *eliminating alternative possibilities in this specific way* (i.e., via a causally deterministic actual sequence)? That is, if it is no problem for moral responsibility that the agent does not have access to alternative possibilities, why would it be a problem that the agent lacks access to alternative possibilities because of a causally deterministic actual sequence?

Of course, there might be something problematic and challenging for moral responsibility in a causally deterministic actual sequence. In other words, it might be that causal determination in the actual sequence rules out moral responsibility for some reason other than that it eliminates access to alternative possibilities. Perhaps actual-sequence determination is incompatible with "initiation" or "sourcehood" or "creativity" or...[10] This claim is important, and raises difficult issues that must be addressed. But here it is important to note that the debate has shifted to a different dialectical terrain—we are here not asking about the threat posed by causal determinism to alternative possibilities; rather, we are asking whether causal determinism *directly* rules out moral responsibility (i.e., whether causal determinism threatens moral responsibility in itself and apart from eliminating access to alternative possibilities). Although in the end I would argue that direct incompatibilism fails, I think it is a perfectly plausible position whose appeal I can understand. What is puzzling to me is how one could accept the first step of the Frankfurt-style compatibilist's argument (i.e., that causal determinism does not threaten moral responsibility by eliminating access to alternative possibilities) but claim that it does threaten moral responsibility by involving a certain path to the ruling out of alternative possibilities—by being a *certain way of eliminating alternative possibilities*. If the elimination of alternative possibilities *in itself* is not problematic, and if the path *in itself* (apart from leading to the elimination of alternative possibilities) is not the source of the problem, how can the problem stem from the fact that causal determinism involves a certain way of eliminating alternative possibilities?

If they are interpreted in this more complex way, it can be seen that the Frankfurt-style examples help a certain sort of compatibilist to make considerable

---

[10] See my *The Metaphysics of Free Will*, pp. 147–154; Fischer and Ravizza, *Responsibility and Control*, pp. 151–169; and my "Frankfurt-Style Compatibilism."

progress. The argumentative strategy of the compatibilist involves more than one step, and it is admittedly not a knockdown argument. But why suppose arguments here must be (maximally) simple and knockdown? My point applies to Speak's replies in this way: Speak insists that the Frankfurt examples are a different sort of context from that of causal determinism, and (relatedly) that PAP must be shown to be false "in the right way" to be any use to the compatibilist. One can think of Speak's view in the following way. In the Frankfurt-style examples, some factor that operates in the alternative sequence, but not in the actual sequence, renders it true that the agent lacks access to alternative possibilities. In contrast, in a case where it is explicitly assumed that causal determinism obtains, some factor (or factors) operate in the actual sequence, and (we can assume) render it true that the agent lacks access to alternative possibilities. So Frankfurt-style examples contain a freedom-undermining factor only in the alternative sequence, whereas causal determinism involves actual-sequence factors that undermine freedom. One cannot therefore straightforwardly apply lessons putatively learned from Frankfurt-style examples to cases in which it is assumed that causal determinism obtains.

I grant this point; one cannot straightforwardly and in one step go from the Frankfurt-style examples to a conclusion about cases in which causal determinism is assumed to obtain. But it does *not* follow that one cannot employ the more nuanced argumentative strategy I sketched above. Here the lesson of the Frankfurt-examples is not straightforwardly applied to contexts of causal determinism, but the argument proceeds in (at least) two steps. Further, it is not alleged by the Frankfurt-style compatibilist that the strategy is *knockdown* or *decisive*. Given a proper understanding of the structure and nature of Frankfurt-style compatibilism, Speak's conclusions that "the famous cases are an irrelevant distraction," that "they make no contribution to the compatibilist issue," and that they "ought simply to be ignored" can be seen to be extreme and certainly unwarranted.

Finally, I shall consider an objection to the argumentative strategy I have suggested on behalf of the compatibilist. I have accepted (for the sake of argument) that an agent such as Paul in a Frankfurt-style case is morally responsible because of (b)—what makes Paul morally responsible is that he did not behave as he did because he could not have done otherwise. Arguably, in a causally deterministic context Paul does indeed behave as he actually behaves because he could not have done otherwise. Thus it appears that the one factor that saved Paul's moral responsibility in the first place (in spite of there being no alternative possibilities open to him) is *missing* in a deterministic scenario. Why, then, should we think that Paul is morally responsible in a causally deterministic scenario?[11]

The dialectical issues here are admittedly subtle. My reply is that it is *not* the case that the one factor that saved Paul's moral responsibility was that he did not

---

[11] I owe this point to David Robb.

do what he did because he could not have done otherwise. Rather, the idea above was this: we can invoke Frankfurt-style examples to show that in principle it is possible for an agent to be morally responsible, even though he lacks alternative possibilities; more specifically, we invoke such examples at a point in the dialectic that does not presuppose causal determinism, and thus the conclusion (that an agent could be morally responsible even in the absence of access to alternative possibilities) should be acceptable even to someone inclined to (or committed to) incompatibilism about causal determinism and moral responsibility. Here it is not being claimed explicitly or implicitly that Paul's not doing what he does because he could not have done otherwise is a factor that "saves his responsibility," or in the absence of which he would not be morally responsible. Rather, the idea was that we can invoke (b) at a particular point in the argument in a way that is dialectically productive—it helps us to make progress in a non-question-begging way. More specifically, the idea is that even someone inclined toward incompatibilism should agree that if causal determinism is false and the relevant agent did not have access to alternative possibilities (because of the existence of a Frankfurt-style counter-factual intervener), the agent might nevertheless be morally responsible—given that the actual sequence proceeds in the right way. So the strategy I suggest does not suppose that (b) specifies a factor that would make a metaphysical difference (in the presence of which an agent is morally responsible and in the absence of which he is not); rather, (b) specifies a factor that is dialectically fruitful in the way sketched above. Of course, a lot then depends on the *second* stage of my argumentative strategy.

VI. CONCLUSION

It seems to me that Speak's critique of Frankfurt-style compatibilism suffers from a certain kind of "all-or-nothing" attitude. He appears to assume that the proponent of Frankfurt-style compatibilism simply asks us to consider the examples and precipitously to conclude that causal determinism is clearly and indisputably compatible with moral responsibility. But I have shown that the Frankfurt-style compatibilist need not pursue this sort of strategy, a strategy that should in any case be highly suspicious to anyone who has thought carefully about free will and moral responsibility (or about any other difficult and contentious philosophical issue). The Frankfurt-style compatibilist can offer an argument *in stages*, and one that does not purport to be impossible to reject (especially by anyone antecedently committed to or strongly inclined to incompatibilism).[12]

---

[12] I am grateful for careful and detailed comments by David Robb and Neal Tognazzini. I thank Daniel Speak for graciously sharing his paper with me and for many illuminating conversations on these topics. I am also indebted to comments by two anonymous referees.

5

Blame and Avoidability: A Reply to Otsuka
Coauthor: Neal A. Tognazzini

Much ink has been spilled over what Harry Frankfurt has dubbed the "Principle of Alternate Possibilities" (henceforth the "Principle of Alternative Possibilities" or PAP).[1] Some compatibilists about causal determinism and moral responsibility have deployed defenses of their view that reject PAP.[2] Others, typically incompatibilists, have vigorously defended PAP.[3] Michael Otsuka seeks to bypass the debates about PAP by presenting and defending a different, but related, principle, which he calls the "Principle of Avoidable Blame:"

> *Principle of Avoidable Blame* (PAB): One is blameworthy for performing an act of a given type only if one could instead have behaved in a manner for which one would have been entirely blameless.[4]

Otsuka contends that PAB is plausible and that it entails incompatibilism (given, of course, the incompatibility of causal determinism and genuine access to alternative possibilities or "could have done otherwise," which we can grant for the sake of the discussion here). Otsuka is willing to concede that Frankfurt-type examples are indeed counterexamples to PAP, but he believes that they do *not* impugn PAB. Here we wish to offer a critical discussion of the core of Otsuka's argument, especially the claim that PAB cannot be refuted by Frankfurt cases. We do not believe that Otsuka has offered good reason to suppose that PAB—and the related incompatibilism—fares any better than PAP.

It will perhaps be helpful first to have before us Otsuka's rendition of a Frankfurt-style counterexample to PAP:

---

[1] Frankfurt (1969). For some of the voluminous literature, see McKenna and Widerker (2003).
[2] See, for example, Fischer (1994, 2006), Fischer and Ravizza (1998).
[3] For a helpful selection, see McKenna and Widerker (2003).
[4] Otsuka (1998).

Suppose an indeterministic world in which people can normally do otherwise. Imagine that somebody in this world named Jones killed an innocent person named Smith, and that he killed him wholeheartedly, with premeditation, for selfish gain, and without any prompting. According to Frankfurt, Jones might be blameworthy for killing Smith even if he could not have refrained from doing so. For we can imagine that Jones could not have refrained for the following reason: had it become clear to somebody named Black (who is an excellent judge of such things) that Jones was about to decide not to kill Smith, then Black would have intervened and forced him to do so. But Black never had "to show his hand because Jones, for reasons of his own, decide[d] to perform, and [did] perform, the very action that Black want[ed] him to perform."[5]

Otsuka takes it that such examples show PAP to be unacceptable, and thus he introduces PAB. In order to evaluate whether PAB fares any better than PAP, we need to be clear on its precise content. In particular, what does it mean to say that "one could instead have behaved in a manner for which one would have been entirely blameless"? Otsuka clarifies this crucial phrase as follows:

> When I say that one could instead have behaved in a manner for which one would have been entirely blameless, I mean that it was within one's voluntary control whether or not one ended up behaving that way.[6]

While this does help clarify PAB a bit, we do not yet have a full understanding of the principle, since we now need to know what it means to say that "it was within one's voluntary control whether or not one ended up behaving in [a blameless] way." Let us imagine that there are (at least) two different ways an agent could behave, "Way1" and "Way2." Let us further suppose that Way1 is a blameworthy way of behaving and that Way2 is a blameless way of behaving. Finally, let us stipulate that the agent voluntarily behaves in Way1, the blameworthy way. Does this—the agent's voluntarily behaving in Way1—suffice for his exercising voluntary control over whether or not he behaves in Way2? There is some reason to think that this *is* enough, since it seems natural to suppose that if the agent voluntarily behaves in Way1, then it was in his voluntary control *not* to behave in Way2, and thus it was in his voluntary control *whether or not* to behave in Way2. Call this the "weak" reading of the relevant phrase.

There is a "strong" reading of the phrase, as well. According to this interpretation, the mere fact that the agent voluntarily behaves in Way1 is *not* sufficient for its being in his voluntary control whether or not he behaves in Way2. Additionally, something like the following counterfactual must be true: if the agent were to have behaved in Way2, the agent would have voluntarily initiated the sequence of events

---

[5] Otsuka (1998, pp. 687–688).
[6] Otsuka (1998, p. 688).

that led to his behaving in Way2. In this stronger reading, what is needed for an agent to have in his voluntary control whether or not he behaved in a certain way is that voluntariness be involved at least in some part of the causal chain leading to the agent's behavior in *both* the actual and the counterfactual circumstances.[7]

Otsuka appears to endorse what we have called the "strong" reading of the phrase "it was within one's voluntary control whether or not one ended up behaving in [a blameless] way," given what he says in a crucial footnote:

> Suppose that someone would have behaved in a manner for which she would have been entirely blameless if and only if she had had a totally unexpected, involuntary, and incapacitating seizure. Suppose that she could have had such a seizure insofar as this was a physiologically live possibility. There is perhaps a sense in which she could have behaved in [a] manner for which she would have been entirely blameless. But for the purpose of interpreting the Principle of Avoidable Blame, she could not have so behaved.[8]

To see why this case seems to support the "strong" reading, consider the two ways of behaving that are open to the woman in Otsuka's scenario: Way1, which is the actual way the woman behaves, and Way2, which is the way the woman would have behaved by being subject to an involuntary and incapacitating seizure. Otsuka states that for the purposes of understanding PAB, this woman could not have behaved in a manner for which she would have been entirely blameless. This must mean, given Otsuka's attempt at clarification above, that he thinks it is not within this woman's voluntary control whether or not she ended up behaving in Way2. But this claim is false if we understand the phrase in the "weak" sense—after all, nothing in the example rules out the possibility that the woman in fact acts in Way1 voluntarily. So Otsuka must think that the example is one in which the agent could not have behaved blamelessly (in the relevant sense) because the agent would not have voluntarily initiated the counterfactual sequence that culminates in her behaving in Way2. It thus appears that we should interpret the relevant phrase in the "strong" sense, requiring some voluntariness in both actual and counterfactual circumstances.[9]

---

[7] Someone might be tempted to interpret the relevant phrase in an even stronger sense. According to this "super-strong" sense, not only must the agent initiate the alternative sequence voluntarily, but she also must end up behaving voluntarily in the alternative sequence. This sense, however, would make (PAB) clearly vulnerable to Frankfurt examples, since Jones does not end up behaving voluntarily in the alternative sequence in which Black forces him to kill Smith. Otsuka does not endorse this "super-strong" sense (see footnote 9).

[8] Otsuka (1998, p. 688).

[9] Importantly, not *every* bit of behavior in the counterfactual sequence must be voluntary. The agent may well "end up" behaving involuntarily, but for PAB to be satisfied, the causal chain leading to the counterfactual upshot must at least have been initiated voluntarily. Otsuka says explicitly that although it must have been in the agent's voluntary control whether or not she ended up behaving in a blameless manner, "I need not claim that the behavior itself must have been voluntary" (Otsuka 1998, p. 688). This shows that Otsuka clearly does not endorse what we called the "super-strong" sense in footnote 7. We are grateful to Otsuka for helping us understand this point.

The problem is that when we interpret PAB this way, it seems clearly vulnerable to Frankfurt-style counterexamples. Recall that in the above counterexample—which Otsuka concedes shows PAP to be false—the counterfactual circumstance in which Black intervenes is not one in which Jones initiates the counterfactual sequence voluntarily. Rather, it is one in which Black notices ahead of time what Jones is going to do and then forces Jones to act as he (Black) wants. Thus, if we are to interpret "it was within Jones's voluntary control whether or not he ended up killing Smith" in the "strong" sense, it looks like this is false in a Frankfurt-style counterexample. And yet, intuitively, Jones is blameworthy for what he does in the actual sequence of events. These two verdicts together yield the falsity of PAB.

But perhaps this is a bit too quick. After all, Otsuka does provide an *argument*, in the form of a dilemma, to the conclusion that Frankfurt-style counterexamples do not succeed against PAB. Otsuka's dilemma argument begins as follows:

> Frankfurt has proposed that Black's intervention would have been triggered by an involuntary twitch that Jones would have registered if and only if he was about to decide to refrain from killing Smith. We are to suppose that this twitch would have been caused by the sort of thought processes that would always and only have preceded a decision on the part of Jones to refrain from killing Smith.
>
> Now the twitch would have been the result of thought processes over which Jones either had voluntary control or not.[10]

Otsuka then goes on to consider both horns of this dilemma, arguing that PAB is not violated on either horn. But we need not consider these arguments, since it seems clear to us that we should reject the proposed dichotomy in the first place. Otsuka seems to think that when Frankfurt proposed that Black's intervention would have been triggered by a twitch, Frankfurt had in mind that this twitch must have been the result of some thought process or other. In fact, however, in the passage from Frankfurt that Otsuka cites, it is unclear whether Frankfurt was thinking that thought processes would cause the twitch.[11] And even if Frankfurt

---

[10] Otsuka (1998, p. 691).

[11] Otsuka cites Frankfurt (1969, p. 835), which reads as follows: "The assumption that Black can predict what [Jones] will decide to do does not beg the question of determinism. We can imagine that [Jones] has often confronted the alternatives—A and B—that he now confronts, and that his face has invariably twitched when he was about to decide to do A and never when he was about to decide to do B. Knowing this, and observing the twitch, Black would have a basis for prediction. This does, to be sure, suppose that there is some sort of causal relation between [Jones's] state at the time of the twitch and his subsequent states. But any plausible view of decision or of action will allow that reaching a decision and performing an action both involve earlier and later phases, with causal relations between them, and such that the earlier phases are not themselves part of the decision or of the action. The example does not require that these earlier phases be deterministically related to still earlier events." It is not clear that this passage posits that the twitch is caused by some thought process or other, of which we then might

did have this in mind, we do not think it is essential to a plausible Frankfurt example. There seems to be no reason why the twitch in question might not be the result of any thought process whatsoever.

We said that Otsuka's dilemma presents a false dichotomy, and we are now in a position to see why. Rather than forcing a choice between the twitch being caused by thought processes over which Jones had voluntary control and the twitch being caused by any thought processes over which Jones did not have voluntary control, we can instead maintain that the twitch is not caused by any thought processes whatsoever. That is, we can envisage a version of the Frankfurt case in which Jones would show a twitch *prior* to the beginning of the relevant thought process just in case he were about to engage in the sort of process that would issue (absent an intervention) in his deciding to refrain from killing Smith. If Black were to see the twitch, he would intervene to block the entire process (including the "thought process"). Thus, given the placement of the twitch *before* the beginning of the thought process, Black is in a position to prevent Jones from even engaging in the relevant thought process, and it becomes irrelevant whether (in the absence of intervention) that thought process would have been voluntary or not. Given the appropriate placement of the "prior sign" (twitch), Otsuka's dilemma becomes irrelevant.

Otsuka does not rest his entire defense of PAB on this dilemma, however. He writes:

> Even if one manages to construct an example that overcomes [the difficulties raised by the dilemma], I do not think that such an example would refute the Principle of Avoidable Blame. Let us assume, for the sake of argument, that it is somehow possible to construct an example in which, unbeknownst to Jones and without actually exerting any influence on him, Black (or someone or something else) closed all possibility that Jones behaved any less badly than he actually behaved. It follows from what I say in the next section that, in this case, Jones would not be worthy of blame for what he has done.[12]

What Otsuka does in "the next section" is provide a positive account of what makes someone blameworthy when someone has acted badly. He then goes on to point out that this positive account is not satisfied in the Frankfurt cases, and hence that Jones is not blameworthy. Since the success of the Frankfurt cases relies crucially on the judgment that Jones *is* blameworthy in the actual sequence, this result would indeed be sufficient to show that PAB is not vulnerable to the Frankfurt cases.

---

wonder whether it is in the agent's control. In particular, it is unclear whether, in speaking of distinct "phases," Frankfurt was thinking of phases of the causal process leading to action or perhaps phases of practical reasoning. If the former, then no thought processes need be involved at all.

[12] Otsuka (1998, p. 694).

But we do not think that Otsuka's argument succeeds here either. To see why, let us first consider his positive account of what grounds blameworthiness in cases where someone has acted badly. He states:

> A person would be worthy of indignation for malevolently inflicting pain only if such infliction was gratuitous—not in the sense that it was done for no reason (he could well have had ample selfish or malevolent reason), but—in the or [sic] sense that it was an expression of the agency of someone who was free, and knew (or ought to have known) that he was free, to behave less badly instead. It is the fact that such a person behaved so badly even though he knew (or ought to have known) that he didn't have to that makes his behavior galling and hence worthy of indignation.[13]

According to Otsuka, for an agent to be blameworthy, she must have known (or at least ought to have known) that she was free to behave less badly (and thus it must have been *true* that she was free to behave less badly). Otsuka continues as follows:

> Take any imagined pair of individuals who have behaved badly (e.g., who have maliciously injured another) and hold everything constant except for the fact that the one could have behaved less badly, and knew that she could have, whereas the other could not have behaved less badly. The fact that the one person behaved as badly as she did even though she knew that she didn't have to provides sufficient grounds for indignation in her case that are lacking in the second case. Moreover, there are no other grounds that are sufficient for indignation in this second case.[14]

In a "prior sign" Frankfurt-style counterexample like the one we discussed before, Jones could not have behaved less badly (in the relevant "strong" interpretation of that phrase), since the counterfactual circumstance is one in which Jones does not voluntarily initiate the causal sequence leading to his killing Smith. Otsuka uses this fact together with his articulated necessary condition on blameworthiness— that one is blameworthy only if one knew that one could have behaved less badly—to conclude that Jones is not in fact blameworthy. Thus, Otsuka concludes that the Frankfurt cases do not impugn PAB after all.

But we fail to see why we should accept Otsuka's proposed necessary condition on blameworthiness. That is, we do not see why we should accept the claim that an agent is blameworthy only if she knew that she could have behaved less badly. After all, Otsuka has not provided any *argument* for this claim; he has merely asserted that "there are no other grounds that are sufficient for indignation in

---

[13] Otsuka (1998, p. 696).
[14] Otsuka (1998, p. 696).

[a case where the agent could not have behaved less badly]." There are plenty of candidates for such grounds, however. To take just one, Jones may well have exercised "guidance control" of his actual behavior, even if it was nevertheless true that he could not have behaved less badly.[15] To convince us that there are no grounds for indignation in a Frankfurt-style counterexample, then, Otsuka would need to argue that the fact that Jones exercised guidance control does not constitute such grounds. Importantly, however, he does not make such an argument. Nor does Otsuka consider any of a range of other possible candidate grounds for indignation in the relevant kind of case—accounts of "acting freely" that do not require "could have done otherwise."

Before we conclude, allow us to consider one further way someone might try to defend PAB, although this is not the route taken by Otsuka. First, recall from above that we distinguished between two senses of the phrase "it was within one's voluntary control whether or not one behaved in [a blameless] way." We argued that Otsuka endorses the "strong" sense, but someone might attempt to defend PAB by endorsing the "weak" sense instead. According to the "weak" sense, it is sufficient for its being in one's voluntary control whether or not one behaved in a blameless way that one voluntarily behaves in the way one actually behaves, regardless of what is true regarding voluntariness in the alternative sequence. Someone might invoke this "weak" sense to argue that in a Frankfurt-style counterexample, it was in fact in Jones's voluntary control whether or not he behaved in a blameless way, and hence that Jones *could* have behaved in a manner for which he would have been entirely blameless. In this reading, it seems that a proponent of PAB could say just the right thing about the Frankfurt cases: that Jones is blameworthy but the consequent of PAB is also true, and hence the cases do not falsify PAB.

But we think that if this is how we are to understand PAB—in the "weak" sense—then PAB would not be fixing on factors that play any explanatory role. It seems that in the alternative sequence of the Frankfurt case, Jones would be avoiding blameworthiness *accidentally*, as it were. After all, Jones would not be acting voluntarily in the alternative sequence. And, as we saw above, this is precisely why Otsuka said that the individual subject to seizures is *not* capable of so acting that she would be blameless, in the sense relevant to PAB. Begin with a case in which the relevant agent is not blameworthy for his behavior. How does posting an alternative possibility *of this sort*—utterly without voluntariness—make it the case that an agent is blameworthy in the actual sequence leading to his behavior? This attempt to get blameworthiness from mere flickers of freedom that lack sufficient robustness would seem to be akin to alchemy.[16]

---

[15] See, for example, Fischer (1994), and Fischer and Ravizza (1998).

[16] To see why this sort of alternative possibility lacks robustness, consider the following account of robustness from Pereboom (2001, p. 26):

Robustness For an alternative possibility to be relevant to explaining why an agent is morally responsible for an action, it must satisfy the following characterization: she could have willed

In conclusion, Otsuka seeks to defend incompatibilism about causal determinism and moral responsibility by offering a variant on PAP. (He also contends that PAB illuminates a wider range of issues in ethics, including "moral dilemmas" or "moral blind alleys.")[17] PAB allegedly avoids the Frankfurt-style counterexamples to PAP. Otsuka interprets PAB as follows: "When I say that one could instead have behaved in a manner for which one would have been entirely blameless, I mean that it was within one's voluntary control whether or not one ended up behaving that way." We have argued that the crucial notion of its being within one's voluntary control whether or not one behaves in a certain way is ambiguous. Given what Otsuka claims about the seizure case, he appears to endorse the strong sense. However, if PAB is interpreted in this way, it seems clearly vulnerable to Frankfurt-style counterexamples. Otsuka constructs a dilemma, however, that is meant to show that PAB is immune to Frankfurt cases. But this dilemma relies on placing the "prior signs" *after* the "thought processes," and there is no reason to place the prior signs after, rather than before, the thought processes. And the cases are potent if they are placed *before* such processes.[18] Finally, Otsuka merely asserts, rather than arguing for, the claim that the Frankfurt cases do not involve any factors that could ground blameworthiness. But we have pointed out at least one factor that could plausibly play this role: guidance control.

In closing we considered an attempt to save PAB by reverting to the "weak" sense of its crucial phrase. But in the weak sense, it seems that PAB loses its explanatory force; more carefully, it would appear that simply adding an alternative possibility in which an agent "accidentally" avoids blame (or the actual level of blame) does not in any way explain the agent's actual blameworthiness. We conclude that

---

something different from what she actually willed such that she understood that by willing it she would thereby be precluded from moral responsibility for the action.

According to this account of robustness, the relevant agent in a Frankfurt case does *not* have a robust alternative possibility. If we interpret PAB according to the "weak" interpretation, then, it is puzzling how the proponent of PAB could support the claim that the agent in a Frankfurt case is blameworthy. For this point in the context of an assessment of PAP, see Fischer (1994, pp. 131–159, 1999a, 2002).

[17] Otsuka (1998, pp. 698–700).

[18] In personal correspondence, Otsuka has suggested that he could modify his dilemma by focusing more generally on the events that precede the twitch, whatever they happen to be, rather than insisting that those events must be thought processes. Interpreted in this way, we would accept the second horn of his dilemma, according to which the events that precede the twitch are not under Jones's voluntary control. Otsuka goes on to argue (Otsuka 1998, p. 692) that this horn is problematic because in order for Black to intervene in such a way that Jones could not have behaved blamelessly, Black would have to set things up such that he would literally *force* Jones to commit the murder in the alternative sequence. Otsuka then observes that Jones would not be blameworthy for the murder in this circumstance, and he concludes that PAB is thus safe from counterexample. But a successful counterexample against PAB does not require that Jones is blameworthy in the *alternative* sequence; rather, blameworthiness in the actual sequence is sufficient. We thus do not see any reason to think that taking the second horn of his dilemma (when the focus is on the events that precede the twitch) is problematic.

PAB does not fare any better than the original PAP, which even Otsuka admits has been shown false by Frankfurt-style counterexamples.[19]

References

Fischer, John Martin. 1994. *The metaphysics of free will: An essay on control.* Oxford: Blackwell Publishers.

Fischer, John Martin. 1999a. Responsibility and self-expression. *The Journal of Ethics* 3: 277–297.

Fischer, John Martin. 1999b. Recent work on moral responsibility. *Ethics* 110: 93–139.

Fischer, John Martin. 2002. Frankfurt-type examples and semi-compatibilism. In *Oxford handbook on free will*, ed. Robert Kane, pp. 281–308. New York: Oxford University Press.

Fischer, John Martin. 2006. *My way: Essays on moral responsibility.* Oxford: Oxford University Press.

Fischer, John Martin, and Mark Ravizza. 1998. *Responsibility and control: A theory of moral responsibility.* New York: Cambridge University Press.

Frankfurt, Harry G. 1969. Alternate possibilities and moral responsibility. *The Journal of Philosophy* 66: 829–839.

Ginet, Carl. 1996. In defense of the principle of alternative possibilities: Why I don't find Frankfurt's argument convincing. *Philosophical Perspectives* 10: 403–417.

Kane, Robert. 1996. *The significance of free will.* Oxford: Oxford University Press.

McKenna, Michael, and David Widerker, eds. 2003. *Moral responsibility and alternative possibilities: Essays on the importance of alternative possibilities.* Aldershot: Ashgate.

Otsuka, Michael. 1998. Incompatibilism and the avoidability of blame. *Ethics* 108: 685–701.

Pereboom, Derk. 2001. *Living without free will.* Cambridge: Cambridge University Press.

Widerker, David. 1995. Libertarianism and Frankfurt's attack on the principle of alternative possibilities. *The Philosophical Review* 104: 247–261.

---

[19] Here we have focused primarily on Otsuka's intriguing suggestion that (PAB) can sidestep the problems (especially those posed by the Frankfurt cases) for PAP. Otsuka concedes that the Frankfurt cases do indeed show the falsity of PAP. There are various objections to the contention that the Frankfurt cases successfully refute PAP, including the vexing "dilemma defense" presented by Kane (1996, pp. 142–145); Widerker (1995) and Ginet (1996). A discussion of such objections is clearly beyond the scope of this critical evaluation of Otsuka. For a preliminary discussion of some of the objections, see Fischer (1999b). It should be noted that placing the prior signs before any of the thought processes raises worries pertinent to the Dilemma Defense; but we believe that such worries can be answered, and, in any case, we are here focusing on whether Otsuka has a *distinct* approach to defending incompatibilism—an approach not identical to or reducible to the invocation of the Dilemma Defense on behalf of PAP.

6

Indeterminism and Control: An Approach to the Problem of Luck

I. The Dilemma of Determinism

William James's famous "Dilemma of Determinism" can be formulated as follows:

1. Either causal determinism is true, or it is false.
2. If causal determinism is true, then I *have* to act as I do, and thus I am not morally responsible for my actions.
3. If causal determinism is false (in a relevant way), then how I act is a matter of luck, and thus I am not morally responsible for my actions.

Therefore:

4. I am not morally responsible for my actions.[1]

Alternatively, the dilemma could be put as follows:

1. Either causal determinism is true, or it is false.
2*. If causal determinism is true, then I cannot do otherwise, and thus I am not morally responsible for my actions.
3*. If causal determinism is false (in a relevant way, i.e., in the sequences leading to my behavior), then my actions are not appropriately connected to my prior states (i.e., "my actions" are not in a genuine sense *my* actions), and thus I am not morally responsible for my actions.

---

[1] William James, "The Dilemma of Determinism," originally an address to Harvard Divinity Students (in Lowell Lecture Hall, Harvard University), published in *The Unitarian Review* (September 1884); reprinted in William James, *The Will to Believe and Other Essays in Popular Philosophy* (New York: Longmans Green and Co., 1907), 145–183.

Therefore:

4. I am not morally responsible for my actions.

The picture behind the Dilemma of Determinism might be thought to be roughly this. To be morally responsible, I must be in control of my behavior. But there are at least two components of the relevant kind of control (or perhaps at least two requirements for such control). First, in order to be in control, it must not be the case that I *have* to do what I actually do; that is, I must have freedom to choose and to do otherwise. Second, the action must be an "outflowing" of *me*—it must be genuinely *my* action in some important sense.[2]

When I am in control of my behavior, in the way required for moral responsibility, I select from among various genuinely open paths into the future through my free choice. Again, there are at least two crucial ideas here: I must *select* from among *various open alternatives*, and *I* must select. As the two formulations of the Dilemma of Determinism indicate, causal determinism would seem to challenge (at least) the notion that I select from among various genuinely open paths into the future, and indeterminism appears to challenge the idea that it is genuinely *I* who selects (or, perhaps, makes a difference).

In this paper I shall focus primarily on the "indeterministic horn," that is, premises (3) and (3*). But I shall begin by considering the "deterministic horn," (premises [2] and [2*]). The proper analysis of the deterministic horn will be illuminating with respect to the indeterministic horn. I shall argue that neither the second premises of the parallel arguments nor the third premises are true, and thus the argument is unsound for two separate reasons. I shall further argue that similar considerations help to establish the failure of *both* the deterministic and indeterministic horns of the dilemma. Not only are the worries similar at a deep level, but the appropriate replies are also based on similar insights.

II. The Deterministic Horn

II.1. THE ARGUMENT FOR THE SECOND PREMISE

Why exactly does it follow from causal determinism that an agent does not have freedom to do otherwise? And why would it follow from an agent's lacking freedom to do otherwise that he is not morally responsible for his actions?

There are various ways to seek to establish that causal determinism implies that we never have the freedom to do other than we actually do. Perhaps the most

---

[2] Timothy O'Connor calls the relevant notion "agent control." As he puts it, agent control is "the manner in which a particular piece of behavior is connected to, controlled by, or an 'outflowing' of 'the agent'": Timothy O'Connor, *Persons and Causes: The Metaphysics of Free Will* (New York: Oxford University Press, 2000), 23.

salient such argument has been dubbed the "Consequence Argument" by Peter van Inwagen.[3] The argument gets its name from the fact that, under causal determinism, every choice and action is the consequence of the past together with the laws of nature. More specifically, if causal determinism is true, every choice and action is the result of a causally deterministic causal sequence. The argument has it that if this is so, we don't ever have a choice about what we do; that is, if causal determinism is true, we never have it in our power to do otherwise than we actually do. As van Inwagen puts it:

> If determinism is true, then our acts are the consequences of the laws of nature and events in the remote past. But it is not up to us what went on before we were born, and neither is it up to us what the laws of nature are. Therefore, the consequence of these things (including our present acts) are not up to us.[4]

Van Inwagen and others have given various more formal versions of this intuitive argument.[5] Here is a still quite informal presentation of the bare bones of the argument. Suppose that causal determinism is true. Given a standard definition of causal determinism, it follows that my current choice to raise my coffee cup (caffeinated, fortunately) is entailed by true propositions about the past and laws of nature. Thus, if I were free (just prior to my actual choice to pick up my coffee cup) to choose (say) to listen to my wife's admonition to drink less coffee and to refrain from picking up the cup, then I must have been free so to act that the past would have been different or the natural laws would have been different. But intuitively the past is "fixed" and out of my control and so are the natural laws. Thus, I cannot now do anything that is such that, if I were to do it, the past would have been different (say, the Spanish Armada never would have been defeated or Napoleon would have been victorious at Waterloo). Similarly, I cannot ever so act that the natural laws would be different (say, some things would travel faster than the speed of light). It appears to follow that, despite the natural impression I have that I am sometimes genuinely free to choose and do otherwise, it turns out that I cannot choose to refrain from picking up the coffee cup (although I won't try that line on my wife) and indeed I am never free to choose and do otherwise, on the assumption of causal determinism.

The Consequence Argument is a "skeptical argument" that challenges our commonsense view that we are often free to do otherwise. As with other skeptical

---

[3] Peter van Inwagen, "The Incompatibility of Free Will and Determinism," *Philosophical Studies* (1975) 27, 185–199; and *An Essay on Free Will* (Oxford: Clarendon Press, 1983).

[4] Van Inwagen, *An Essay on Free Will*, 56.

[5] For just a small selection, see van Inwagen, *An Essay on Free Will*, 55–105; Carl Ginet, *On Action* (Cambridge: Cambridge University Press, 1990); John Martin Fischer, *The Metaphysics of Free Will: An Essay on Control* (Oxford: Blackwell Publishers, 1994); and J. Howard Sobel, *Puzzles for the Will* (Toronto: University of Toronto Press, 1998).

arguments, it gets its bite from intuitively plausible ingredients, such as the idea that the past and natural laws are fixed and out of our control. Of course, one needs to be considerably more careful in developing a definition of causal determinism and in specifying the relevant senses in which the past and natural laws are indeed fixed; but I am confident that the intuitive ideas can be crystallized in such a way as to yield a powerful and highly plausible argument for the incompatibility of causal determinism and freedom to do otherwise. If the Consequence Argument is indeed sound, and if moral responsibility requires freedom to do otherwise, then it would follow that the premises that present the deterministic horn of the Dilemma of Determinisms (2) and (2*) are true.

II.2. A REPLY TO THE ARGUMENT FOR THE SECOND PREMISE

As developed above, there are two steps in the argument for premises (2) and (2*). First, the Consequence Argument seeks to establish that if causal determinism is true, then I cannot choose and do otherwise. Second, the Principle of Alternative Possibilities (PAP) is invoked, according to which moral responsibility requires precisely the freedom to choose and do otherwise.[6] Each step of the argument can be called into question.

Some philosophers have rejected the Consequence Argument. Philosophers such as Keith Lehrer, Terence Horgan, and John Perry have denied that the past is fixed in any sense strong enough to yield the incompatibilistic result.[7] They are willing to say that the past is fixed in *one* sense; that is, no one can initiate a causal chain extending into—and altering—the past. But they are quick to point out that this point, in itself, does not yield a result strong enough to yield incompatibilism via the Consequence Argument. What would be strong enough is the contention that no one can ever so act that the past would have been different from what it actually was; and this, they say, is simply not true. One might think it true by not distinguishing it from the uncontroversial sense in which the past is fixed.

Other philosophers, such as David Lewis, have rejected the fixity of the natural laws.[8] (Actually, David Lewis would reject both the fixity of the past and the natural laws.) Lewis is willing to say that the natural laws are fixed in *one* sense; as he puts it, we are not free to *violate* a natural law. But it does not follow that we are never free

---

[6] The Principle is introduced by Harry Frankfurt in "Alternate Possibilities and Moral Responsibility," *Journal of Philosophy* (1969) 66, 829–839. Actually, Frankfurt dubs the principle, "The Principle of Alternate Possibilities."

[7] See, for example, Keith Lehrer, "'Can' in Theory and Practice: A Possible Worlds Analysis," in (eds.) Myles Brand and Douglas Walton, *Action Theory: Proceedings of the Winnipeg Conference on Human Action* (Dordrecht: D. Reidel, 1976), 241–270; and Terence Horgan, "'Could,' Possible Worlds, and Moral Responsibility," *Southern Journal of Philosophy* (1979) 17, 345–358; John Perry, "Compatibilist Options," in (eds.) Joseph Keim Campbell, Michael O'Rourke, and David Shier, *Freedom and Determinism* (Cambridge, MA: Bradford/MIT Press, 2004), 231–254.

[8] David Lewis, "Are We Free to Break the Laws?" *Theoria* (1981) 47, 113–121.

so to act that some proposition expressing a natural law *would not* have expressed a natural law. Lewis argues that the uncontroversial truth is not enough to support the Consequence Argument, and the contention that *would* be enough is false.

These debates are highly contentious, and I have argued that they end up in what I have called "Dialectical Stalemates."[9] I prefer to address the second step of the argument for premises (2) and (2*). That is, although it is useful to note that the Consequence Argument is not entirely persuasive, I find it more appealing to attack the contention that moral responsibility requires freedom to choose and do otherwise (PAP).

Again, there are various routes to a rejection of PAP. I have focused primarily on the Frankfurt-style counterexamples to PAP—examples that were originally introduced in contemporary philosophy by Harry Frankfurt and that purport to impugn PAP.[10] Here is an updated version of a Frankfurt example:

> Because Black dares to hope that the Democrats finally have a good chance of winning the White House, the benevolent but elderly neurosurgeon, Black, has come out of retirement to participate in yet another philosophical example.[11] (After all, what would these thought-experiments be without the venerable *eminence grise*—or should it be *noir*?) He has secretly inserted a chip in Jones's brain which enables Black to monitor and control Jones's activities. Black can exercise this control through a sophisticated computer which he has programmed so that, among other things, it monitors Jones's voting behavior. If Jones were to show any inclination to vote for McCain (or, let us say, anyone other than Obama), then the computer, through the chip in Jones's brain, would intervene to assure that he actually decides to vote for Obama and does so vote. But if Jones decides on his own to vote for Obama (as Black, the old progressive, would prefer), the computer does nothing but continue to monitor—without affecting—the goings-on in Jones's head.
>
> Now suppose that Jones decides to vote for Obama on his own, just as he would have if Black had not inserted the chip in his head. It seems, upon first thinking about this case, that Jones can be held morally responsible for this choice and the act of voting for Obama, although he could not have chosen otherwise and he could not have done otherwise.[12]

---

[9] Fischer, *The Metaphysics of Free Will: An Essay on Control*, 83–85.

[10] Frankfurt, "Alternate Possibilities and Moral Responsibility." For a selection of papers on Frankfurt-style examples, see David Widerker and Michael McKenna (eds), *Moral Responsibility and Alternative Possibilities: Essays on the Importance of Alternative Possibilities* (Aldershot, UK: Ashgate, 2003).

[11] Obviously, the specifics of the case are now out of date, but what matters is the structure of the example.

[12] I originally presented such an example in John Martin Fischer, "Responsibility and Control," *Journal of Philosophy* (1982) 79, 24–40.

Notoriously (in some quarters), there has been much discussion of the Frankfurt-style examples and their implications in the years subsequent to the publication of Frankfurt's 1969 paper, "Alternate Possibilities and Moral Responsibility." I certainly will not go into the details here. For my purposes it is enough to distill a few (admittedly controversial) lessons. First, it seems to me that Black's presence (as described in the example), perhaps together with other features, makes it the case that Jones cannot choose or do other than he actually does. Further, it seems to me that Black's presence (in the context of those other features) is *irrelevant* to Jones's moral responsibility. Both of these contentions would need to be defended, and, perhaps, qualified.[13] But for the purposes of this paper, I will take them as working hypotheses.

It might be helpful to have before us Frankfurt's statements on behalf of the contention that Black's presence is irrelevant to Jones's moral responsibility:

> The fact that a person could not have avoided doing something is a sufficient condition of his having done it. But, as some of my examples show, this fact may play no role whatever in the explanation of why he did it. It may not figure at all among the circumstances that actually brought it about that he did what he did, so that his action is to be accounted for on another basis entirely… Now if someone had no alternative to performing a certain action but did not perform it because he was unable to do otherwise, then he would have performed exactly the same action even if he *could* have done otherwise. The circumstances that made it impossible for him to do otherwise could have been subtracted from the situation without affecting what happened or why it happened in any way. Whatever it was that actually led the person to do what he did, or that made him do it, would have led him to do it or made him do it even if it had been possible for him to do something else instead… When a fact is in this way irrelevant to the problem of accounting for a person's action it seems quite gratuitous to assign it any weight in the assessment of his moral responsibility.[14]

Although I recognize that further argumentation would be required to convince skeptics, I agree with Frankfurt's intuition that it would be "quite gratuitous" to assign any weight to Black's presence in assessing Jones's moral responsibility. After all, Black did not play any role in the "actual sequence"—the actual causal pathway to Jones's choice and action; Black's device, although present, is *untriggered*. I think that the Frankfurt-style examples help to provide motivation for an "actual-sequence" approach to moral responsibility, according to which moral responsibility

---

[13] See chap. 2 of this book, reprinted from John Martin Fischer, "The Frankfurt Cases: The Moral of the Stories," *Philosophical Review*, 119 (2010): 315–336.

[14] Frankfurt, "Alternate Possibilities and Moral Responsibility," 836–837.

attributions depend on (possibly dispositional or modal) features of the actual sequence, rather than on the availability of genuinely open alternative possibilities. The mere presence of certain sorts of *untriggered ensurers* (such as Black's device) rules out alternative possibilities without in any way affecting the actual sequence that issues in the relevant behavior. In my view, this is the fundamental reason to reject the deterministic horn of the dilemma, as expressed by premises (2) and (2*). Of course, there might well be *other* reasons (not captured in these premises) to suppose that causal determinism rules out moral responsibility; but, here I am focusing primarily upon the specific reasons featured in the premises of the Dilemma of Determinism as presented earlier.[15]

III. The Indeterministic Horn

III.1. THE ARGUMENT FOR THE THIRD PREMISE

I suggested that the intuitive idea of control that underwrites moral responsibility requires that an agent selects from among genuinely open alternatives and thereby makes a difference through his free choice (and action). The Consequence Argument calls into question whether an agent can select from among open alternatives, if causal determinism is true. But if causal determinism is false (in the relevant way), an interestingly similar argument—The Rollback Argument—calls into question whether it is *the agent* who makes the difference. In order to have the requisite control, the choices and actions must flow from the *agent* in the right way—it must be genuinely *the agent's* action. And, as suggested above, in order for the choice and action to be genuinely the agent's, they must be suitably related to the agent's prior mental states. If it is purely a matter of chance or luck that an individual chooses as he does, then the choice in question would not appear to be related to the agent's prior mental states—including his desires, beliefs, intentions, and acceptances of values—in the right way. And, according to the Rollback Argument, if causal indeterminism is true, then an agent's choices are—in a sense to be specified—purely a matter of luck. Thus, the Consequence Argument and the Rollback Argument play parallel roles in purporting to support the second and third premises.

More specifically, the Rollback Argument seeks to explain precisely *why* it would follow from causal indeterminism (in the relevant places) that the choices and actions would not be an outflowing of the agent in the required sense; that is, it seeks to pinpoint the reason why, if indeterminism were to obtain, the required *relationship* between the agent's prior mental states and his choice (and action) would not be present. For ease of discussion, let us call this relationship, the "responsibility-grounding relationship."

---

[15] For a discussion of the "sourcehood" worry, see John Martin Fischer, "Compatibilism," in John Martin Fischer et al., *Four Views on Free Will* (Oxford: Blackwell Publishers, 2007), 44–84, esp. 61–71.

Peter van Inwagen gives a particularly clear presentation of the Rollback Argument, and thus I ask the reader's patience with the following lengthy quotation:

> Let us suppose undetermined free acts occur. Suppose, for example, that in some difficult situation Alice was faced with a choice between lying and telling the truth and that she freely chose to tell the truth—or, what is the same thing, she seriously considered telling the truth, seriously considered lying, told the truth, and was able to tell the lie she had been contemplating. And let us suppose that... Alice's telling the truth, being a free act, was therefore undetermined. Now suppose that immediately after Alice told the truth, God caused the universe to revert to precisely its state one minute before Alice told the truth (let us call the first moment the universe was in this state "t1" and the second moment the universe was in this state "t2") and then let things go forward again. What would have happened the second time? What would have happened after t2? Would she have lied or would she have told the truth? Since Alice's "original" decision, her decision to tell the truth, was undetermined—since it was undetermined whether she would lie or tell the truth—her "second" decision would also be undetermined, and this question can therefore have no answer; or it can have no answer but, "Well, although she would either have told the truth or lied, it's not the case that she would have told the truth and it's not the case that she would have lied; lying is not what she would have done and telling the truth is not what she would have done. One can say only that she *might* have lied and she *might* have told the truth."
>
> Now let us suppose that God *a thousand times* caused the universe to revert to exactly the state it was in at t1 (and let us suppose that we are somehow suitably placed, metaphysically speaking, to observe the whole sequence of "replays"). What would have happened? What should we expect to observe? Well, again, we can't say what would have happened, but we can say what would *probably* have happened: sometimes Alice would have lied and sometimes she would have told the truth. As the number of "replays" increases, we observers shall—almost certainly— observe the ratio of the outcome "truth" to the outcome "lie" settling down to, converging on, some value... [L]et us imagine the simplest case: we observe that Alice tells the truth in about half the replays and lies in about half the replays. If, after 100 replays, Alice has told the truth 53 times and has lied 48 times, we'd begin strongly to suspect that the figures after a 1,000 replays would look something like this: Alice has told the truth 493 times and has lied 508 times. Let us suppose that these are indeed the figures after 1,000 replays. Is it not true that as we watch the number of

replays increase, we shall become convinced that what will happen on the *next* reply is a matter of chance?"[16]

Van Inwagen goes on to state that our inclination to say that what will happen on the "next replay" is a matter of chance will not be different, if we change the probabilities that Alice will tell the truth (as long as this objective probability is under 100 percent). Van Inwagen adds, "Nothing we could possibly learn, nothing God knows, it would seem, should lead us to distrust our initial inclination to say that the outcome of the next replay will be a matter of chance."[17] Van Inwagen goes on to conclude from the fact that the action is a matter of chance that Alice lacked a kind of dual ability: the ability to tell the truth and the ability to lie. It might be said that Alice lacked the ability to guarantee (in advance) which action would occur, where this ability included the power to guarantee either that she would lie or that she would not lie.

It should be noted that van Inwagen himself does not accept that the Rollback Argument decisively shows that indeterminism implies that the responsibility-grounding relationship fails to hold (and thus that premises [3] and [3*] are true). Rather, he thinks that the Rollback Argument presents a significant challenge to the coherence of libertarianism—a challenge that he thinks can be met. Van Inwagen does not see *how* the challenge can be met, so he must accept what he calls the "puzzling" view that indeterminism does not rule out the responsibility-grounding relationship, rather than the "inconceivable" view that causal determinism is compatible with freedom to do otherwise. Van Inwagen famously says, "I must choose between the puzzling and the inconceivable. I choose the puzzling."[18] In the discussion in the previous section of this chapter, I sought to call into question the contention that the compatibility of causal determinism and certain notions of freedom and moral responsibility is inconceivable. In the following I shall seek to diminish at least some of van Inwagen's puzzlement.

It is interesting to note that, not only do the Consequence Argument and the Rollback Argument play similar roles in putatively supporting the relevant premises in the Dilemma of Determinism, but they can be seen to share an abstract form. The problem raised by the Consequence Argument is that if one were to roll back the universe to the relevant prior instant a thousand (or a million or...) times, the agent would *always* make the same choice. This calls into question the notion that the agent has the power to *select* from among *more than one* path that are *genuinely available* to him. And, as we have seen above, the problem raised by the Rollback Argument is that if one were to roll back the universe to the relevant prior instant a thousand (or a million or...) times, the agent would *not* always

---

[16] Peter van Inwagen, "Free Will Remains a Mystery," reprinted in John Martin Fischer, ed., *Critical Concepts in Philosophy: Free Will Volume IV* (London: Routledge, 2005), 173–192; the quotation is from 187–188, and citations of page numbers below are from the Fischer volume.

[17] Van Inwagn, "Free Will Remains a Mystery," 189.

[18] Van Inwagen, *An Essay on Free Will*, 150.

make the same choice. This calls into question the notion that the *agent* has it in his power to make the relevant selection; that is, it calls into question whether the responsibility-grounding relationship obtains. The Rollback and Consequence Arguments can thus be seen to share a common structure; but they are, as it were, "inverses" or mirror-images of each other. And, of course, they target different aspects of the basic idea that when I am morally responsible, it is *I* who *select* from among various open options.[19]

III.2. CRITIQUE OF THE ARGUMENT FOR THE THIRD PREMISE

Recall the (reformulated) third premise of the Dilemma of Determinism:

> 3*. If causal determinism is false (in a relevant way, i.e., in the sequences leading to my behavior), then my actions are not appropriately connected to my prior states (that is, "my actions" are not in a genuine sense *my* actions), and thus I am not morally responsible for my actions.

Note that the Rollback Argument is supposed to establish that (or give a reason for) the contention that if causal determinism is false, then my actions are not appropriately connected to my prior states; that is, the Rollback Argument is supposed to show exactly why the responsibility-grounding relationship would not obtain, if causal determinism were false.

I now wish to call into question the efficacy of the Rollback Argument in establishing that causal indeterminism rules out the responsibility-grounding relationship. (After my discussion of the Rollback Argument, I shall go on to show how my critique can be *generalized* to various other plausible ways of defending the third premise.) Imagine a causally deterministic world (W1) in which everything goes as it is supposed to in the sequence issuing in a given human choice and action. That is, suppose causal determinism obtains and Jones chooses (for his own

---

[19] Perhaps it is not surprising that the Rollback Argument and The Consequence Argument have a common structure insofar as it might be argued that, at a deep level, they both rely on the notion of luck. Indeed, Saul Smilansky has argued that the problem with the fact that, under causal determinism, all our choices and behavior would be the consequences of the past and laws of nature, is precisely the problem of luck. See Saul Smilansky, *Free Will and Illusion* (Oxford: Clarendon Press, 2000); and "Compatibilism: The Argument from Shallowness," *Philosophical Studies* (2003) 115, 257–282.

In simple form, Smilansky's argument is as follows. If causal determinism is true, then all our deliberations, choices, and behavior are the result of causally deterministic sequences that began well before we were even born (or had any sense of the relevant options and the values that might be brought to bear on them, etc.). Since we are not responsible for initiating these sequences, and since our decisions and behavior are the necessary results of them, we are not "ultimately" in control of our deliberations and actions in the sense relevant to robust moral responsibility and ethical desert. If causal determinism is true, then it can be seen from a more objective or expansive perspective that what we choose to do, and in fact do, are purely a matter of "luck": what we choose may be "up to us" in a superficial sense, but what we choose is causally determined by our values and background dispositions, which are causally determined by our previous experiences, and so forth.

reasons, in the "ordinary way") at t2 to raise his hand at t3, and Jones does in fact raise his hand at t3. Imagine, further, that whatever is required for the responsibility-grounding relationship between prior states of Jones and his choice at t2 to raise his hand at t3 is present; that is, let us say that the *requisite glue* that connects the agent's prior states with his choice at t2 is present. I am not sure exactly what this glue consists in; that is, I am not exactly sure what is required for the responsibility-grounding relationship. But we can suppose that in W1 it—whatever it is—obtains in the case of Jones's choice at t2 to raise his hand at t3.[20] (Of course, it is not enough for Jones's freely choosing at t2 to raise his hand at t3 that this glue be present; but at least we cannot say in W1 that Jones does not freely choose at t2 to raise his hand at t3 because the glue is absent.)

Now imagine another possible world (W2) in which everything is the same as W1 in respect of the way the causal sequence that actually leads to Jones's choice at t2 to raise his hand at t3 (everything, that is, apart from causal determination). In W2, as in W1, Jones chooses for his own reasons, in the "normal way," at t2 to raise his hand at t3 (and Jones does indeed raise his hand at t3). In general, whatever exactly it is that makes it the case that the responsibility-grounding relationship is present in the actual sequence flowing through Jones to his choice at t2 (and action at t3)—everything, that is, apart from causal determination—is also present in the sequence that takes place in W2.

But now we add that there is a genuinely random machine in W2, but not in W1. Let's say that Jones begins his deliberations at t1 about whether to raise his hand; his last moment of deliberation is t1.9, and he makes his choice at t2. The random machine "operates" in W2 between times t1 and t2. (By "operating" I simply mean that the machine goes through a series of internal states culminating in either M1 or some other state at t1.9.) For our purposes, we can focus on state M1. That is, if the machine is in state M1 at t1.9, there are two possibilities, each with a 50 percent objective probability attached to it. The first possibility is that the machine does nothing—it "goes to sleep," as it were, and does not trigger any causal interaction with the world (including Jones). The second possibility is that it will initiate a causal sequence that would *preempt* Jones's choice at t2 to raise his hand at t3. That is, on the second possibility, the machine would trigger a causal sequence that would terminate in (say) a direct electronic stimulation of Jones's brain sufficient to ensure that Jones chooses at t2 to *refrain* from raising his hand at t3. It is assumed that the process involving the machine in W2 is genuinely random

---

[20] Note that this case, as I've presented it in the text, will not move a committed *skeptic* about whether the glue can be present *ever*—even in a causally deterministic context. Rather, my primary target in this paper is a theorist who thinks that *indeterminism* poses a special problem for moral responsibility in virtue of posing a special challenge to the possibility of the glue's obtaining. That is, there are philosophers who do not worry about the choice and action's being an "outflowing" of the agent under causal determinism, but *do* worry that *indeterminism* would call into question the contention that the relevant behavior is an outflowing of the agent. It is to such philosophers that I address my argument.

(whatever is required for genuine randomness). Further, let us suppose that, as things actually go in W2, the machine's state at t1.9 is indeed M1, and, further, the machine simply "goes to sleep" and never triggers any causal interference in the sequence flowing through Jones to his choice at t2 to raise his hand at t3. (I.e., the machine is in M1 at t1.9 and the first possibility is realized—no intervention in the causal sequence flowing through Jones.)

In both worlds W1 and W2, Jones chooses and does exactly the same thing (type-identical choices and actions), as a result of relevantly similar processes. More specifically, we have assumed that the causal process linking Jones's prior states and his choice is the same in relevant respects in both worlds; thus, if the requisite glue connecting the prior states with the choice obtains in W1, it also obtains in W2. Presumably, the mere existence and operation of the machine in W2 should not in any way threaten these claims about the responsibility-grounding relationship. How could the mere existence of such a machine affect the responsibility-grounding relationship, given that the machine does not causally interact with the sequence flowing through Jones and issuing in the choice at t2?[21] Indeed, it should be intuitively obvious that the mere existence and operation of the machine in W2 is *irrelevant* to whatever it is that makes it the case that the responsibility-grounding relationship obtains in the sequence flowing through Jones.

Notice, however, that W2 is causally indeterministic during the relevant interval. Indeed, W2 is causally indeterministic in the relationship between the prior states of Jones at t1.9 and Jones's choice at t2; after all, Jones's actual deliberations could have been preempted by a causal sequence that was not in fact triggered in W2. So we could obviously run the Rollback Argument with respect to W2: if we were to roll back the universe to t1.9 and allow it to go forward a thousand times, then in say 467 "replays" Jones will choose at t2 to raise his hand at t3, and in say 533 replays Jones will be caused to choose at t2 to refrain from raising his hand at t3. The Rollback Argument clearly "applies" to the conditions of W2, as W2 is explicitly an indeterministic world.

But the key point is that intuitively it is obvious, as I claimed before, that the mere existence and operation of the machine in W2 cannot in itself show that

---

[21] As Randy Clarke has reminded me, there are tricky issues here. Is the machine not entering state M2 a cause? If so, it might not be exactly right to say that the machine doesn't causally interact with Jones. Still, I here rely on some intuitive notion—difficult to specify—according to which the machine does not actually causally interact with the sequence flowing through Jones.

Note that similar worries come up in the context of evaluating the classical Frankfurt cases (and variations on them). For example, the untriggered machine in W2 is parallel to resting Black in the original Frankfurt case. In both cases my contention is that they (resting Black and the untriggered machine) are (in some sense) *not* part of the actual sequence flowing through Jones and thus are *irrelevant* to Jones's moral responsibility. In the context of a defense of their version of a Frankfurt case, Alfred Mele and David Robb discuss such issues: Alfred R. Mele and David Robb, "BBs, Magnets and Seesaws: The Metaphysics of Frankfurt-style Cases," in Widerker and McKenna, eds., *Moral Responsibility and Alternative Possibilities: Essays on the Importance of Alternative Possibilities*, 127–138.

the requisite glue is not present in W2—it cannot show that whatever underwrites the responsibility-grounding relationship is missing. (Recall, again, that the machine's "operating" refers simply to its going through a sequence of internal states; it does *not* imply the triggering of its capacity to initiate a preempting sequence.) Perhaps my point could be put as follows. Whatever underlies the responsibility-grounding relationship—whatever constitutes the relevant glue that binds together the prior states of the agent with his choice—is a matter that is *intrinsic* (in some sense) to the relevant causal sequence. It is a matter of *the way the prior states of the agent lead to the choice in question,* and this cannot be affected by the mere presence of something (such as the random machine in W2) that *plays no role in the causal sequence flowing through the agent.* And if this is correct, then the *mere fact* that the Rollback Argument can successfully be run cannot *in itself* show that the responsibility-grounding relationship is not present. After all, in W2 the responsibility-grounding relationship is indeed present; it is present to the same extent that it is present in W1. Yet we can run the Rollback Argument relative to the conditions present in W2.

In a nutshell, then, my argument is as follows. Let's suppose, what is not implausible, that we have some sufficiently determinate intuitive notion of "the way a causal sequence goes," where this notion abstracts away from whether causal determinism obtains or not. We now suppose that in W1 the actual causal sequence goes in the "normal" way typically thought to ground attributions of moral responsibility, apart from considerations pertinent to causal determination. Now add to W1 that causal determinism does in fact obtain. It should be widely accepted that, whatever the requisite glue (the responsibility-grounding relationship) is, it obtains in W1. Given that the responsibility-grounding relationship is present in W1 and intuitively cannot be expunged simply because of the existence of the genuinely random machine in W2, it also is present in W2. But we can successfully run the Rollback Argument with respect to the conditions present in W2; indeed, the mere existence of the machine in W2 makes it the case that the relationship between Jones's prior mental states and his choice at t2 is *indeterministic* (even though "the way the causal sequences go" in W1 and W2, as defined above, is the same). Thus, the mere fact of the application of the Rollback Argument does *not* show what it is intended to show, namely, that the responsibility-grounding relationship is absent. So the application of the Rollback Argument cannot be the reason why causal indeterminism threatens the responsibility grounding relationship—threatens to make us come unglued, as it were.

Above I noted that the Consequence Argument and the Rollback Argument have the same abstract structure. It is interesting to notice, also, that the responses to the two threats—the threat from causal determinism and the threat from causal indeterminism—employ similar ingredients.

To explain. Recall that Frankfurt pointed to an important intuition about Black (the counterfactual intervener) in the Frankfurt cases. As Frankfurt noted, Black didn't play any role in how the actual sequence unfolds; as he put it, we could "subtract" Black from the story and everything would proceed in just the same way. Frankfurt then said, as quoted previously, "When a fact is in this way irrelevant to the problem of accounting for a person's action it seems quite gratuitous to assign it any weight in the assessment of his moral responsibility." Black is merely a counterfactual intervener; he is, as I described him, an "untriggered ensurer." Frankfurt's point, and it is an intuitively compelling point, is that a merely *counterfactual* intervener—an individual or device not actually triggered to have any effect on the causal sequence in question—is *irrelevant* to an agent's moral responsibility.[22]

Now the random machine in W2 is also a *merely counterfactual* intervener. The random machine in W2 is an *untriggered preemptor*. But both untriggered ensurers (such as Black) and untriggered preemptors (like the random machine) are equally *untriggered*; that is, they are *merely counterfactual* interveners, and, as such, they are plausibly thought to be *irrelevant* to attributions of moral responsibility. Thus, just as the Consequence Argument and the Rollback Argument are structurally similar at an abstract level, so are the responses to the threats they underwrite from causal determinism and causal indeterminism; both responses rely on a basic intuition, first formulated by Harry Frankfurt, to the effect that mere counterfactual interventions are irrelevant to ascriptions of moral responsibility. As I would put it, moral responsibility is a matter of what happens in the *actual sequence*.

The Rollback Argument is only one way of seeking to support Premise 3 of the Dilemma of Determinism; I have contended that the possibility of certain sorts of untriggered preemptors shows that the Rollback Argument cannot in fact support Premise 3. As far as I can tell, various of the most salient ways of attempting to support Premise 3 fall prey to the possibility of untriggered preemptors (and the associated argumentation). I turn in the next section to a brief defense of this claim.

IV. Other Arguments for the Third Premise

There is a large literature surrounding the "Luck Problem." This problem is, after all, why some compatibilists have claimed that not only is moral responsibility

---

[22] Classical Frankfurt cases involve untriggered ensurers (such as Black). I have presented what I have somewhat immodestly called, "Fischer-type cases," in which (say) Jones would be instantaneously annihilated, if he were about to choose to do otherwise. These somewhat chiliastic cases involve what might be dubbed "untriggered destroyers." Untriggered destroyers are equally as efficacious as untriggered ensurers in challenging the notion that moral responsibility requires alternative possibilities. See John Martin Fischer, "Responsibility and Agent-Causation," in Widerker and McKenna, eds., *Moral Responsibility and Alternative Possibilities: Essays on the Importance of Alternative Possibilities*, 235–250; reprinted in John Martin Fischer, *My Way: Essays on Moral Responsibility* (New York: Oxford University Press, 2006), 143–158.

compatible with causal determinism, but moral responsibility *requires* causal determinism.[23] This is not, however, the direction I would take, because it would imply that our moral responsibility would, as it were, hang on a thread—just as much as it would if moral responsibility were deemed *incompatible* with causal determinism. Rather, I have sketched (in the previous section) a response to the problem of luck—or at least a response to one version of it. I think the response can be generalized to various other versions of the argument from luck, and it will be helpful simply to consider a few other versions here.[24]

Ishtiyaque Haji has presented what might be called the "ensurance formulation" of the Luck Problem. The basic idea is that indeterminism implies that an agent cannot ensure or guarantee, just prior to her choice and action, that she would make that choice and act in that way. Given this lack of capacity to ensure, it allegedly follows that the agent is not in control of her behavior—some factor *outside the agent* makes the difference, in the end. That is, given that (under indeterminism) the agent herself cannot guarantee the outcome, it is only when some external factor is added that the outcome ensues, and thus it is not *the agent* who makes the difference; *she* does not control the outcome. It is, then, a matter of luck whether the agent chooses and acts as she does, rather than choosing and acting in some other way.

Robert Kane also takes it that causal indeterminism entails that agents lack the capacity to ensure or guarantee the behavior in question prior to it. Kane calls this capacity, "antecedent determining control," and he says that "...the ability to be in, or bring about, conditions such that one can guarantee or determine which of a set of outcomes is going to occur *before* it occurs, whether the outcomes are one's own actions, the actions of others, or events in the world generally" is something the libertarian agent cannot have.[25]

Kane however goes on to say:

No doubt, such "antecedent determining control" as we might call it, is valuable in many circumstances; and we cannot help but value it by virtue of an evolutionary imperative to seek security and get control of our surroundings. But it does not follow that because you cannot determine which of a set

---

[23] Peter van Inwagen calls the argument that moral responsibility *requires* causal determinism the "*Mind* Argument" because many of the important presentations and discussions of this argument appeared in *Mind*. See, for example, R. E. Hobart (whose given name was Dickenson S. Miller), "Free Will as Involving Determinism and Inconceivable Without It," *Mind* (1934) 58, 1–27. Van Inwagen's discussion of the *Mind* Argument is in van Inwagen, *An Essay on Free Will*, 126–152.

[24] In thinking about the various versions of the Luck Problem, I have benefited greatly from reading unpublished material by Christopher Franklin, in particular, "Farewell to the Luck (and *Mind*) Argument," *Philosophical Studies* (forthcoming).

[25] Robert Kane, *The Significance of Free Will* (New York: Oxford University Press, 1996), 144. See also Robert Kane, "Responsibility, Luck, and Chance: Reflections on Free Will and Determinism," *Journal of Philosophy* (1999) 96, 217–240.

of outcomes occurs *before* it occurs, you lack control over which of them occurs, *when* it occurs. When the conditions of plural voluntary control are satisfied, agents exercise control over their future lives *then and there* in a manner that is not antecedently determined by their pasts.[26]

Kane's view, then, is that we do not need antecedent determining control—the capacity to ensure our choices and actions prior to them—in order to exercise a kind of control that would render us morally responsible. My argument in the previous section can be construed as a defense of Kane's position. Clearly, there is no reason to suppose that in W1 Jones lacks the power prior to t2 to ensure or guarantee his choice at t2 (and action at t3); but in W2 he does lack this power. Thus, in W1 he has antecedent determining control, whereas in W2 he lacks it. But, as argued previously, the requisite glue—whatever it is about the relationship between Jones's prior states and his choice at t2 that underwrites the view that he is in control—is present in W2, just as much as in W1. Thus, the mere fact that an agent lacks antecedent control does not in itself show that he is not in control in the sense required for moral responsibility.

Alfred Mele has developed another version of the Luck Problem.[27] In Christopher Franklin's terminology, this is the "Explanatory Formulation." As many philosophers have pointed out, it appears that if causal indeterminism obtains, then we cannot give a *contrastive explanation* of an agent's choices and behavior. (I do not include Mele himself in this group, although he gives a version of what might be called the Explanatory Formulation.) That is, it seems that we cannot give an explanation of why (say) Jones chooses as he actually does *rather than making a different choice*. Given the putative lack of availability of contrastive explanations under indeterminism, many have concluded that agents in causally indeterministic worlds cannot have the sort of control required for moral responsibility; after all, if we cannot even in principle explain why the agent chooses *X* rather than *Y*, it does not seem that it is genuinely *up to the agent* whether to choose *X* rather than *Y*.

Mele brings out this sort of worry by considering a goddess Diana who is creating agents who satisfy event-causal libertarian conditions. She worries, however, about the luck problem:

> Her worry, more specifically, is that if the difference between the actual world, in which one of her agents judges it best to *A* straightaway and then, at *t*, decides accordingly, and any possible world with the same past up to *t* and the same laws of nature and he makes an alternative decision while the judgment

---

[26] Robert Kane, *The Significance of Free Will*, 144.

[27] Alfred Mele, *Free Will and Luck* (New York: Oxford University Press, 2006). Here again I am indebted to chapter 4 of Christopher Franklin's dissertation.

persists is just a matter of luck, then he does not freely make that decision in that possible world, W. Diana suspects that his making that alternative decision rather than deciding in accordance with his best judgment—that is, the difference between W and the actual world—is just a matter of bad luck, or, more precisely, of worse luck in W for the agent than in the actual world. After all, because the worlds do not diverge before the agent decides, there is no difference in them to account for the difference in decisions.[28]

Mele's contention is the cross-world difference between the actual world and W is just a matter of luck, and thus the existence of luck poses a significant challenge to the agent's being free in either world. Just as Robert Kane seeks to address the problem of the lack of antecedent determining control, Alfred Mele goes on to address the problem posed by the apparent fact that the relevant cross-world differences are just a matter of luck.[29]

Again, the argument of the previous section shows that the mere lack of the availability of a contrastive explanation (of the relevant kind) does *not* in itself show that an agent does not possess the sort of control required for moral responsibility. After all, in W_1, but not in W_2, it is presumably possible to provide a contrastive explanation of Jones's behavior by reference to states "internal to Jones" in the relevant sense—his motivational states and whatever particular states realize or constitute them. Similarly, in W_2 (but not W_1) Mele could run his argument from cross-world differences. But, as we have seen above, the responsibility-underwriting glue is present in W_2, just as much as in W_1. I thus conclude that the mere fact that the relevant cross-world differences are purely a matter of luck does not in itself show that the agent's behavior results from luck in a sense that would rule out his moral responsibility.

Consider the pair of worlds, W_2 and W_2^*. As we know, in W_2 the state of the machine at $t_{1.9}$ is M_1 and the machine "goes to sleep." Imagine that in W_2^* the state of the machine at $t_{1.9}$ is M_1, and it swings into action (the other possible result of being in M_1). Nothing else is different about W_2 and W_2^* (up to $t_{1.9}$). Thus, Mele's argument applies: if it is sound, one could conclude that the difference between W_2 and W_2^* is just a matter of luck. But (as above) if the responsibility-underwriting glue is present is W_1, it is present in W_2. So, although Mele's argument applies to W_2, the glue is nevertheless present in W_2. Mele's argument thus cannot in itself show that there is an insuperable problem (pertaining to luck) with causal indeterminism.

---

[28] Alfred Mele, *Free Will and Luck*, 8.

[29] John Martin Fischer, "Review of Alfred Mele's, *Free Will and Luck*," *Mind* (2008) 117, 187–191; also, see Kane, "Responsibility, Luck, and Chance: Reflections on Free Will and Determinism."

V. Conclusion: An Approach to the Problem of Luck

A traditional conception of moral responsibility has it that in order to be morally responsible, I must make a difference to the unfolding world by selecting one from various genuinely open alternatives. There are two crucial ideas here. First, I must have alternative possibilities; I must select from among genuinely available options. Second, the path taken must be an outflowing of me—it is *I* who makes a difference by selecting the path. The two key premises of the Dilemma of Determinism call into question each of these ideas. The second premise states that if causal determinism is true, then I don't have alternative possibilities, and thus I do not select from among more than one genuinely available path into the future. The third premise states that if causal determinism is false, then it is not *I* who makes the selection.

It is interesting that the Consequence Argument (underwriting the second premise) and the Rollback Argument (supporting the third premise) have a similar abstract structure; in both cases we are essentially asked to imagine that the universe is rolled back. In the case of the Consequence Argument, we note that no matter how many times we allow it to go forward, it will take the same path. In the case of the Rollback Argument, we note that the universe will *not* take the same path every time we allow it to go forward. Both observations can be disturbing.

I have sketched replies to both premises (both horns of the dilemma). First, I have argued that moral responsibility does not require alternative possibilities. Here the Frankfurt cases are helpful; they are cases involving counterfactual interveners (such as Black) who are *untriggered ensurers*. Second, I have argued that indeterminism does not by itself entail the absence of the control required for moral responsibility. Here the genuinely random machine is helpful; it is a counterfactual intervener that is an *untriggered preemptor*. In both cases it is crucial that we have a *counterfactual* intervener—an individual or device that is poised to intervene but remains dormant. I have contended that the basic intuition elicited by Harry Frankfurt in his famous challenge to the second premise—that moral responsibility ascriptions are based on the actual sequence and thus mere untriggered devices or causally dormant individuals (counterfactual interveners) are not relevant to ascriptions of moral responsibility—also plays a crucial role in addressing the problem of luck. This basic intuition, after all, drives my argument that employs the genuinely random machine.[30]

---

[30] I think that Frankfurt is basically correct that mere counterfactual interveners or untriggered factors are irrelevant to ascriptions of moral responsibility. But this simple, important point needs to be interpreted and perhaps even qualified in light of cases such as "Shark," which are discussed in John Martin Fischer and Mark Ravizza, *Responsibility and Control: A Theory of Moral Responsibility* (New York: Cambridge University Press, 1998), 127–128. See also the fascinating (as yet unpublished) paper by Carolina Sartorio, "Actuality and Responsibility," *Mind* (forthcoming). Although Sartorio rejects the simple formulation of the point—that counterfactual interveners are irrelevant to ascriptions of moral responsibility—she does formulate and defend an alternative way of capturing the basic insight. I believe that the basic insight (articulated suitably) is all that is needed for my purposes in the text.

Think of it this way. Assume (for simplicity's sake) that the counterfactual intervener, Black, in the Frankfurt example makes it the case that Jones cannot do otherwise. (More carefully, it would be Black together with other factors that would have this implication, but put this aside for now.)[31] Frankfurt's point is that insofar as Black's presence is irrelevant to Jones's moral responsibility, it follows that the fact that Jones cannot do otherwise is similarly irrelevant to Jones's moral responsibility. Now assume (again, for simplicity's sake) that the genuinely random machine makes it the case that the Rollback Argument applies in my example above (and that Jones lacks antecedent determining control, etc.). Insofar as the mere presence of the machine is irrelevant to Jones's moral responsibility in the example, it follows that the fact that the Rollback Argument applies (and that Jones lacks antecedent determining control, etc.) is irrelevant to Jones's moral responsibility.

In previous work, I have urged that we focus like a laser on the "actual sequence" that issues in the behavior in question. In developing an account of the control that grounds moral responsibility, I have suggested that we prescind from counterfactual interveners, such as Black, and attend to the properties of Jones as manifested in the unfolding actual sequence of events. In identifying those properties, we pretend that Black does not exist; as it were, we put him in a box. (As Frankfurt put it, if we were to "subtract Black away," the flow of the actual sequence would be exactly the same.) Similarly, in evaluating the relationship between indeterminism and control-grounding moral responsibility, we need to have a laserlike focus on the actual sequence. And when we "subtract away" the genuinely random machine, we see clearly that the sequence issuing in the relevant behavior in W2 is exactly the same as in W1. Thus, insofar as the presence of the machine is irrelevant to Jones's responsibility, Jones has exactly the same glue in W2 as in W1.

I have then sketched an approach to the problem of luck. I do not call it a "solution" to this problem, in part because of a natural conservatism about such claims, but also in part because I do not give an *account* of the responsibility-underwriting glue. Also, I have not argued that *no* articulation of the problem of luck can avoid the sort of strategy of response I have sketched.[32] It should be noted

---

[31] For further discussion, see chap. 2 of this book.

[32] If one is not convinced by my strategy that *no* articulation of the problem of luck will be forceful, then perhaps one can see my paper as forcing the proponent of (say) the Rollback Argument (or various of the other arguments) to be clearer and more precise as to how exactly to formulate the worry. For example, a proponent of the Rollback Argument might seek to place some constraints on the admissible scenarios that would rule out cases such as W2, where the "randomness" is installed in a place that is "external to and independent of" the agent. Both Anthony Brueckner and Tim O'Connor have suggested the possibility of such strategies to me. Brueckner notes that in my example of W2 the randomness is "injected" into the machine (but not the brain), and O'Connor wonders whether we can put aside "environmental wildcards" (such as meteorites, lightning bolts, and, presumably, causal sequences initiated by distill and causally independently triggered machines), in evaluating agency.

Recall, however, that the machine's randomness makes it the case that the connection between Jones's prior mental states and his choice is indeterministic in W2, so there is indeterminacy in just the

that my suggestion does not vindicate indeterminism in a context in which the agent has "dual control"—that is, moral-responsibility conferring control in both the actual sequence and the alternative sequence. Insofar as certain libertarians adopt the dual-control picture, my solution does not in itself provide a full defense against the problem of luck that could be invoked by all libertarians.[33] Instead, I have had the more modest project of arguing that *if* the requisite glue is indeed present in a context of causal determination, then it is *also* present in *certain contexts* under causal indeterminism. It would seem to follow that causal indeterminism *per se* does not rule it out that we are glued together as morally responsible agents. That is, the mere possibility of running the Rollback Argument *in itself* does not threaten moral responsibility.[34]

In defending a compatibilist account of moral responsibility (elsewhere), I have contended (as any compatibilist must) that not all causally deterministic sequences are created equal.[35] That is, I have contended that it is not the case that all causally deterministic sequences crowd out moral responsibility; causal determination *qua* causal determination does not rule out moral responsibility. Similarly, here I have argued that not all contexts of causal indeterminism threaten the responsibility-underwriting relationship; thus, causal indeterminism *qua* causal indeterminism does not rule out moral responsibility.[36]

"right spot" in W2. That is, by "injecting randomness" into the machine in W2, we *thereby* inject indeterminacy into the relevant place in the sequence flowing through Jones. Perhaps one could reformulate the Rollback Argument to require that we only consider scenarios where the indeterminacy in the agent is somehow "non-derivative"—it is, as it were, injected *directly* in the agent. I do not here argue that one could not seek to reformulate the Rollback Argument in this way, although I am somewhat skeptical about this possibility; here I am simply claiming that it is important to note that it *must* be reformulated. Further, such a reformulation, if it can be given, should help us to see more precisely what the real basis of the Rollback Argument is.

[33] I am indebted to Dana Nelkin and David Brink for this point.

[34] I believe that this is an important *first step* in a more complete defense of the coherence of indeterministic control. Just as with the Frankfurt examples, I would counsel patience and at least a *two-step* argument. Here, the first step is to show that the mere applicability of the Rollback Argument does not in itself establish that the control required for moral responsibility is absent. One can then offer *additional* argumentation for the particular model of indeterministic control one wishes to defend. Thus, even though the first step of the argument cannot in itself establish an indeterministic "dual-control" model, this step is entirely consistent with going on to defend just such a model. From the fact that my Random Machine Argument does not provide a model in which there is dual control, it does *not* follow that it could not be an important first step in the defense of such a model. (Again, the dialectical situation here is analogous to the two-step approach I have defended with respect to the Frankfurt examples. This is yet another way in which the two dialectical contexts exhibit a striking symmetry.)

[35] See, for example, John Martin Fischer, *The Metaphysics of Free Will: An Essay on Control*; John Martin Fischer and Mark Ravizza, *Responsibility and Control: A Theory of Moral Responsibility* (New York: Cambridge University Press, 1998); John Martin Fischer, *My Way: Essays on Moral Responsibility*; and John Martin Fischer et al., *Four Views on Free Will*.

[36] Indeed, my account of moral responsibility is consistent with either causal determination or indeterminism: John Martin Fischer and Mark Ravizza, *Responsibility and Control: A Theory of Moral Responsibility*, 253.

Insofar as we have good responses to both of the horns of the Dilemma of Determinism, moral responsibility does not hang on a thread. This is a good thing, since it does not seem to be a comfortable position to have to proclaim from our armchairs that we know that causal determinism is false. And it would appear to be equally uncomfortable to feel the need to pronounce, from our philosophical La-Z Boys, that causal determinism is true. It is thus a good thing that we have found plausible and "independent" arguments for the *resilience* of moral responsibility to the truth or falsity of causal determinism—arguments that are not simply statements of the desirability of such resilience. In the end, then, moral responsibility is neither inconceivable nor puzzling.[37]

---

[37] I have benefited from giving versions of this paper at the Law and Neuroscience Conference, Faculty of Laws, University College, University of London; University of California, San Diego; University of Colorado, Boulder (Keynote Address, Rocky Mountain Ethics Congress); University of Indiana, Bloomington (Bo Clark Lecture); University of Texas, Austin; University of Notre Dame, and the American Philosophical Association Pacific Division Meetings (San Diego) [Special Session in Honor of Paul Hoffman]. I am extremely grateful for comments by Neal A. Tognazzini, Christopher Franklin, Ben Mitchell-Yellin, Justin Coates, Patrick Todd, Garrett Pendergraft, Paul Hoffman, Randolph Clarke, Anthony Brueckner, Dana Nelkin, Michael Hardimon, David Brink, Walter Sinnott-Armstrong, Michael Tye, Robert Kane, and Mark Sainsbury.

PART TWO

The Middle Path: Guidance Control

7

The Direct Argument: You Say Goodbye,
I Say Hello

I. Widerker's Critique of the Direct Argument: The Lure of Liberty

In a provocative and important article, "Farewell to the Direct Argument," David
Widerker argues that the direct argument for the incompatibility of causal determinism and moral responsibility is not helpful in advancing the debate.[1] More
specifically, he contends:

> [T]he direct argument is not an improvement over the traditional argument.
> Not only are some standard versions of it invalid; but even if one were to come
> up with a flawless version, its plausibility would still depend on the traditional
> assumption that determinism rules out avoidability. Ultimately, the direct
> argument cannot do the work its proponents wanted it to do.[2]

Widerker characterizes the direct argument as follows:

> [The direct argument] does not employ the notion of avoidability, but argues
> "directly" for [the conclusion that moral responsibility and causal deter-
> minism are incompatible] from some general and allegedly uncontroversial
> assumptions about moral responsibility and determinism.
>
> An incompatibilist like Peter van Inwagen, who introduced this type of
> argument into the literature on free will, has done so to show that one could
> establish the incompatibility of moral responsibility and determinism *without*
> the "avoidability" or "could-have-done-otherwise" notion of free will.[3]

---

[1] Widerker, "Farewell to the Direct Argument," *Journal of Philosophy* 6 (2002): 316–324.
[2] Ibid., p. 317.
[3] Ibid., p. 316, emphasis in the original. Peter van Inwagen introduced the direct argument in "The
Incompatibility of Responsibility and Determinism," in Michael Bradie and Myles Brand (eds), *Action*

Although the argument can be given different (and more careful) regimentations, we can understand it informally as follows. It employs the Principle of Transfer of Non-Responsibility. This is the principle (roughly) that if no one is morally responsible for p, and no one is morally responsible for "if p, then q," then no one is morally responsible for q. If we assume that no one is morally responsible for the remote past, and no one is morally responsible for the laws of nature or anything entailed by the laws of nature (or, more specifically, any instance of the laws of nature), then it appears as if causal determinism implies that no human being is morally responsible for anything.[4]

Widerker brings out some complexities which suggest that the Principle of Transfer of Non-Responsibility needs to be "improved," and, for the sake of discussion, he accepts a modified version proposed by Carl Ginet.[5] For my purposes, I will put these details to the side; none of the discussion here will depend on them, or on adopting the "improved" version of the principle. Widerker contends that any modification of the principle will be subject to the following sort of criticism:

> [C]onsider again Jones, who deliberately murders Smith for some selfish reason, knowing very well that in doing so he is acting immorally. Suppose further that Jones lives in a deterministic world. Is Jones morally blameworthy for what he did? Proponents of the direct argument will want to answer this question negatively. But suppose that their opponent disagrees, claiming that Jones *is* blameworthy, since he knew that he was acting wrongly and *could* have avoided acting as he did. What can the defender of the direct argument say in reply? It seems that his only and obvious response would be to say that, in the deterministic world under consideration, Jones could *not* have avoided killing Smith. Otherwise, there would be no reason to regard the improved version of transfer NR as valid, as it would be rendered invalid by the deterministic scenario under consideration. But notice that the dialectical situation has changed. For now it is clear that the validity of the improved version of transfer NR (transfer NR*) requires that determinism

---

and Responsibility, Bowling Green Studies in Applied Philosophy, vol. 2 (Bowling Green, OH: Bowling Green State University Press, 1980), pp. 30–37; this piece is reprinted in John Martin Fischer (ed.), *Moral Responsibility* (Ithaca, NY: Cornell University Press, 1986), pp. 241–249. Also, see Peter van Inwagen, *An Essay on Free Will* (Oxford: Clarendon Press, 1983), pp. 182–188. I have discussed the direct argument in John Martin Fischer and Mark Ravizza, *Responsibility and Control: A Theory of Moral Responsibility* (Cambridge: Cambridge University Press, 1998), pp. 151–169; Fischer, "The Transfer of Non-Responsibility," in Joseph K. Campbell, Michael O'Rourke, and David Shier (eds), *Freedom and Determinism* (Cambridge, MA: MIT Press, 2004), pp. 189–209; and Eleonore Stump and John Martin Fischer, "Transfer Principles and Moral Responsibility," *Philosophical Perspectives* 14 (2000): 47–56.

    [4] Widerker lays out the argument more carefully (following van Inwagen) in "Farewell to the Direct Argument," pp. 317–318.

    [5] Widerker, "Farewell to the Direct Argument," pp. 322–323, esp. fn. 14, p.322.

rules out avoidability. In response to this objection, the proponent of the direct argument may argue that he is more sure of the validity of transfer NR* than he is of the assumption that

(M) Someone who knowingly acted in a morally wrong way, and believed correctly that he could have avoided acting as he did, is blameworthy for his act

and, therefore, he does not see a reason not to use transfer NR*. But such a reply would be implausible. Surely, (M), which is explicative of the very notion of blameworthiness, enjoys a degree of certainty that does not fall below that of transfer NR*. Hence, (M) can certainly be viewed as a defeater of that principle.[6]

Widerker concludes, among other things, that "the direct argument... depends for its plausibility on the assumption... of the incompatibility of determinism with the freedom to avoid acting as one did. Hence, it cannot do the work its proponents wanted it to do."[7]

II. Discussion of Widerker

It is, however, puzzling that Widerker takes (M) as even potentially a defeater of transfer NR*. This is because (M) would have it (in Widerker's example) that Jones is blameworthy for murdering Smith, insofar as he could have done otherwise (given that certain other conditions are met). So, in the example, perhaps Jones would be morally responsible for the *connection* (posited by causal determinism) between the relevant antecedent state of the universe and his murdering Smith. In this approach, the critic of the direct argument who adopts (M) would be denying the nonresponsibilty-for-the-laws premise. Or perhaps the critic of the direct argument (who adopts [M]) will deny the nonresponsibilty-for-the-past premise. (In this sort of view, Jones could have done otherwise, and thus could have so acted that the past would have been different from what it was. Hence, Jones can be morally responsible for *p* [stating that some past event occurred]). In these two approaches, which I believe are the most attractive for the critic of the direct argument, the modal transfer principle, transfer NR*, would *not* be impugned; Widerker's case would *not* be an example in which an agent (Jones) is not morally responsible for the relevant antecedent state of the universe and also not morally responsible for the connection between that state of the universe and his murdering Smith, and yet morally responsible for murdering Smith.

---

[6] Ibid., pp. 322–323, emphases in the original.
[7] Ibid., p. 323.

The example is not even of the form that would call transfer NR* into question (quite apart from the issue of whether [M] could be invoked legitimately within this dialectical niche).

As it is not at all evident how the example above supports a denial of the modal transfer principle, let me suggest a possible way of supporting this interpretation. Michael Slote argues that a compatibilist about causal determinism and free will (in the sense that involves genuine metaphysical access to alternative possibilities) may accept the fixity of the past and the fixity of the laws but deny the modal transfer of powerlessness principle.[8] Note that this modal transfer principle is employed in certain versions of the Consequence Argument—the argument that causal determinism and free will (in the sense that involves access to alternative possibilities) are incompatible.[9] The transfer of powerlessness principle is structurally similar to the modal transfer of nonresponsibility principle(s), but the relevant modality is powerlessness (or lack of access to alternative possibilities), rather than nonresponsibility. Someone who accepts Slote's approach could deny the validity of the Consequence Argument (by rejecting the transfer of powerlessness principle) and thus deny the transfer of nonresponsibility principle (without denying either of the premises of the direct argument). Adopting Slote's approach (or a similar approach) would thus support the denial of transfer NR* in the context of the direct argument for incompatibilism about causal determinism and moral responsibility.

But I find this sort of move unattractive for two reasons. First, I am not convinced by Slote.[10] Note that there is no indication in Widerker's "Farewell to the Direct Argument" that he is relying on Slote's approach; more important, there is no discussion of how Slote's approach is related to Widerker's rejection of transfer NR*. Slote can be seen as pointing to a certain analogy between the phenomena pertinent to knowledge and those pertinent to power. Given this putative parallelism, together with Slote's contention that knowledge involves a kind of "selectivity" that allows for the rejection of the Principle of Closure of Knowledge Under Known Implication, Slote concludes that we should also reject the parallel principle of transfer of powerlessness (van Inwagen's Principle Beta).

But even on the hypothesis that Slote is correct about his analysis of contexts of knowledge, I have argued that there is no reason to suppose that the contexts of power attributions are relevantly similar to the contexts of knowledge attributions (with respect to "selectivity").[11] Additionally, I see no argument in Widerker's "Farewell to the Direct Argument" for the contention that contexts of

---

[8] Michael Slote, "Selective Necessity and the Free-Will Problem," *Journal of Philosophy* 79 (1982): 5–24.

[9] Peter van Inwagen dubbed the argument the "Consequence Argument" in *An Essay on Free Will*.

[10] For an extended critical discussion of Slote, see John Martin Fischer, *The Metaphysics of Free Will: An Essay on Control* (Oxford: Blackwell Publishers, 1994), pp. 29–45.

[11] Fischer, *The Metaphysics of Free Will*, pp. 29–45.

responsibility attribution involve the relevant sort of "selectivity." Absent such an argument, it is puzzling to me how it could be maintained that Jones is not morally responsible for p, and Jones is not morally responsible for the connection between p and q, but nevertheless that Jones *is* morally responsible for q (in virtue of being able to bring about not-q). Here it would seem that, given that Jones is not morally responsible for p, if one says that Jones is morally responsible for q (in virtue of being able to bring about not-q), one ought to say that Jones is morally responsible for the *connection* between p and q.

Perhaps Widerker has in mind some reason to suppose that the phenomena pertinent to moral responsibility ascriptions are relevantly similar to the phenomena pertinent to knowledge ascriptions with respect to Slote's notion of selectivity; or perhaps Widerker is not relying on a Slote-type approach at all. In either case, additional argumentation is clearly needed in order to dispel the mystery associated with Widerker's contention that acceptance of (M) should lead one to reject the relevant *transfer* principle. Further, I do not believe that the Consequence Argument depends essentially on a modal "transfer of powerlessness" principle.[12] That is, I believe that the Consequence Argument can be formulated in such a way that it does not depend—either explicitly or implicitly—on such a principle. If this is correct, then a critic of the direct argument (who accepts [M]) *must* deny either the fixity-of-the-past premise or the fixity-of-the-laws premise.

A critic of the direct argument *might* find fault with the modal transfer principle (such as transfer NR*), but he certainly need not. Widerker should not have taken the critic to hold that it is the transfer principle that is at fault. Rather, the point of the objector (who accepts [M]) is that *either* one of the premises of the direct argument is false *or* the transfer principle is invalid.

In the final section of Widerker's paper, in which he purports to raise a "Further Objection," he essentially raises the sort of issue I have just raised:

> [T]he hope of the proponents of the direct argument to be able to prove that determinism excludes moral responsibility without the notion of avoidability was unrealistic in the first place. To see this, it is enough to consider one central assumption of the direct argument, to wit, that no one is morally responsible for the laws of nature. Why should one accept it if not for the fact that no one could have prevented them for obtaining?[13]

I agree with Widerker that the proponent of the direct argument would insist on the fixity of the natural laws—the idea that we do not have power over the laws of

---

[12] See John M. Fischer and Mark Ravizza, "When the Will Is Free," *Philosophical Perspectives* 6 (1992): 423–452; Fischer and Ravizza, "Free Will and the Modal Principle," *Philosophical Studies* 83 (1996): 213–230; and Fischer, "A New Compatibilism," *Philosophical Topics* 24 (1998): 49–66.

[13] Widerker, "Farewell to the Direct Argument," p. 324. Note that section II is called "A Stronger Objection" whereas section III is called "Three Morals and a Further Objection." Clearly, Widerker thinks of the objections of sections II and III as different.

nature (or their instances). Without this assumption (and the assumption of the fixity of the past), the argument would not be obviously sound (although, as I argued above, the modal principle would not thereby be impugned). I believe that the upshot of Widerker's argument (together with the ruminations I offered above) is that the best argument for either premise of the direct argument or for its transfer principle will involve a premise about the unavoidability of a certain relevant thing (e.g., the laws of nature). This is a worthwhile and significant point, with which I agree.[14]

Widerker's insight shows that van Inwagen was mistaken in his statement of the dialectical role of the direct argument. In his early paper on these topics, van Inwagen distinguishes two propositions:

i. Determinism is incompatible with free will.
ii. Moral responsibility is impossible without free will.[15]

Although van Inwagen points out that he accepts both (i) and (ii), he says:

> Because (i) is so very controversial, however, I propose in this paper to investigate the question whether moral responsibility is compatible with determinism *independently* of (i). I shall argue that determinism and responsibility are incompatible, and not only shall I make no use of proposition (i) in my argument, I shall make no mention whatever of free will other than a very brief one ... the concept of free will, will not *figure* in my argument.[16]

Given the upshot of Widerker's argument, van Inwagen is incorrect in supposing that he has given an argument (the direct argument) that avoids considerations pertinent to (i).

III. A Different Motivation for the Direct Argument

I believe that van Inwagen should have said that the direct argument avoids considerations pertinent to (ii), rather than (i). That is, I believe that the proper way to understand the direct argument is an attempt to argue for the incompatibility of causal determinism and moral responsibility without invoking the putative requirement of alternative possibilities for moral responsibility.

---

[14] Randolph Clarke has pointed out in his comments on the discussion thread of a previous version of this paper in the Online Philosophy Conference 2 (OPC2), posted May 23, 2007, that Peter van Inwagen (who introduced the direct argument) simply takes it as obvious that no one is responsible for the laws or the past, offering no argument appealing to their fixity to back up these claims (see van Inwagen, *An Essay on Free Will*, pp. 184–185).

[15] Van Inwagen, "The Incompatibility of Responsibility and Determinism," p. 241.

[16] Ibid., pp. 241–242, emphases in the original.

Indirect arguments go via the Principle of Alternative Possibilities, according to which moral responsibility requires avoidability.[17] In contrast, direct arguments do not invoke this principle or any other principle that posits the requirement of avoidability or alternative possibilities for moral responsibility. Given the huge debate about Frankfurt-style counterexamples to the Principle of Alternative Possibilities, it is at least interesting, and arguably attractive, to explore whether one could construct an argument for incompatibilism that does not depend on the Principle of Alternative Possibilities.[18]

Now someone might object as follows. Let us grant that the explicit purpose of the proponent of the direct argument is to construct an argument that does not depend on the requirement of avoidability for moral responsibility. But he has constructed an argument that depends (for example) on the contention that instances of the laws of nature are such that we cannot falsify them. But this will be contested by a compatibilist about causal determinism and avoidability. Since typically a compatibilist about causal determinism and avoidability would also be a compatibilist about causal determinism and moral responsibility, the argument will not make any progress.

Note that a similar move might be made in the context of the argument for the incompatibility of causal determinism and the sort of freedom that involves avoidability or genuine metaphysical access to alternative possibilities, the Consequence Argument.[19] That is, the fixity of the laws is an assumption of the Consequence Argument. It could be said, as above, that certain compatibilists are committed to the falsity of the assumption of the fixity of the natural laws, and thus such an assumption cannot legitimately be employed in the Consequence Argument. Although there are very complex and delicate issues about burden of proof and begging the question lurking here, it suffices for my purposes to note that it is not obviously a fair criticism of the Consequence Argument that the argument employs an assumption that would be (and, indeed, would have to be) resisted by a compatibilist, if it arguably has some *independent plausibility*.

The points above seem to me to reflect the fact that at bottom the incompatibilist believes that the laws of nature exert a "push" or contain a kind of "compulsion" that is incompatible with moral responsibility. In the direct approach, the push directly rules out moral responsibility; in the indirect approach, the push rules out avoidability, which is required for moral responsibility. One could say that this common source—the "pushing" or "compelling" feature of natural

---

[17] The principle is criticized in Harry Frankfurt, "Alternate Possibilities and Moral Responsibility," *Journal of Philosophy* 66 (1969): 828–839.

[18] Frankfurt hoped we could dispense with the Principle of Alternative Possibilities and thus sidestep certain traditional puzzles. A proponent of the direct argument might wish to sidestep the debates about the Frankfurt-style examples!

[19] For discussions, see van Inwagen, *An Essay on Free Will*; Carl Ginet, *On Action* (Cambridge: Cambridge University Press, 1990); and Fischer, *The Metaphysics of Free Will*.

laws—is an important ingredient in both the direct and indirect arguments for incompatibilism.

It does *not* however follow, as Widerker puts it, that "the direct argument... cannot usefully advance the debate between incompatibilists and their opponents."[20] As I have suggested above, the motivation of the proponent of the direct argument need *not* be to expunge the notion of avoidability (despite van Inwagen's claim to the contrary); rather, the idea is to jettison the Principle of Alternative Possibilities. Sidestepping debates about this principle may be attractive. Further, it may be appealing to focus on the nature of natural laws and to seek to make dialectical progress in that way, rather than attempting decisively to resolve issues pertaining to the relationship between moral responsibility and alternative possibilities.[21] Apart from the question of whether success (or even progress) is in the offing, it is certainly the case that the proponent of the direct argument would have shifted the debate to different territory.

I have argued that, although he mistakenly identifies the culprit in the direct argument as (exclusively) the transfer of nonresponsibility principle, Widerker is onto something important: the direct argument can only be defended by presupposing important claims about unavoidability. Further, in contrast to van Inwagen, I have suggested that the proper way to understand the motivation of the proponent of the direct argument is to seek to argue for the incompatibility of causal determinism and moral responsibility without invoking the Principle of Alternative Possibilities (the requirement of alternative possibilities for moral responsibility). I have suggested that, given this motivation, the direct argument arguably makes progress, at least in the sense of shifting the dialectical terrain in a way that some will find fruitful and promising.

Ultimately, however, I do not know whether this apparent shift helps us to make genuine philosophical progress. I (and Mark Ravizza) have argued that examples structurally similar to Frankfurt-style counterexamples to the Principle of Alternative Possibilities show that transfer NR* and related principles are invalid.[22] It may be, then, that the evaluation of transfer NR* depends on precisely the same sorts of considerations as the evaluation of the Principle of Alternative Possibilities; in this case it would seem that no dialectical progress would have been made by employing the direct argument.

There are, however, philosophers who accept that Frankfurt-style counterexamples show the falsity of the Principle of Alternative Possibilities, and yet also

---

[20] Widerker, "Farewell to the Direct Argument," p. 324.

[21] In Laura Ekstrom's view, the laws of nature compel or "push": "Protecting Incompatibilist Freedom," *American Philosophical Quarterly* 35 (1998): 281–291. In contrast, Bernard Berofsky defends a view according to which the laws of nature do not compel: *Freedom from Necessity* (London: Routledge and Kegan Paul, 1987).

[22] Fischer and Ravizza, *Responsibility and Control*, pp. 151–169, and Fischer, "The Transfer of Non-Responsibility." The latter paper is a reply to Michael McKenna, "Source Incompatibilism, Ultimacy, and the Transfer of Non-Responsibility," *American Philosophical Quarterly* 38 (2001): 37–52.

accept that some suitably revised transfer of nonresponsibility principle is valid (and can be employed in a sound argument for the incompatibility of causal determinism and moral responsibility).[23] It may thus be essentially contentious whether in the end the move to the direct argument is helpful.

IV. Different Families of Direct Arguments

I believe we should distinguish different "families" of direct arguments. The family we have been considering employs some sort of modal transfer of nonresponsibility principle. It appears to be controversial whether this sort of direct argument can help us to make dialectical progress. But other families of direct arguments do not employ modal transfer principles; rather, they invoke notions such as "sourcehood," "origination," and so forth. Whereas these may be no more successful in the end, it seems that they employ genuinely different ingredients than the indirect arguments.[24]

Consider, for example, Derk Pereboom's famous "four-case argument."[25] Pereboom begins by constructing an example in which there is significant manipulation in virtue of which he takes it that most people would say that there is no moral responsibility. He then proceeds step by step to construct other examples that do not appear to differ in any relevant way from the first case; by the time Pereboom gets to the end of the sequence of four cases, he is describing an ordinary

---

[23] See Eleonore Stump, "The Direct Argument for Incompatibilism," *Philosophy and Phenomenological Research* 61 (2000): 459–466, and "Control and Causal Determinism," in Sarah Buss and Lee Overton (eds), *Contours of Agency: Essays on Themes from Harry Frankfurt* (Cambridge, MA: The MIT Press, 2002), pp. 33–60. For a reply, see John Martin Fischer and Mark Ravizza, "Reply to Stump," *Philosophy and Phenomenological Research* 61 (2000): 477–480.

Derk Pereboom is also precisely this sort of incompatibilist about causal determinism and moral responsibility. In *Living Without Free Will* (Cambridge: Cambridge University Press, 2001), he accepts that Frankfurt-style counterexamples (suitably developed) show the falsity of the Principle of Alternative Possibilities, but he nevertheless holds that causal determinism would rule out sourcehood (in the sense required for moral responsibility). Note that transfer principles are often stated in terms of the notions of entailment, sufficiency for, or rendering inevitable. Pereboom's preferred incompatibilist claim can't be stated in terms of any of these notions. By virtue of accepting standard Frankfurt-style arguments, source incompatibilists like Pereboom agree that it is possible that conditions hold that are sufficient for or entail that an action is performed, or render it inevitable, while the agent can still be responsible for this action. But crucially there is a distinction between conditions holding that are sufficient for or entail that an action is performed, or render it inevitable, and those conditions causally determining the action. For the latter point, see John Martin Fischer, "Responsibility and Control," *Journal of Philosophy* 79 (1982): 24–40.

[24] For a more detailed discussion of "source incompatibilism," see Fischer, *The Metaphysics of Free Will*, pp. 147–154; and "Frankfurt-Style Compatibilism," in Buss and Overton (eds), *Contours of Agency*, pp. 1–26, reprinted in G. Watson (ed.), *Free Will*, 2nd ed. (Oxford: Oxford University Press, 2003), pp. 190–211. Also see John Martin Fischer, "Compatibilism," in John Martin Fischer, Robert Kane, Derk Pereboom, and Manuel Vargas, *Four Views on Free Will* (Oxford: Blackwell Publishers, 2007), esp. pp. 61–71.

[25] Pereboom, *Living Without Free Will*, pp. 110–117.

scenario under causal determinism. Pereboom's point is that there is no principled way of distinguishing the problematic—responsibility-undermining—sorts of causation from "mere" causal determination. Insofar as he is confident that the sort of manipulation in the first case expunges any thread of moral responsibility, he concludes that causal determination would rule out moral responsibility.

Now this is an interesting and important argument; I have sought to address it elsewhere.[26] I focus here on the apparent fact that this argument does not seem to employ any sort of modal transfer principle (such as transfer NR or its relatives). Whereas it might be thought that some such principle is lurking in the background, Pereboom says:

> [Consider the principle] "[I]f one's action results from a deterministic causal process that traces back to factors beyond one's control, to factors that one could not have produced, altered or prevented, then one is not free in the sense required for moral responsibility."
>
> I think that this principle is not employed by my manipulation argument as a premise. Rather, it is drawn from the argument as a general conclusion, and it is in this sense that ... [it is] right to say that it underlies the argument. Without presupposing this claim, interested parties are asked to reflect on the manipulated agents, to ask whether they are intuitively morally responsible, and if not, whether there is a difference between the manipulated agents and the ordinary determined agent that can explain a difference in responsibility. This procedure does not presuppose the truth of the quoted principle, and one would not want to craft a manipulation argument against compatibilism in such a way as to presuppose the truth of the key incompatibilist claim.[27]

Similarly, consider the already famous "Zygote Argument" of Alfred Mele.[28] Mele says:

> Diana creates a zygote Z in Mary. She combines Z's atoms as she does because she wants a certain event E to occur thirty years later. From her knowledge of the state of the universe just prior to her creating Z and the laws of nature of her deterministic universe, she deduces that a zygote with precisely Z's constitution located in Mary will develop into an ideally self-controlled agent who, in thirty years, will judge, on the basis of rational deliberation, that it is best to A and will A on the basis of that judgment,

---

[26] See especially John Martin Fischer, "Responsibility and Manipulation," *The Journal of Ethics* 8 (2004): 145–177, reprinted in John Martin Fischer, *My Way: Essays on Moral Responsibility* (New York: Oxford University Press, 2006), pp. 223–250; and Fischer et al., *Four Views on Free Will*, pp. 185–188.

[27] Derk Pereboom, in comments on the discussion thread of a previous version of this paper in the Online Philosophy Conference 2 (OPC2), posted May 23, 2007. Pereboom was responding to comments in the same thread by Joseph Campbell.

[28] Alfred Mele, *Free Will and Luck* (New York: Oxford University Press, 2006), 188–195.

thereby bringing about E…Thirty years later, Ernie [the individual who develops from Z] is a mentally healthy, ideally self-controlled person who regularly exercises his powers of self-control.[29]

The Zygote Argument begins with the intuition that, when the process issuing in behavior is initiated by an agent with the intention to produce just that behavior (as in the example of Diana), the behavior in question cannot be free in the relevant sense, and the agent cannot be morally responsible. The proponent of the argument proceeds to contend that there is no significant difference between this sort of process (beginning with the intentions of an agent such as Diana) and ordinary sequences under causal determinism. The conclusion is that causal determinism rules out freedom and moral responsibility. Although Mele does not endorse the argument or its conclusion, he is sufficiently worried about it that he remains an agnostic about the compatibility of causal determinism and moral responsibility. He contends that the Zygote Argument is an improvement on various "manipulation arguments," such as Pereboom's four-stage argument.

Being a bit more careful, Mele regiments the core of the argument as follows:

1. Because of the way his zygote was produced in his deterministic universe, Ernie is not a free agent and is not morally responsible for anything.
2. Concerning the free action and moral responsibility of the beings into whom the zygotes develop, there is no significant difference between the way Ernie's zygote comes to exist and the way any normal human zygote comes to exist in a deterministic universe.
3. So determinism precludes free action and moral responsibility.[30]

As far as I can see, no transfer principle is explicitly invoked or implicitly relied upon here. As Randolph Clarke puts it, "No transfer principle is in sight. Is one hidden somewhere? Not that I can determine."[31]

Of course, one can articulate some sort of general principle, such as a modal transfer of nonresponsibility principle, and point out that it provides support for premise (1). But this, even if true, does not in itself show that invocation of such a principle is *necessary* for providing support for premise (1). Just as in Pereboom's description of his procedure, we need not invoke general principles in support of our intuitions about the relevant premises of the Zygote Argument. Rather, we are supposed to rely on reflective judgments about the history of Ernie's zygote (and the relationship of such a history to moral responsibility). Randolph Clarke puts this point nicely:

---

[29] Ibid., p. 188.

[30] Ibid., p. 189.

[31] Randolph Clarke, in comments on the discussion thread of a previous version of this paper in the OPC2, posted May 23, 2007.

What would make Premise 1 of the zygote argument true is that Ernie isn't responsible for what he does, because of the way his zygote was produced. The preplanning of his life by Diana is supposed to get us to see this. Then, with premise 2, we are supposed to see that subtracting the preplanning makes no moral difference.[32]

In this section I have pointed to what I take to be direct arguments for the incompatibility of causal determinism and moral responsibility that do not (at any level) rely upon a modal principle such as transfer NR. Various philosophers might well resist my contention; they would insist that at some level—perhaps not readily accessible on initial inspection—the arguments all rely upon some principle such as transfer NR.[33] It is difficult to provide a decisive refutation of this view. I note, again, that the mere fact that one *can* regiment a particular intuitive line of reasoning so that it relies upon a certain general principle does not show that one *must* so regiment it! It is interesting that the debates here reinscribe parallel debates about whether the principle of transfer of powerlessness is necessary—either explicitly or implicitly—for all versions of the Consequence Argument.[34]

V. Conclusion

The direct argument for the incompatibility of causal determinism and moral responsibility is really an extended family of "direct arguments"—arguments that do not proceed via the Principle of Alternative Possibilities (according to which moral responsibility requires the sort of control or freedom that involves genuine metaphysical access to alternative possibilities). Some members of the family employ modal transfer principles (such as transfer NR*), whereas others do not (arguably, at least).

I began by disagreeing with Widerker's contention that acceptance of (M) would "defeat" the relevant transfer of nonresponsibility principle (such as transfer NR*). I argued for a more refined analysis of the implications of accepting (M). But my analysis led me to agree with Widerker about his fundamental diagnosis of the problem with the entire family of direct arguments—that they do not in fact prescind from considerations pertinent to the sort of control or freedom that

---

[32] Randolph Clarke, OPC2, May 23, 2007. Clarke goes on to say, "Once we see this second point, we might want to return to premise 1 and reject it. We needn't call it question-begging; we can just say we disagree."

I am inclined to agree that the Zygote Argument does not appear to rely upon a modal transfer of nonresponsibility principle. For a discussion of the argument, including my reasons for rejecting it, see John Martin Fischer, "Review of Alfred Mele, *Free Will and Luck*," *Mind* 117 (2008): 195–201.

[33] For such suggestions, see the contributions to the OPC2 discussion thread on a previous version of this paper by Joseph Campbell, Eddy Nahmias, and Ted A. Warfield.

[34] See Fischer and Ravizza, "When the Will Is Free" and "Free Will and the Modal Principle," and Fischer, "A New Compatibilism."

involves access to alternative possibilities. In fact, the argument crucially assumes certain views about the relationship between causal determinism and such freedom or "avoidability."

Further, I have suggested that we not follow van Inwagen in thinking of the significance of the direct arguments as prescinding from avoidability *in general*; rather, I have suggested that their significance is that they proceed without requiring the *specific* sort of avoidability encoded in the Principle of Alternative Possibilities. An argument that does not require this sort of principle would be attractive to certain philosophers. In the end, however, I am not inclined to think that the move to the family of direct arguments is promising. First, I believe that there are fatal counterexamples to any of the proposed modal transfer principles that play the crucial role in certain of the direct arguments. Second, I believe that none of the direct arguments that purport to do without such modal principles is attractive.[35]

---

[35] For a helpful discussion of related issues, see Michael McKenna, "Saying Goodbye to the Direct Argument in the Right Way," *Philosophical Review* 117 (2008): 349–383. I am especially indebted to extremely helpful and insightful comments by Carl Ginet and Derk Pereboom. I am also very grateful to generous and insightful comments in the Online Philosophy Conference 2 by David Widerker and Randolph Clarke. Additionally, I have benefited from various contributions to the OPC2 discussion thread, including those of Joseph Campbell, Ted A. Warfield, Derk Pereboom, and Eddy Nahmias. Thanks to OPC2 organizers Thomas Nadelhofer and Eddy Nahmias for inviting me to participate.

8

Conditional Freedom and the Normative Approach to Moral Responsibility

I. Introduction

Many (although certainly not all) philosophers have thought that moral responsibility requires freedom (or control).[1] But even those philosophers who accept this association of responsibility and control have differed with respect to what sort of freedom is required for moral responsibility. These disagreements are not just between compatibilists and incompatibilists; as a matter of fact, the disagreements cut across the compatibilism/incompatibilism divide. Additionally, the disagreements pertain to a number of different specific issues. One disagreement is about whether the sort of freedom required for moral responsibility is an "alternative-possibilities" or "actual-sequence" sort of freedom (or control). Within each of these camps, there are disagreements about how precisely to analyze the relevant notion of freedom. Finally, there is some sort of disagreement—at least at some level—about whether the relevant notion of freedom is (in some sense) fundamentally "metaphysical" or "normative." The latter debate appears to have some relationship to the former disagreements, but it is frankly somewhat unclear precisely what the debate consists in and what the relationship is. In this paper I shall explore some aspects of this interrelated web of issues.

---

[1] See, for example, Peter van Inwagen, *An Essay on Free Will* (Oxford: Clarendon Press, 1983); Robert Kane, *The Significance of Free Will* (Oxford: Oxford University Press, 1996); John Martin Fischer, *The Metaphysics of Free Will: An Essay on Control* (Oxford: Blackwell Publishers, 1994); and John Martin Fischer and Mark Ravizza, *Responsibility and Control: A Theory of Moral Responsibility* (Cambridge: Cambridge University Press, 1998). For examples of philosophers who deny the association of responsibility and freedom, see Robert Adams, "Involuntary Sins," *The Philosophical Review* 85 (1994), 3–31; and Angela M. Smith, "Responsibility for Attitudes: Activity and Passivity in Mental Life," *Ethics* 115 (2005), 236–271.

II. The Consequence Argument and the "Well, Duh! Objection"

Let us start with the basic assumption that moral responsibility requires freedom in the sense of genuine metaphysical access to alternative possibilities. Typically, such freedom or control is picked out by such expressions as "freedom to choose otherwise" and "freedom to do otherwise;" I have dubbed this sort of control, "regulative control."[2] So, for the sake of the discussion here, I am assuming the truth of something like what Harry Frankfurt called the "Principle of Alternate Possibilities" (PAP): moral responsibility requires freedom to do otherwise (at some suitable time).[3]

But how is such freedom—the freedom to do otherwise—to be understood? And how does it fit with the doctrine of causal determinism? The "Consequence Argument" purports to show that causal determinism is incompatible with the freedom to do otherwise, quite apart from the details of particular analyses of such freedom.[4] The argument was dubbed the "Consequence Argument" by Peter van Inwagen, because it exploits the fact that, under causal determinism, all our choices and behavior are the *consequences* of the past plus the laws of nature. The argument proceeds from this fact and the assumptions that the past is fixed and the laws of nature are fixed to the conclusion that, if causal determinism is true, we lack freedom to do otherwise. The argument can be developed as rigorously as you would like, and I believe that it can be given in different valid forms.[5] Here I shall simply assume that the Consequence Argument—in some formulation—is valid.

But is it sound? It is sound only if all of its premises are true. A crucial premise is some version of the intuitive idea that the past is "fixed" and out of our control now—presumably it is now fixed because it is, in Nelson Pike's phrase, "over and done with."[6] More specifically, the proponent of the Consequence Argument embraces a particular interpretation of the fixity of the past—an interpretation that is, charitably put, congenial to incompatibilism. In this interpretation, all (temporally nonrelational) features of the past must be held fixed. This interpretation, together with the associated view about the fixity of the natural laws, *straightforwardly forces* the incompatibilist conclusion.

---

[2] Fischer, *The Metaphysics of Free Will*, and Fischer and Ravizza, *Responsibility and Control*.

[3] Harry G. Frankfurt, "Alternate Possibilities and Moral Responsibility," *The Journal of Philosophy* 66 (1969), 829–839, reprinted in John Martin Fischer, ed., *Moral Responsibility* (Ithaca, NY: Cornell University Press, 1986), 143–152.

[4] Van Inwagen, *An Essay on Free Will*; Carl Ginet, *On Action* (Cambridge: Cambridge University Press, 1990).

[5] See, for example, van Inwagen, *An Essay on Free Will*; Carl Ginet, *On Action* (Cambridge: Cambridge University Press, 1990); and Howard Sobel, *Puzzles for the Will* (Toronto: University of Toronto Press, 1998).

[6] Nelson Pike, "Divine Omniscience and Voluntary Action," *The Philosophical Review* 74 (1965), 27–46.

To see this, consider the following version of the Principle of the Fixity of the Past and Laws of Nature:

> An agent S can at t do X at t only if there exists a possible world with the same past relative to t and the same natural laws as in the actual world and otherwise "suitably related" to the actual world in which S does X at t.[7]

Now let us be a bit more explicit about the doctrine of causal determinism. No matter how we define it, causal determinism will entail that, for any given time, a complete statement of the (temporally nonrelational) facts about that time, together with a complete statement of the laws of nature, entails every truth as to what happens after that time. So if causal determinism obtains in possible world p, then any possible world with the same past and laws as p will have exactly the same present and future as p. The Consequence Argument essentially employs the Principle of the Fixity of the Past and Natural Laws, in conjunction with the definition of causal determinism, to get to the incompatibilist conclusion. Intuitively, the argument is very straightforward; in fact, one wonders why it should require a great deal of technical machinery or sophisticated argumentation at all!

This is precisely what Gary Watson has said, and it motivates him to point out that it is just *obvious* that freedom to do otherwise, understood in a way that requires the fixity of *all* features of the past and *all* the laws, is incompatible with causal determinism.[8] Watson puts the point as follows:

> It is more common, perhaps, to think of the traditional issue as "purely metaphysical." Certainly Fischer's explicit formulation of incompatibilism (that determinism is inconsistent with the belief in "genuinely open alternative possibilities") is not stated in normative terms. But everyone knows that determinism is inconsistent with alternative possibilities construed in an absolute sense.[9]

Watson here seems to conflate—or at least associate—the "metaphysical" interpretation of the freedom to do otherwise with an "absolute" conception of such freedom; he goes on to recommend what he calls a "normative" conception which is "conditional." I am puzzled as to why exactly we should associate the metaphysical with the absolute approach, and the normative with the conditional; I shall return to this point later in the paper. But I believe that Watson's fundamental point is worth careful consideration: that it would be odd to interpret the compatibilist as saying that freedom, understood both "absolutely" (non-conditionally) and also in the specific way embraced in the Consequence Argument (according to which *all* features of the past are to be held fixed) is compatible with causal determinism.

---

[7] Fischer, *The Metaphysics of Free Will*, 91.

[8] Gary Watson, "Some Worries about Semi-Compatibilism: Remarks on John Fischer's *The Metaphysics of Free Will*," *Journal of Social Philosophy* 29 (1998), 135–136.

[9] Watson, "Some Worries about Semi-Compatibilism," 135–136.

After all, it is just *obvious* that such freedom is incompatible with causal determinism. One might dub Watson's point the "Well, duh! Objection."

Given that it is obvious that causal determinism is incompatible with a certain sort of "absolute" conception of freedom to do otherwise, Watson suggests that the thoughtful compatibilist will adopt a "conditional" conception of such freedom—a conception he deems more congenial to the "normative background" against which discussions of freedom typically take place. He says:

> [W]e have a number of related concepts of freedom; if incompatibilism is the view that at least some of these conflict with determinism, everyone is an incompatibilist. The issue is: which of those concepts are implicated in the central values of our lives?[10]

Watson goes on to suggest that a "conditional" conception of freedom is centrally important in various "normative contexts," including deliberation and situations in which we make attributions of moral responsibility. About deliberation, he says:

> One thing that deliberating whether or not to take door A or B *clearly* presupposes is the belief that which door you take depends on your will (on the upshot of deliberation)—that is, that if you decide to take B, you will take B.[11]

Watson additionally suggests that a conditional notion of freedom is central to our attributions of moral responsibility, suggesting that in attempting to ascribe moral responsibility to someone, we naturally tend to adopt that individual's deliberative perspective.[12] And, as we have seen, Watson thinks a conditional notion of freedom is centrally important within the deliberative context. Note that Watson does *not* say that conditional freedom is *all* the freedom we want or need for deliberation or responsibility; rather, his contention is that it is an important part of ordinary thought about these matters.

I wish to focus here on the suggestion that the conditional notion of freedom is the "freedom-relevant condition" necessary for moral responsibility; more specifically, I want to consider the idea (perhaps suggested by some of Watson's formulations, but, as I stated, not specifically endorsed by him) that conditional freedom is all the freedom required for moral responsibility. That is, I wish to evaluate the suggestion that what plays the crucial role in PAP is conditional freedom, and thus that conditional freedom is the sort of freedom about which we should be concerned in evaluating the Consequence Argument. Perhaps I could put the

---

[10] Watson, "Some Worries about Semi-Compatibilism," 136.

[11] Watson, "Some Worries about Semi-Compatibilism," 138.

[12] Watson, "Some Worries about Semi-Compatibilism," 138. One finds a similar approach, especially in adopting a (roughly speaking) "normatively motivated" conditional analysis of freedom (suitably revised) in Hilary Bok, *Freedom and Responsibility* (Princeton, NJ: Princeton University Press, 1998).

point as follows. Watson suggests that it is just *obvious* that absolute freedom (of a certain sort) is incompatible with causal determinism, so the proponent of compatibilism must have some other notion of freedom in mind. More specifically, Watson suggests that this notion plays a central role in various "normative contexts," such as deliberation and responsibility attribution; thus, Watson's suggestion (or perhaps the suggestion that emerges from much of Watson's discussion) is that the compatibilist must have conditional freedom in mind when he contends that freedom—the sort that's relevant to PAP—is compatible with causal determinism.[13] And, of course, the Consequence Argument is not sound, if the relevant sort of freedom is conditional freedom; the truth of the relevant conditionals does not require that all features of the past (together with the natural laws) be held fixed.

III. A Nasty Problem for Conditional Freedom: The Frankfurt Cases

Watson makes a fair point in wondering who the target of the Consequence Argument is. We all know, or should know, that causal determinism straightforwardly rules it out that we are free to do otherwise, where this sort of freedom requires that all the past and laws be held fixed. How could a compatibilist have been thought to disagree with this? Further, Watson's suggestion that we take the compatibilist to have in mind conditional, rather than absolute, freedom is helpful in providing a possible interpretation of compatibilism, according to which it is not obviously and straightforwardly problematic. But I shall argue in this section that there is a fatal problem for the suggestion that conditional freedom is the freedom linked with moral responsibility. Insofar as the Consequence Argument treats the freedom-relevant condition that is necessary and sufficient for moral responsibility, it cannot be conditional freedom.[14]

---

[13] Note that there is a bit of a tension in Watson's views here. On the one hand, he is contending that it is conditional freedom that plays the relevant role in our thinking about moral responsibility, but on the other hand he hesitates to say that conditional freedom is all the freedom required for moral responsibility. Indeed, he is quite aware of the problems for taking subjunctive conditionals to provide sufficient conditions for the sort of freedom at stake in attributions of moral responsibility. Now I take it that it is a presupposition of the Consequence Argument that it is discussing the freedom-relevant component of moral responsibility—not just a part of it or a condition that must be combined with other conditions to get it. Perhaps Watson is simply saying that conditional freedom plays an important role in ordinary thought, but must be supplemented to get a theoretically acceptable specification of the freedom-relevant condition on moral responsibility. Please interpret my use of "Watson's suggestion" as "a suggestion that emerges from much of Watson's discussion, but may not in the end be endorsed by Watson himself."

[14] Again, although this claim is suggested by some of what Watson says, he explicitly denies that he is claiming or presupposing that conditional freedom is *all* the freedom required for moral responsibility. What matters to me here is an evaluation of the idea, not whether Watson himself is to be associated with the idea.

In his famous paper, "Alternate Possibilities and Moral Responsibility," Harry Frankfurt built on an example suggested by John Locke that appears to call into question PAP. In Locke's example, a man voluntarily decides to stay in a room whose door is, unbeknownst to him, locked. In Frankfurt's example, the locked door is, as it were, taken into the man's mind; although Frankfurt left the precise details aside, the idea is that another person—named "Black," in Frankfurt's presentation—stands ready to intervene if the man tries to leave the room, or even begins to consider choosing to leave the room. Black is merely a counterfactual intervener; Frankfurt's view was that Black's presence *ensures* that the actual choice and behavior occur, but, since Black never plays any role in how the actual sequence unfolds, the man can be morally responsible for what he chooses and for his behavior (say, staying in the room).[15]

To make the discussion here a bit more concrete, it will be helpful to have a specific version of a Frankfurt case:

> Jones has left his political decision until the last moment, just as some diners leave their decision about what to order at a restaurant to the moment when the waiter turns to them. In any case, Jones goes into the voting booth, deliberates in the "normal" way, and chooses to vote for the Democrat. On the basis of this choice, Jones votes for the Democrat. Unbeknownst to Jones, he has a chip in his brain that allows a very nice and highly progressive neurosurgeon (Black) to monitor his brain. The neurosurgeon wants Jones to vote for the Democrat, and if she sees that Jones is about to do so, she does not intervene in any way— she merely monitors the brain. If, on the other hand, the neurosurgeon sees that Jones is about to choose to vote for the Republican, she swings into action with her nifty electronic probe and stimulates Jones' brain in such a way as to ensure that he chooses to vote for the Democrat (and goes ahead and votes for the Democrat). Given the set-up, it seems that Jones freely chooses to vote for the Democrat and freely votes for the Democrat, although he could not have chosen or done otherwise... The neurosurgeon's chip and electronic device has brought Locke's locked door into the mind. Just as the locked door plays no role in Locke's man's choice or behavior but nevertheless renders it true that he could not have done otherwise, Black's set-up plays no role in Jones' actual choice or behavior, but it apparently renders it true that he could not have chosen or done otherwise.[16]

How exactly does the neurosurgeon Black "know" what Jones is about to do? This is left vague, just as Frankfurt left it vague in his original presentation. But there are

---

[15] Frankfurt, "Alternate Possibilities and Moral Responsibility."
[16] John Martin Fischer, "Compatibilism," in John Martin Fischer, Robert Kane, Derk Pereboom, and Manuel Vargas, *Four Views on Free Will* (London: Blackwell Publishers, 2007), 44–84; the quotation is from p. 58.

various ways of attempting to resolve the vagueness and filling in the details. This is a big part of the impetus for the huge literature surrounding the Frankfurt cases.[17]

It is (mercifully!) not necessary to go through the details of the debates about the Frankfurt cases or to evaluate the issues they raise. Rather, I shall distill just a few central points that emerge from the literature on these examples and apply them to the issues pertinent to this paper—in particular, the suggestion that the compatibilist should embrace a "normatively inspired" conditional conception of the freedom relevant to moral responsibility.

Return to the troubling vagueness in the presentation of the Frankfurt examples above. How exactly does Black know what Jones is about to choose (and do)—and thus how does Black know when to intervene, if at all? What triggers the intervention? If Black must wait until Jones begins to make a choice or decision, that is too late, because the beginning of a choice or decision seems to be a voluntary mental act, truncated as it may be. Here, as elsewhere in life, size is not what really matters; even a small alternative possibility may have the requisite "oomph." So if Black must wait until Jones begins to make a choice, Jones would seem to have an alternative possibility of the relevant sort, that is, one that involves voluntariness. In this version of the Frankfurt case, the responsibility intuition is elicited, but it is not the case that alternative possibilities are expunged.

One can understand much of the literature surrounding the Frankfurt examples as (sometimes elaborate) attempts to construct versions of the cases in which the responsibility intuition is maintained but the alternative possibilities are successfully expunged—along with replies to these attempts. It is difficult to defend the contention that *both* of Frankfurt's key intuitions hold in any one example: that the relevant agent is morally responsible, and that he lacks alternative possibilities.

Here is a way of understanding the challenge for a proponent of the claim that the Frankfurt cases impugn PAP. Given the vagueness in the "standard" presentation of the examples, one might ask, "What exactly triggers Black's intervention?" And the answer—the triggering event—would seem to be an alternative possibility. Thus one would not have entirely eliminated alternative possibilities. Now one promising answer to the question about what triggers the intervention posits a "prior sign"—a completely involuntary indication of a future choice to do otherwise (if left unmolested); if Black sees the prior sign, he can intervene prior to any voluntary activity (even mental activity) by Jones. Thus, although the prior sign would be an alternative possibility of sorts, it would not involve voluntariness, and thus arguably would not be of the *right kind* to ground ascriptions of moral respon-

---

[17] For the tip of the iceberg, see John Martin Fischer, "Recent Work on Moral Responsibility," *Ethics* 110 (1999), 93–139, and David Widerker and Michael McKenna (eds.), *Moral Responsibility and Alternative Possibilities: Essays on the Importance of Alternative Possibilities* (Aldershot, U.K.: Ashgate, 2003).

sibility. In this view, it is not the case that *any old* alternative possibility will do the trick (in grounding attributions of moral responsibility); rather, such an alternative possibility must be sufficiently *robust*.[18]

Again, it is not necessary (here) to explore whether this view is defensible. Nor is it necessary to evaluate the various versions of proposals for Frankfurt cases in which it is putatively the case that both the relevant agent is morally responsible and there are no suitably robust alternative possibilities. It is sufficient here to note that there is considerable controversy over whether any such example has been—or even could be—presented.

To see why the Frankfurt-case skeptics resist the contention that both the responsibility intuition and the no-alternative-possibility intuition can be simultaneously defended (defended as true in the same example), consider the following dilemma.[19] Return to the "prior sign" version of the cases, just to fix ideas. Now either the prior sign is not causally sufficient for the subsequent voluntary beginning of (say) choice or it is causally sufficient for the subsequent mental activity in question. Suppose, first, that the prior sign is not causally sufficient. Now it emerges that nothing rules it out that (say) Jones can indeed begin to choose otherwise at the subsequent time; and this is evidently a robust alternative possibility. No matter how closely Black hovers over Jones (or watches the screen of the computer that is monitoring Jones's brain), he cannot intervene so quickly that he does not leave in place a robust (albeit truncated) alternative possibility. Darn! The situation is kind of like a border patrol agency that is authorized to apprehend individuals *only after they have crossed a border*; they can legally prevent individuals from getting very far, but they cannot entirely preempt any crossing at all. Black is kind of like a border control agent; he can prevent Jones from acting on his choice or even completing his choice; but he cannot preempt entirely the beginnings of choice.

It seems that the only way to get rid of such an alternative possibility is to accept the second horn of the dilemma: that the prior sign is causally sufficient for the subsequent mental activity. But now the Frankfurt-case skeptic will point out that it would be question-begging to say that Jones is morally responsible for his

---

[18] For the original suggestion, see John Martin Fischer, "Responsibility and Control," *The Journal of Philosophy* 79 (1982), 24–40; for further discussion, see Fischer, "Recent Work on Moral Responsibility," and John Martin Fischer, (adapted from chapter 7 of Fischer, *The Metaphysics of Free Will*), in Widerker and McKenna (eds.), *Moral Responsibility and Alternative Possibilities: Essays on the Importance of Alternative Possibilities*, 27–52.

[19] Roughly this sort of argument is in Robert Kane, *Free Will and Values* (Albany: State University of New York Press, 1985) and Robert Kane, *The Significance of Free Will* (New York: Oxford University Press, 1996), esp. 142–145; David Widerker, "Libertarian Freedom and the Avoidability of Decisions," *Faith and Philosophy* 12 (1995), 113–118, and David Widerker, "Libertarianism and Frankfurt's Attack on the Principle of Alternative Possibilities," *The Philosophical Review* 104 (1995), 247–261; Carl Ginet, "In Defense of the Principle of Alternative Possibilities: Why I Don't Find Frankfurt's Argument Convincing," *Philosophical Perspectives* 10 (1996), 403–417; and Keith Wyma, "Moral Responsibility and Leeway for Action," *American Philosophical Quarterly* 34 (1997), 57–70.

choice and behavior; after all, if the context of debate is one in which it is contested whether causal determinism is compatible with moral responsibility, one would not be entitled to posit causal determination in the example. The upshot of the dilemma is that either there emerge robust alternative possibilities, or the moral responsibility intuition cannot be sustained; again, it apparently emerges that it is difficult simultaneously to sustain *both* the responsibility intuition and the no-alternative-possibilities intuition.

The complexities and difficulties I have charted (in a rather schematic way) show at least part of the reason why the Frankfurt cases are contentious. I do not here wish to go any further into the details of these debates, or to indicate what I take to be the most promising routes to a satisfying analysis of the examples.[20] Rather, here I simply wish to argue that, once one shifts from an absolute to a conditional notion of freedom (along the lines of Watson's suggestion above), the Frankfurt cases are completely decisive. That is to say, the main points of controversy in the debates about the Frankfurt cases become entirely irrelevant, and the Frankfurt cases retain their full efficacy in oppugning PAP. Whatever inadequacies the Frankfurt-type cases are alleged to possess, these do not obtain in the context in which a conditional conception of freedom is employed in PAP.

To explain. The proponent of the conditional notion of freedom (as pertinent to both deliberation and moral responsibility) will insist that it is important that our actions (and, more generally, behavior of various kinds) are dependent on our choices (or perhaps evaluations or judgments of certain sorts).[21] So, for the proponent of conditional freedom, what is essential is that one's (say) bodily movements be dependent on (or a certain kind of "function of") one's choices (decisions, willings, etc.). More specifically, the kind of dependence involved is articulated by suitable subjunctive conditionals. Whatever else must be the case when one has conditional freedom, it must be the case that one's bodily movements "track" one's choices in roughly the following way: if one were to choose to do X, one would do X, and if one were to choose to do something else, Y, one would do Y. The proponent of conditional freedom typically points out that it is not much of a consolation that we can will certain bodily movements, if we cannot *translate* our wills into action; what we care about, according to such a theorist, is (among other things) that there be a suitable *connection* between what we choose to do and what we in fact do. In this view, our behavior must be choice-dependent in the specified way.

Now it should be clear that Frankfurt cases decisively show that conditional freedom is *not* the freedom linked to moral responsibility. This is because the

---

[20] For recent attempts, see John Martin Fischer, "Free Will and Moral Responsibility," in D. Copp (ed.), *Oxford Handbook of Ethical Theory* (Oxford: Oxford University Press, 2006), 321–354; reprinted in an expanded form in John Martin Fischer, *My Way: Essays on Moral Responsibility* (Oxford: Oxford University Press, 2006), 182–216. Also, see chapter 2 of this book.

[21] I shall explore the idea that the crucial notion of freedom is some sort of "judgment-sensitivity" in the next chapter; this view is associated primarily with Thomas Scanlon.

"counterfactual intervener" Black can always swing into action based on the triggering event of an agent's choice (or decision or act of will) to do otherwise; given this triggering event, presumably it is straightforward that Black can *block* the crucial connection between it and the chosen behavior. We saw that the vagueness in the standard description of the Frankfurt cases leaves it somewhat unclear how Black can foresee what Jones is about to do (or choose to do); this situation leads to complicated and delicate debates about whether Black can actually expunge all alternative possibilities. But, on the assumption that it is conditional freedom that matters, it is quite clear that Black can use the relevant choice (decision, act of will, etc.) as the triggering event, and he can then sever the intended connection between the choice and behavior.

Given the conditional conception of freedom, there is no problem with finding a triggering event. We thus clearly avoid most of the salient problems for the Frankfurt cases; indeed, I think we avoid them all. It is as though the conditional analysis gives rise to a "no-man's land;" this space separates the "border" from the "protected territory." So, as soon as an individual crosses the border and goes into the no-man's land, he can be apprehended by the border patrol *prior to arriving in the protected territory*. The no-man's land is a kind of buffer zone. Given the existence of this sort of buffer zone, we do not have to get into fine issues about border crossings; the protected territory is, as it were, safe.

My conclusion is that the Frankfurt cases decisively show that the conditional conception of freedom is not the sort of freedom linked to moral responsibility; it is clearly not the sort of freedom that plays the crucial role in PAP. Of course, there are well-known problems about the sufficiency of the subjunctive conditionals for true freedom.[22] It is frequently noted that intuitively one cannot do *Y* if one cannot choose to do *Y* (perhaps because of a pathological aversion, phobia, or other sort of volitional incapacity); but this situation is entirely consistent with the truth of the conditional, "If one were to choose to do *Y*, one would do *Y*." Thus, it is widely acknowledged that the subjunctive conditional is not sufficient for the relevant power.

Now in light of such problems various proponents of the conditional conception of freedom have sought to offer more refined conditional analyses. In some such analyses, what is taken to be sufficient is not a simple conditional, but a set of interlocking conditionals of a certain sort.[23] Other philosophers have sought to offer conditions that specify that the agent's actual choice not have been the result of some factor such as a pathological aversion, phobia, and so forth.[24] These

---

[22] Gary Watson is well aware of such difficulties, and he never asserts that the subjunctive conditionals specify *all* the freedom we need. For a more detailed discussion of the conditional analysis, see John Martin Fischer, "Compatibilism," in John Martin Fischer, et al., *Four Views on Free Will* (London: Blackwell Publishers, 2007), 48–53.

[23] Keith Lehrer, "Preferences, Conditionals, and Freedom," in Peter van Inwagen (ed.), *Time and Cause: Essays Presented to Richard Taylor* (Dordrecht: D. Reidel Publishing Co., 1980), 187–201.

[24] See, for example, Richard Foley, "Compatibilism," *Mind* 87 (1978), 421–428.

proposals all have their detractors. But I believe that the Frankfurt cases can help us to sidestep such disagreements insofar as they decisively show that conditional freedom cannot be the sort of freedom that plays a crucial role in PAP. Even if one were to solve all the problems that were classically raised against the conditional analysis of freedom, the Frankfurt examples show that such freedom is not the freedom linked to moral responsibility.

Perhaps it should be noted that various philosophers have recently offered sophisticated "dispositional" or "conditional" accounts of the freedom that is putatively linked to moral responsibility; Randolph Clarke calls these views the "New Dispositionalism."[25] A careful analysis of this literature is beyond the scope of this paper, but I will say at least a few words to locate the New Dispositionalism within the context of my discussion here.

The New Dispositionalists are united in presenting sophisticated analyses of freedom in terms of conditionals—perhaps, in Vihvelin's term, "bundles of conditionals." Further, they contend that this notion of freedom is linked to moral responsibility (via PAP) and that it is present in the Frankfurt examples. That is, the New Dispositionalists contend that the agents in Frankfurt cases possess an important kind of freedom—the freedom linked to moral responsibility. I must say that I find this view somewhat puzzling.

We all agree that agents in Frankfurt examples keep their "general capacities" of the relevant sort, just as we do not lose our general capacities when we are temporarily unconscious, asleep, and so forth. For example, I do not lose the general capacity to speak English when I am asleep. Similarly, we can all agree that the relevant general capacities are not lost by the agent (say, Jones) in the Frankfurt cases; Jones has the general capacity to vote for a Republican, even in the Frankfurt case described earlier. But I would insist that Jones *cannot* in the circumstances vote for a Republican, where this "can" includes or presupposes both a general capacity and the *genuine opportunity to exercise the capacity.*[26]

The New Dispositionalists evidently wish to say that there exists a kind of power (corresponding to the relevant notion of "can") that is "in-between" a general capacity and a power expressed by "can in the circumstances" (where "can in the circumstances" entails not just a general capacity but the genuine opportunity to exercise it), and, further, that *this* is the power that is linked to moral responsibility (via PAP). It is this "in-between" power that they seek to analyze via their sophisticated conditionals (or bundles of such conditionals).

---

[25] Kadri Vihvelin, "Free Will Demystified: A Dispositional Account," *Philosophical Topics* 32 (2004), 427–450; Michael Smith, "Rational Capacities, or: How to Distinguish Recklessness, Weakness, and Compulsion," in Sarah Stroud and Christine Tappolet, (eds.), *Weakness of Will and Practical Irrationality* (Oxford: Clarendon Press, 2003), 17–38; and Michael Mara, "Dispositions and Habituals," *Nous* 39 (2005), 43–82. Clarke's extremely penetrating critical discussion is in Randolph Clarke, "Dispositions, Abilities to Act, and Free Will: The New Dispositionalism," *Mind* 118 (2009), 323–351.

[26] For a discussion, see John Martin Fischer and Paul Hoffman, "Alternative Possibilities: A Reply to Lamb," *Journal of Philosophy* 91 (1994), 321–326.

But what exactly is this "in-between" power? Randolph Clarke has insight-fully pointed out that whatever power is linked with moral responsibility (via PAP), it must have certain characteristics we associate with something's being "up to the agent."[27] In Clarke's analyses, it would follow that it is *not* up to Jones whether or not he votes for the Democrat (in the Frankfurt case above). I think it is indis-putable that Clarke is correct to contend that our idea of the power linked to moral responsibility implies "up-to-us-ness." So, whatever precisely the "in-between" power is, it would seem that either it is *not* the power relevant to moral responsi-bility, or the New Dispositionalists are incorrect in supposing that agents in the Frankfurt cases have this sort of power. It is clear, after all, that it is *not* up to Jones whether he votes for the Democrat. So, despite the considerable subtlety and sophistication of the New Dispositionalism, the proposed conditional analyses cannot accommodate the extremely plausible judgment that the agents in Frankfurt cases do *not* have it in their power, in the sense relevant to moral responsibility, to do otherwise. I think that it is very implausible to suppose that in the Frankfurt cases it is up to the agent (say Jones) whether he will behave as he actually does, and thus, despite my considerable admiration for the subtlety and ingenuity of its proponents, I agree with Clarke's assessment that "the new dispositionalism leaves unresolved many of the long-standing problems of freedom and responsibility, and indeed fails to address many of the main points of contention."[28]

The New Dispositionalists apparently have the intuition that in the Frankfurt cases the agent (say Jones) *can* indeed do otherwise, in the relevant sense of "can." While it is delicate to say what the relevant sense of "can" is, I think it is about as clear as anything can be in this realm of discussion that the agents in the Frankfurt cases *cannot* do otherwise, in the relevant sense of "can"—the sense typically asso-ciated with moral responsibility. Recently in conversation Manuel Vargas informed me that this is a "mere intuition," and I suppose I do not dispute that it is an intui-tion. But I take it that it is a datum that should be accommodated by any adequate account of moral responsibility; although I do not subscribe to the view that every intuitive judgment should be preserved by a general theory of responsibility, this would be the sort of datum that, I should have thought, would be difficult to "overturn."[29]

Return briefly to Watson's suggestion (or the suggestion derived from Watson) discussed above. The suggestion was that we take it that the compatibilist adopts a "normatively inspired" conditional conception of freedom, rather than the sort of "absolute" conception that would be straightforwardly ruled out by causal deter-minism. This was supposed to help us see how a compatibilist could resist the conclusion of the Consequence Argument. We have seen that such a move is not

[27] Randolph Clarke, "Dispositions, Abilities to Act, and Free Will: The New Dispositionalism."
[28] Randolph Clarke, "Dispositions, Abilities to Act, and Free Will: The New Dispositionalism, 348–9."
[29] For a preliminary discussion of the sort of "wide reflective equilibrium" methodology I find congenial, see Fischer and Ravizza, *Responsibility and Control*, 10–11.

promising, quite apart from general problems with the idea that the relevant sub-junctive conditionals are sufficient for the sort of freedom in question; the Frankfurt cases show that conditional freedom just cannot be the freedom linked to moral responsibility (via PAP). Whereas it is contentious whether the Frankfurt cases show that freedom to do otherwise (quite generally) is not required for moral responsibility, it should be uncontroversial that they show that *conditional freedom* is not a necessary condition of moral responsibility. So the compatibilist who adopts the suggestion that conditional freedom is the freedom relevant to moral responsibility (as specified in PAP) is out of the frying pan and into the fire.

IV. Normative Conceptions of Moral Responsibility

I have pointed out that Watson tends to associate the conditional analysis of free-dom with a "normative" approach to the conditions for moral responsibility. This is apparently because Watson thinks that in typical "normative contexts"—contexts of assessment of action—we tend to assume some sort of conditional analysis of the relevant kind of freedom. Also, Watson holds that the notion of freedom in question is linked importantly to deliberation—to our conception of agents as practical reasoners or deliberators—and he believes that the conditional analysis captures an important component of our views about deliberation.

It is noteworthy that various philosophical approaches to the conditions for moral responsibility are classified as "normative," whereas others are deemed fun-damentally "metaphysical." But the basis for this differentiation has never been entirely clear to me. Here I do not have the space to go into this matter in detail; rather, I will lay out in a sketchy and preliminary fashion various different ways in which a theory might be deemed "normative." Perhaps it will be illuminating to note that there are very different features in virtue of which various theories have been considered "normative"; I am here simply assembling notes with the hope of turning to a more careful consideration of these issues in the future (or, better yet, spurring others to undertake this project!).

Note first that Gary Watson himself is often thought to be the "pioneer" in contemporary philosophy of the "normative" approach to moral responsibility. His pioneering contribution can be traced to his classic article, "Free Agency."[30] Here Watson makes the distinction between "values" and mere preferences, and he argues that acting freely is a matter of acting in accordance with one's values, rather than mere preferences. The view is highly suggestive, but frustratingly, Watson does not develop it in great detail or with much precision. In an important passage, Watson states:

---

[30] Gary Watson, "Free Agency," *Journal of Philosophy* 72 (1975), 205–220; reprinted in John Martin Fischer, ed., *Moral Responsibility* (Ithaca, NY: Cornell University Press, 1984), 81–96.

It is not easy to give a nontrivial account of the sense of "to value" in question... We might say that an agent's values consist in those principles and ends which he—in a cool and non-self-deceptive moment—articulates as definitive of the good, fulfilling, and defensible life...

The valuational system of an agent is that set of considerations which, when combined with his factual beliefs (and probability estimates), yields judgments of the form: the thing for me to do in these circumstances, all things considered, is *a*. To ascribe free agency to a being presupposes it to be a being that makes judgments of this sort. To be this sort of being, one must assign values to alternative states of affairs, that is, rank them in terms of worth.[31]

One might simplify (and, no doubt, oversimplify) Watson's view as stating that an agent values something insofar as he takes it to be "normatively defensible," that is, defensible in light of relevant normative considerations. Plugging this into a biconditional purporting to give an account of moral responsibility (again, no doubt in a Procrustean fashion), one gets: an agent "acts freely" or is morally responsible for his behavior if and only if he takes it to be normatively defensible (i.e., defensible in light of various considerations, including normative considerations). Here, and in what follows, I am assuming that whatever *other* conditions there are for moral responsibility (e.g., epistemic conditions) are satisfied; in this section I am focusing on what might be called the "freedom" condition of moral responsibility.

This is a normative account of moral responsibility to the extent that normativity or normative considerations play a certain kind of role in the *analysans* (the right side of the biconditional). (It is not straightforward to characterize in a general way what this distinctive kind of role is; obviously, mere use of the term, "normativity," or some other similar term will not necessarily provide the right sort of account.) An initial point is simply that this is a normative conception of moral responsibility in a different way in which the conditional view of freedom is a normative approach to moral responsibility. Here (but not in the case of the conditional analysis) it is matter of normativity playing a certain sort of role on the right side of the biconditional. Note also that Watson's account sketched in his landmark essay "Free Agency" does not entail a belief by the agent in "objective" value in any sense; also, the agent may well be incorrect in his relevant belief, but this would not in itself bear on his moral responsibility (according to the account sketched above).

Of course, there are well-known problems with the biconditional suggested by Watson's early account, one of which stems from the apparent fact of "weakness of the will"—acting freely but against what one believes is all-things-considered defensible (in light of the relevant considerations). Although Watson has wrestled

---

[31] Watson, "Free Agency," 91 in Fischer 1984.

with these issues over the years, it is not clear that he has come up with a refinement of the original view with which he is satisfied. In more recent work, Watson has emphasized the notion of "normative competence" as playing a crucial role on the right side of the moral responsibility-analyzing biconditional. Note that this is yet another specific way in which a theory of moral responsibility might be deemed "normative"; that is, it shares with the previous suggestion the feature that normativity plays a certain role in the right side of the biconditional, but the instantiation of this role is different. Here, Watson invokes a more complex notion of "normative competence," rather than a simple belief with normative content. I shall return to the notion of normative competence below.

Susan Wolf follows Gary Watson in presenting a "normative" approach to moral responsibility, but her specific approach is interestingly different from any of the models suggested by Watson. In a nutshell, Wolf defends the "Reason View," according to which "the freedom necessary for responsibility consists in the ability (or freedom) to do the right thing for the right reasons...to choose and to act in accordance with the True and the Good."[32] The Reason View implies an "Asymmetry Thesis": whereas one cannot be morally responsible for a bad action that one could not have avoided, one can be morally responsible for a good or right action that one could not have avoided.[33]

Here I do not wish to engage in a critical evaluation or discussion of Wolf's interesting views.[34] My purpose is simply to point out that the specific instantiation of normativity's role in the right side of the biconditional is here distinctive; indeed, it issues in what might be called a "valence-dependent" account of moral responsibility, according to which the conditions differ if the behavior is right or wrong. In contrast, all of the normative models suggested by Watson are valence-independent. Additionally, unlike in Watson's approach, Wolf contends that her model presupposes the "objectivity" of normativity, at least in some sense of objectivity.[35]

---

[32] Wolf, *Freedom Within Reason*, 94. Other contemporary "normative" theorists have similarly defined moral responsibility in terms of a capacity to be guided by "the good." Eleonore Stump follows Aquinas, whereas Gideon Yaffe follows Locke: Eleonore Stump, "Sanctification, Hardening of the Heart, and Frankfurt's Concept of Free Will," *Journal of Philosophy* 85 (1988), 395–420, reprinted in John Martin Fischer and Mark Ravizza, eds., *Perspectives on Moral Responsibility* (Ithaca, NY: Cornell University Press), 211–234; and Gideon Yaffe, "Free Will and Agency at Its Best," *Philosophical Perspectives* 14 (2000), 203–229; and *Liberty Worth the Name* (Princeton, NJ: Princeton University Press, 2000).

[33] Wolf makes it clear that the notion of "could" that plays a role in the Asymmetry Thesis does not correspond exactly to the notion traditionally and typically thought to be relevant to moral responsibility; rather, she has in mind her notion of "psychological possibility." Wolf, *Freedom Within Reason*, 94–116.

[34] Elsewhere, I have discussed Wolf's views about free will and moral responsibility: John Martin Fischer and Mark Ravizza, "Responsibility, Freedom, and Reason," *Ethics* 102 (1992), 368–389; and Fischer and Ravizza, *Responsibility and Control: A Theory of Moral Responsibility*, 55–61.

[35] Wolf, *Freedom Within Reason*, 117–131.

Another normative approach to moral responsibility is developed by Angela Smith.[36] Smith presents her view in the context of a critique of what she calls the "volitional" model. In the volitional view of moral responsibility, susceptibility to voluntary control (typically via choice or decision) is necessary for moral responsibility. Smith points to a broad range of mental states over which we appear to lack voluntary control and for which we seem to be legitimately considered morally responsible; involuntary emotional reactions, things that simply occur to us (or don't), features of situations we happen to notice (or don't), and so forth. These phenomena, according to Smith, present a strong case for rejecting the control model. In contrast to the volitional or control model, Smith defends the "rational relations" model, according to which moral responsibility for a mental state or condition requires that it depend upon and reflect a person's evaluative judgment. In her view, the state in question need not have arisen from an explicit judgment; rather, it must be reasonable to take the state in question to reflect an evaluative judgment on the part of the person—a judgment that it is appropriate, in principle, to ask the individual to defend. The view is developed and defended with considerable care and philosophical subtlety, and it represents yet another specific way in which a theory of moral responsibility might be deemed "normative."

One of the most salient and influential of the putatively normative approaches to moral responsibility has been presented by R. Jay Wallace.[37] It is however not obvious exactly in what sense Wallace's view is properly deemed normative, as there are various different ideas that appear to be suggested by Wallace. Once we sort these ideas out in a provisional way, it may emerge (depending on the interpretation of Wallace) that his is a normative approach in an interestingly different way from the ways in which previously discussed theories are normative.

To simplify (and, no doubt, to oversimplify), in Wallace's view an agent is morally responsible for his behavior if and only if it would be fair to hold him responsible for it. That is, the right side of the biconditional includes the normative notion of fairness, and the approach embodies the priority of "holding" to "being" morally responsible.

Near the beginning of his book, Wallace writes, "if we wish to make sense of the idea that there are facts about what it is to be a responsible agent, it is best not to picture such facts as conceptually prior to and independent of our practice of holding people responsible."[38] Later he reiterates the claim:

[I]n the normative approach, the facts about whether people are morally responsible are not yet available to be appealed to at this stage in the inquiry. Those facts are fixed by the answer to the question of when it is appropriate to

---

[36] Angela Smith, "Responsibility for Attitudes: Activity and Passivity in Mental Life," *Ethics* 115 (2005), 236–71.

[37] R. Jay Wallace, *Responsibility and the Moral Sentiments* (Cambridge, MA: Harvard University Press, 1994).

[38] Wallace, *Responsibility and the Moral Sentiments*, 1.

hold people responsible, and so they cannot be invoked to decide that very question.[39]

The point is presumably that we cannot replace the right side of the biconditional above with any purely descriptive condition (any condition in which normativity does not play a certain distinctive role). The priority of holding responsible to being responsible, together with the non-reductionist claim (non-reductionism of the normative to the non-normative) gives yet another specific way a theory of moral responsibility could be normative. Of course, all normative approaches would accept the claim of non-reductionism; Wallace's specific contribution is the analysis of being responsible in terms of the fairness of holding responsible.

Although Wallace's views are suggestive and intriguing, I find the issues puzzling in some ways. First, I frankly do not see any *argument* in Wallace for the claim of the impossibility of replacement or reduction. Of course, one cannot argue for everything, and perhaps Wallace is simply presenting a hypothesis that should be evaluated as part of a holistic methodology. In an insightful discussion, Manuel Vargas seems to confirm my diagnosis here, saying, "Wallace's main argument for a normative practice-based interpretation of our commonsense convictions is the fruitfulness of his account."[40]

But why exactly is it fruitful to assume, without argumentation, that there is no reductive specification of the right side of the biconditional? Why exactly does this help to illuminate the phenomena of responsibility? Does Wallace think that it is "fruitful" in the sense that accepting his claim will help us to avoid wasted time in seeking to systematize our considered judgments via specifications that are non-normative? But why would it be fruitful to truncate exploration of such specifications *in advance*?

But perhaps I have been operating with an unfair or at least uncharitable reading of Wallace's "fruitfulness" claim, which is, after all, a claim *attributed to Wallace by Vargas*. Perhaps Wallace is simply pointing to the fruitfulness of examining our actual practices of responsibility ascription (including our practices of excusing, exempting, and justifying) to seek to understand the nature of moral responsibility, including whether such responsibility presupposes a general condition such as PAP. I have absolutely no disagreement with this point, and if this is all Wallace would wish to assert, if he were to talk about the "fruitfulness" of his account, then I have no objection to the assertion. But then it is still unclear what the *argument* is for Wallace's important claim—the claim that moral responsibility is irreducibly normative (in the sense that one cannot "replace" the right side of his biconditional [An agent is morally responsible for his behavior if and

---

[39] Wallace, *Responsibility and the Moral Sentiments*, 92–93.

[40] Manuel Vargas, Responsibility and the Aims of Theory: Strawson and Revisionism," *Pacific Philosophical Quarterly* 85 (2004), 218–241, esp. 226. Vargas says in footnote 18, 239, "In conversation Wallace has confirmed that he has not given a 'direct' argument for the practice-based conception."

only if it would be fair to hold him responsible for it] with a purely non-normative specification).[41]

Maybe the following passage provides a clue to a more charitable and accurate interpretation of Wallace's point:

> Incompatibilists often appeal to our distinctively moral interest in *fairness*, suggesting that it would be unfair to hold people responsible if determinism is true. For instance, many of us are tempted, in reflective moments, to think that it would somehow be unfair to treat people as morally responsible if they are deprived of alternate possibilities for action. A common incompatibilist strategy is to elaborate this thought, arguing that determinism would make it unfair ever to hold people morally responsible, because it would deprive us universally of alternate possibilities for action. But if this is the form that incompatibilist arguments take, then compatibilists need to mount a similarly moral kind of inquiry. Specifically, they need to show that our moral norms of fairness do not commit us to any condition of responsibility that would be universally defeated if determinism is true—that, for instance, it can be fair to hold people responsible even if they do not have alternate possibilities for action.[42]

This passage suggests that Wallace's main point is that we need to look at our responsibility practices carefully and engage in what will be at least in part a *normative* analysis of the presuppositions and framing principles of these practices. As before, I would not disagree with this claim, but I would also insist that it does *not* follow that in the end we will not be able to replace the right side of the biconditional with entirely non-normative ingredients. After all, the conclusion of our (in part) normative inquiry might lead to precisely this sort of replacement; at least is seems inappropriate *to rule out this possibility in advance.*

Wallace seems to be aware of this sort of objection, or something similar:

> Some incompatibilists will perhaps resist this way of characterizing the debate. They will maintain that, though fairness is part of what is at stake in the debate about responsibility, it cannot be the whole story; distinct from the question of the fairness of our practice of holding people responsible, there is the further issue of whether it is true that people are morally responsible agents. Moreover, this truth will only be secured if there actually obtains an objective fact in the world, prior to and independent of our practices, which our judgments of moral responsibility track and reflect: the

---

[41] I believe that there is much of value in Wallace's highly intelligent and illuminating work; here I am simply homing in on his specific claim that the right side of the relevant biconditional is irreducibly normative (in the specific way he suggests), that is, the claim that we cannot replace the condition of the fairness of holding responsible with a purely descriptive, non-normative condition.

[42] Wallace, *Responsibility and the Moral Sentiments*, 94.

fact, namely, that responsible agents have strong freedom of will. But nothing I have said so far rules out the possibility that responsibility requires strong freedom of will; nor have I denied that there is an objective fact of the matter, prior to and independent of our moral practices, about whether people have freedom of will in the strong sense. My concern in this section has been to understand a different class of facts, about moral responsibility. I have claimed that we make best sense of these facts by interpreting them non-metaphysically, taking them to be bound up with our practice of holding people responsible. And we do this in a way that most sympathetically captures the traditional incompatibilist's concerns, I have suggested, by focusing on the question of whether determinism would render it unfair to hold people responsible for what they do. If incompatibilists wish to maintain that judgments of responsibility should track prior and independent facts about strong freedom of will, they will need to establish the normative significance of such facts by showing that it is only fair to hold people responsible when those facts obtain.[43]

I am frankly not sure I understand what Wallace means by "strong" freedom of the will, and how to distinguish such freedom from Wallace's "different class of facts about moral responsibility." If by "strong freedom of the will" Wallace means a kind of freedom that involves freedom to do otherwise (regulative control), then his view here would agree with mine. And even if Wallace is correct about the incompatibilist's burden here—that he must establish that it is only fair to hold people responsible when they have "strong freedom of the will"—it would *not* follow that (perhaps after such argumentation is complete) we could not replace the right side of Wallace's biconditional with ingredients that are entirely non-normative. Again, this is a quite separate point.[44]

Return to Wallace's biconditional, "S is morally responsible for his behavior just in case it would be fair to hold S morally responsible for it." Although I have interpreted Wallace as arguing for a certain sort of non-replacement thesis with respect to the right side of the biconditional, it is interesting to note that Wallace also would appear to argue for the contention (which he spells out in admirable detail and nuance) that it would be fair to hold an agent morally responsible for his behavior if and only if he acts while in possession of certain general capacities of practical rationality. In short, Wallace's view is that it is fair to hold an agent responsible for his behavior insofar as the agent has a certain sort of "normative competence." This suggests that Wallace would countenance the following sort of biconditional (resulting from the appropriate replacement): "S is

---

[43] Wallace, *Responsibility and the Moral Sentiments*, 95.

[44] The analysis in the text suggests yet another way in which a theory of moral responsibility might be deemed "normative"; in this approach, it is not so much that the right side of the relevant biconditional has irreducibly normative ingredients, but that the argumentation for the specification must in part be normative.

morally responsible for his behavior just in case S acts while in possession of the relevant sort of normative competence." Of course, the replacement that issues in this new biconditional is entirely compatible with Wallace's non-reductionist replacement theses, as it is obvious that normativity has a crucial role in the right side of the biconditional.

The new biconditional however raises a question about the distinction between "normative" and "metaphysical" approaches to moral responsibility. Typically, Wallace's approach (and Watson's) would be deemed a normative approach, whereas my (and Mark Ravizza's) would be deemed "metaphysical." I have never quite understood the basis for pigeon-holing the views in this way, and perhaps we can now see a bit more clearly why this pattern of classifications should be puzzling. After all, my view posits guidance control on the right side of the relevant biconditional, and guidance control includes (moderate) reasons-responsiveness. Whereas I invoke the notion of "reasons-responsiveness" and such philosophers as Watson and Wallace talk of "normative competence," there does not seem to be any interesting difference, with respect to the issue of irreducible normativity! It would then seem to be a mystery as to why the Fischer-Ravizza approach would be considered "metaphysical," whereas the Watson-Wallace approach would count as "normative." Perhaps this is as it should be; that is, perhaps my approach *should* be considered to be "normative," as distinct (say) from approaches that posit a requirement of "freedom to do otherwise" or "regulative control." It would be fine with me finally to be considered a member of the Normativity Club! Here I simply note that this result may be surprising to those who are inclined to invoke the distinction between "metaphysical" and "normative" approaches to moral responsibility and to categorize approaches in light of this distinction.

Finally, someone might insist that Wallace's approach is fundamentally different (say) from mine in giving analytic hegemony to the (explicitly normative) notion of "fairness."[45] Wallace, it might be thought, is fundamentally interested in the normative justification—the fairness—of our responsibility practices. Now this might be true, but how exactly is it different from my approach (or those of others who write about moral responsibility—even such "metaphysicians" as Kane, van Inwagen, and O'Connor)? I take it that we are *all* fundamentally interested in the normative issue of whether our responsibility practices are *justified* in light of skeptical worries issuing from both causal determinism and various forms of indeterminism.

For example, I began my book, *The Metaphysics of Free Will: An Essay on Control*, with a set of thought experiments involving clandestine manipulation.[46]

---

[45] Here (as elsewhere in this section) I am indebted to a very helpful conversation with Manuel Vargas.

[46] Fischer, *The Metaphysics of Free Will: An Essay on Control*, esp. 1–22.

I then pointed out that it can seem that the situation under causal determinism would be the *same* as that under the envisaged sorts of manipulation. I set myself the task of explaining why this is *not* the case; that is, I undertook to *answer* the skeptical worry that our responsibility practices would *not* be *justified* or *normatively defensible*, given the similarity between causal determination and clandestine manipulation of certain sorts. How is this project—which has motivated me in *all* of my work on the various facets of free will (even the traditional problem of the relationship between God's omniscience and human freedom)—different from Wallace's? Similarly, I take it that libertarians offer their (various) accounts of free will precisely because they do *not* think that our responsibility practices would be *normatively defensible* or *fair*, given causal determinism. I believe that Wallace himself would agree with this conceptualization of the dialectic; that is, I think that Wallace would agree that we *all* are interested in the normative foundations of our responsibility practices, but we come to different conclusions about the conditions for the normative defensibility of these practices. Note that, whereas Wallace emphasizes the notion of "fairness," Ravizza and I talk of moral responsibility involving (say) being an "apt" or "appropriate" candidate for the reactive attitudes; but we are clear that such "appropriateness" may involve considerations of fairness. It would be dubious to place significant weight on the difference between the role of "fairness" in Wallace's model and the role of "appropriateness" in the Fischer-Ravizza model; how could such a fine distinction be so important? And how could it line up with a putative distinction between a normative and metaphysical approach to moral responsibility?

In this section I have frankly just scratched the surface of a set of issues pertaining to the alleged distinction between "metaphysical" and "normative" approaches to the sort of freedom that grounds ascriptions of moral responsibility. Here I have just attempted to begin to chart some of the territory, that is, to give a preliminary and admittedly sketchy articulation of different ways in which various theories of moral responsibility may count as "normative." Of course, we all agree that the concept of moral responsibility is essentially normative; after all, moral responsibility is, as it were, the gateway to reactive attitudes, moral praise and blame, moral evaluations, and so forth. But the distinctive contention under consideration here is not about the *concept* of moral responsibility, but its *conditions of application*. At the very least, I hope to have shown that various theories of moral responsibility that are classified as "normative" count as normative for *different specific reasons*. Apparently, then, "normative approach to moral responsibility" is not a phrase that picks out a natural kind, so to speak.

V. Conclusion

It is plausible to associate moral responsibility with *some kind of freedom*. Indeed, the Principle of Alternative Possibilities (PAP) makes this sort of association explicit; according to PAP, it is a necessary condition of moral responsibility that the relevant agent had been "free" to do otherwise. But exactly what notion of freedom is involved in PAP, and, more generally, what sort of freedom is associated with moral responsibility? I have begun an inquiry into these questions in this paper. I have presented the "Well, duh? Objection," which challenges us to specify the notion of freedom that plays a crucial role in PAP. I have pointed out that if in response to this objection one adopts a conditional conception of freedom, the Frankfurt examples provide decisive and *uncontroversial* counterexamples to PAP. That is, whatever general problems the Frankfurt cases face in calling into question the association of moral responsibility and freedom do *not* apply to the context of *any* conditional analysis of the freedom in question. In part because the conditional analysis has been deemed a "normative" approach to moral responsibility, I have made a preliminary attempt to chart the contours of a heterogeneous mélange of theories that have been considered "normative." In the following chapter, I will continue the inquiry into what sort of freedom is associated with moral responsibility, and I shall further discuss certain models that are deemed "normative."

In a wonderful footnote (the first) in his great article, "Alternate Possibilities and Moral Responsibility," Harry Frankfurt says, "The two concepts employed in the principle of alternate possibilities [PAP] are 'morally responsible' and 'could have done otherwise.' To discuss the principle without analyzing either of these concepts may well seem like an attempt at piracy. The reader should take notice that my Jolly Roger is now unfurled."[47] As Bertrand Russell famously said, "The method of 'postulating' what we want has many advantages; they are the same as the advantages of theft over honest toil."

In this chapter I have begun the process of investigating both of the key notions in PAP: moral responsibility and freedom to do otherwise. In the following chapter I intend to continue seeking some of the fruits of honest toil, although in this age of increasing piracy on the high seas, I should perhaps note that I am not immune to the blandishments of theft.

---

[47] Harry Frankfurt, "Alternate Possibilities and Moral Responsibility," in Fischer, *Moral Responsibility*, 148.

9

Judgment-Sensitivity and the Value of Freedom

I. Scanlon's Approach to Moral Responsibility

T. M. Scanlon has developed a distinctive and illuminating approach to moral responsibility.[1] Scanlon's view is highly nuanced, and much of his discussion is beyond the scope of this paper. It will, however, be helpful to have at least a bare sketch of some of Scanlon's main theses. It will be evident that an analysis of Scanlon's approach to moral responsibility should build on the analysis of "Watson's suggestion" in the previous chapter.

Scanlon distinguishes between two different notions of moral responsibility: responsibility as attributability and substantive responsibility.[2] Responsibility as attributability is present when some action (or behavior in general) can be attributed to an agent in the way that is required in order for it to be a basis for moral appraisal. Substantive responsibility (in Scanlon's view) involves claims about what people are required or not required to do for each other; when someone is responsible in this sense for an outcome, he cannot complain of the burdens or obligations that result. According to Scanlon, these two different notions of responsibility have different but related moral roots. He says:

> These two notions of responsibility are linked by the fact that both concern the moral significance of our judgment-sensitive attitudes and other responses. But they are distinguished by the fact that two different kinds of significance are involved. Conditions of responsibility in the first sense depend on the

---

[1] See T. M. Scanlon, "The Significance of Choice," in Sterling McMurrin (ed.), *The Tanner Lectures in Human Values*, Volume 8 (Salt Lake City: University of Utah Press, 1988), pp. 149–216; and T. M. Scanlon, *What We Owe to Each Other* (Cambridge: Harvard University Press, 1998), pp. 248–294.
[2] Scanlon, *What We Owe to Each Other*, pp. 248–251.

importance, for moral appraisal of an agent, of determining whether a given action did or did not reflect that agent's judgment-sensitive attitudes. Standards of responsibility in the second sense arise in large part from the importance, for agents themselves, of having their actions and what happens to them depend on and reflect their choices and other responses.[3]

Scanlon's term for the value we place on having what happens to us depend on our choices is the "Value of Choice;" more specifically, he defines this value as "the reasons we have for wanting what happens to us to depend on the way in which we respond when presented with the relevant alternatives."[4]

In the previous chapter, I argued that the Frankfurt cases provide decisive reason to reject a conditional conception of freedom. It should be evident that these cases present similar problems for Scanlon's approach. In particular, the analysis in the previous section should cast considerable doubt on whether responsibility is based on judgment-sensitivity. It is also perhaps a bit unclear whether we do in fact place value on (roughly speaking) having our actions depend counterfactually on our judgments.

The main objection I have to Scanlon's approach is his linking responsibility as attributability with judgment-sensitivity; more specifically, the objection is to the suggestion that the basis for such moral responsibility is to be found in judgment-sensitive attitudes. Sometimes Scanlon writes of moral responsibility for the attitudes themselves, whereas on other occasions he discusses moral responsibility for actions that are the results of the relevant attitudes. In any case, Scanlon emphasizes the importance of distinguishing features such as height, which are presumably not judgment-sensitive, with other attitudes, such as concern or indifference to another person, which are presumably judgment-sensitive. He says:

> Moral criticism claims that an agent has governed him- or herself in a manner that cannot be justified in the way morality requires, and it supports demands for acknowledgement of this fact, and for apology, or for justification or explanation. It would make no sense to criticize someone in this way, or to demand such responses, for something that is not even in principle sensitive to his or her judgment. "Why are you so tall?" cannot be a moral criticism.[5]

But it is clear that a Frankfurt-case "counterfactual intervener," such as Black, could render it true that a particular attitude is not judgment-sensitive without intervening in the scenario at all. Just as such an intervener could straightforwardly employ the "decision" as a triggering event (as discussed previously on the conditional analysis of freedom), he could similarly use the relevant judgment as a

---

[3] Scanlon, *What We Owe to Each Other*, p. 290.
[4] Scanlon, *What We Owe to Each Other*, p. 290.
[5] Scanlon, *What We Owe to Each Other*, p. 272.

triggering event. He could thus block the *connection* between an alternative judgment and different attitudes and behavior.

In a suitably revised Frankfurt case, the agent (say Jones) makes a judgment as to what is best based on his own reasons, and he is in no way impaired or interfered with. Further, this judgment issues in an appropriate attitude and also subsequent behavior. Intuitively, Jones acts freely and is morally responsible. But, given the presence of Black, it is true that had Jones judged differently, Black would have swung into action and induced the very same attitude and behavior that occur in the actual sequence of events. Thus, Jones's attitude is not judgment-sensitive (where judgment-sensitivity is defined in terms of subjunctive conditionals of the sort employed in the conditional analysis of freedom), and his behavior does not flow from a judgment-sensitive attitude.

Exactly the same considerations appear to apply to judgment-sensitivity as to the conditional conception of freedom. We can grant that the Frankfurt cases are contentious in their application to an absolute notion of freedom. But they are uncontroversial in showing that the conditional conception of freedom is inadequate to play the required role in responsibility attributions, and they are similarly efficacious in exhibiting the inadequacy of the notion of judgment-sensitivity as providing the basis of moral responsibility.[6]

My main point here is that the Frankfurt cases call into question Scanlon's contention that responsibility as attributability rests on judgment-sensitivity. I shall return to this point below, but I wish now to explore Scanlon's related idea that standards related to the notion of substantive responsibility depend on the Value of Choice. I will seek to clarify the sense in which this is true and to argue that it no way supports the linkage of responsibility as attributability with judgment-sensitivity.

Recall that the Value of Choice is the value we place on its being the case that what happens to us depends on the way in which we respond when presented with the relevant alternatives. I believe that this can be understood in terms of the value we place on counterfactual dependence of outcomes on choice. So, for example, a restaurant patron appears to have an interest in its being the case that if here were to order fish, he would get fish; and if he were to order turkey, he would get turkey; and if he were to order the vegetarian dish, he would get the vegetarian dish, and so forth. That is, the restaurant patron appears to have an interest in its being the case that what he gets is counterfactually dependent upon his choices.

In his illuminating and subtle analysis, Scanlon argues that the reasons we have for endorsing the Value of Choice can be divided into "instrumental" (or

---

[6] Of course, if Scanlon wishes to offer a more refined analysis of the concept of "judgment-sensitivity," this might help him to avoid the problems I have developed in the text. This might, however—depending on the particular refinements—bring Scanlon's analysis quite close to my notion of "reasons-responsiveness."

"predictive"), "representative," and "symbolic."[7] To oversimplify, instrumental value pertains to maximization of preferences over time; the idea is (roughly) that if things are set up so that outcomes are counterfactually dependent on our choices, we are more likely to maximize the satisfaction of our preferences over time. The latter two categories of reasons for valuing counterfactual dependence of outcome on choice have to do with the "meaning" of our actions. Scanlon writes:

> On our anniversary, I want not only to have a present for my wife, but also to have chosen that present myself. This is not because I think that I am more likely to come up with a present she will like (as far as that goes it would be better to have her choose the present herself). The reason is rather that the gift has a different meaning if I choose it myself—both the fact that I chose it and the choice that I make reflect my thoughts about her and about the occasion.[8]

I agree with Scanlon about the various reasons we value some sort of dependence of outcomes on choice. In my subsequent discussion, I shall simply focus on something like "instrumental" value (for simplicity's sake). But I think an interesting point emerges about the precise way in which we value such dependence. Consider, first, an ordinary choice and action. Let us go back to the example of Jones and Black, but subtract Black. That is, let us begin by supposing that Jones deliberates in the "ordinary" way and decides for his own reasons (whatever they are) to vote for the Democrat, and that as a result of the "normal mechanism" (whatever it is), he goes ahead and votes for the Democrat. We do not make any special assumptions about causal determinism or particular impairments; indeed, we assume that Jones' choice and action spring from the normal, unimpaired operation of the human deliberative mechanism. Here there is no reason to suppose that Jones lacks judgment-sensitivity. Call this the "Jones Scenario."

Now add Black again, changing nothing else. That is, go back to the Frankfurt case in which Black is a *counterfactual intervener*: he plays no actual role in the unfolding of the sequence that issues in Jones's voting for a Democrat. Call this the "Jones/Black Scenario." My clear intuition is that Jones is fully morally responsible for his choice and act of voting for the Democrat in both scenarios, although his behavior stems from judgment-sensitivity in the Jones Scenario, but *not* the Jones/ Black Scenario. So, in terms of what we care about in caring about moral responsibility, nothing is lost when we go from the Jones Scenario to the Jones/Black Scenario.[9] I believe that the value of acting so as to be deemed morally responsible

---

[7] Scanlon, *What We Owe to Each Other*, pp. 251–256.

[8] Scanlon, *What We Owe to Each Other*, p. 251.

[9] Indeed, nothing of value—or, more specifically, nothing we care about in caring about moral responsibility—gets lost in going from what we take to be "ordinary contexts" to contexts in which there are *global* Frankfurt-case counterfactual interveners. Here we would compare possible worlds or scenarios in which there is (sometimes at least) judgment-sensitivity with possible worlds or scenarios in which there is *never* judgment-sensitivity.

is the value of a distinctive kind of self-expression.[10] And it is clear that whatever precisely this self-expression consists in, it is exactly the same in the Jones and Jones/Black scenarios; moving from the Jones to the Jones/Black scenario does not have any effect on the relevant instances of self-expression.

If I am correct about the claim that we do not lose anything of value (in terms of what we care about in caring about moral responsibility) in moving from the Jones to the Jones/Black scenario, this simply highlights the fact that responsibility as attributability does not have its basis in judgment-sensitivity. But this claim might appear to call into question Scanlon's idea that standards related to the notion of substantive responsibility depend on the Value of Choice. Given that we do not affect what we care about in a particular case of behavior for which an agent can be deemed morally responsible in moving from a context of judgment-sensitivity to a context of no judgment-sensitivity, how can Scanlon's point about substantive responsibility be defended?

I believe that consideration of the transition from the Jones Scenario to the Jones/Black Scenario points to the fact that in defending the Value of Choice for substantive responsibility, we are adopting a different standpoint from the standpoint from which we evaluate the relationship between judgment-sensitivity and responsibility as attributability. So not only are the notions of responsibility different, but the perspectives from which the relevant assessments are to be made are fundamentally different. It is perfectly appropriate to evaluate the claim that responsibility as attributability can be linked to judgment-sensitivity by considering scenarios such as Jones and Jones/Black; here the consideration assumes full knowledge (by the evaluator) of how things actually go in Jones's deliberations, and so forth. One could perhaps call this a more "concrete" evaluation.

In seeking to defend the contention that judgment-sensitivity is an important basis of substantive responsibility, I believe one is (perhaps implicitly) engaging in a more "abstract" evaluation. That is, one is adopting a different standpoint—one that abstracts from particular cases and asks about general institutions. So I might ask myself why in general I would prefer to have institutions and practices that allow outcomes to be counterfactually dependent on choices, abstracting away from specific knowledge about what my particular preferences will be. That is, not knowing what my preferences will be, I would presumably prefer that my situation be such as to allow for the pertinent kind of judgment-sensitivity, since this will probably maximize my chances of having my preferences satisfied over time. (Again, for simplicity's sake, I am simply focusing on what Scanlon calls the "instrumental/predictive" reason for valuing the relevant kind of counterfactual dependence; I believe that the same analysis will apply, *mutatis mutandis*, to the other reasons.) More specifically, it is plausible that *ex ante*—that is, prior to

---

[10] See John Martin Fischer, "Responsibility and Self-Expression," *The Journal of Ethics* 3 (1999), pp. 277–297; reprinted in Fischer, *My Way, Essays on Moral Responsibility* (New York: Oxford University Press, 2006), pp. 106–123.

knowing what my particular preferences, commitments, and projects are or are likely to be—I can see that it is in my interest that things be set up so that what happens to me is counterfactually (or perhaps subjunctively) dependent on my choices.

Think of it this way. Suppose you know that there might be individuals such as Black, who will let people alone, as long as they choose on their own to vote for the Democrat, but who will intervene, if the individual shows signs of choosing to vote Republican. Further, you do not know what your political views are—for all you know, you might be a card-carrying and committed Republican. Given this lack of knowledge, presumably you would prefer that there not exist individuals such as Black; after all, if you are a Republican in a world in which Black is around you will not be allowed to give effect to your "real values." *Ex ante* it would be very plausible to prefer that outcomes depend on choices, since the chances of getting whatever we care about in caring about moral responsibility would thus be maximized.

To take stock, in thinking concretely about Jones's moral responsibility, there is no difference between the Jones Scenario and the Jones/Smith Scenario. If Jones is morally responsible in the Jones Scenario, he is equally morally responsible in the Jones/Smith Scenario. Thus, instances of moral responsibility cannot be traced back to instances of judgment-sensitivity in the way suggested by Scanlon. But it does not follow that we do not place a value on judgment-sensitivity and the related notion of counterfactual dependence of outcomes on choice. This value can be seen to issue from a different, more abstract perspective. *Ex ante* one would rationally prefer to have outcomes depend counterfactually on choices (and judgments); from this more abstract standpoint in which one doesn't know one's particular normative orientation, one would prefer to live in a world in which one can satisfy his (relevant) preferences, whatever they turn out to be. The Value of Choice emerges from the more abstract perspective; it cannot be maintained from the more concrete standpoint of evaluation. Thus, what is plausible and attractive in Scanlon's analysis of the Value of Choice and its relationship to substantive responsibility cannot be translated into a defense of his suggestion that responsibility as attributability is based in judgment-sensitivity.

Perhaps the point I am making—or a related point—can be put in slightly different terms. We can distinguish between freedom to choose and do otherwise (regulative control) and choosing and acting freely (guidance control). The fact that we do not change our responsibility attributions in going from the Jones Scenario to the Jones/Black Scenario indicates that guidance control is all the freedom required for moral responsibility. But there might be a lingering feeling that if one has guidance control but not regulative control, something is missing—something of value is somehow left out. Perhaps I can capture this point by invoking the idea that *ex ante* (i.e., from a perspective that abstracts away from knowledge of one's actual motivational states, projects, commitments, etc.) one would rationally prefer that one's environment be set up to allow for regulative control; this is because *ex ante* having such an environment would maximize one's chances of exhibiting guidance control and thus getting whatever it is we value in acting so as to be deemed morally responsible.[11]

In the preceding paragraphs, I have contended that the Value of Choice (and the value of having regulative control) emerges from the abstract rather than the concrete context of evaluation. I wish now to offer a qualification to the contention that we would value regulative control from the abstract perspective. Black—the "counterfactual intervener" in the standard presentation of the Frankfurt cases—is presented as having an antecedently fixed orientation. That is, Black is presented as wishing to ensure that Jones vote for the Democrat; it just so happens that there is a felicitous coincidence of Black's antecedent and fixed goal and Jones's ultimate decision (and action). Let us call an intervener with an antecedently fixed orientation—a set of relevant goals that do not depend on the agent's actual preferences, decisions, and behavior—a "rigid intervener." Jones—in the standard Frankfurt case—is fortunate that Black is a mere counterfactual intervener.

In contrast, we can imagine a "flexible intervener." Such an intervener would simply stand by and ensure that an agent act as he actually does—whatever that turns out to be. That is, a flexible intervener waits until the relevant agent (say, Jones) "leaves the *ex ante* situation," to speak metaphorically; given Jones's actual preferences, he can ensure that Jones does not act contrary to them. One need not speculate on the motivations of such an intervener; maybe he is by nature a philosophical sort, and he wishes to highlight that there can be situations in which an agent acts freely (however he wishes to act) and yet cannot choose or do otherwise. From the *ex ante* perspective—from which one does not know one's actual preferences—one could know that, whatever one's preferences actually turn out to be, the counterfactual intervener would allow one to decide and act freely (exhibit guidance control), but would ensure that one is unable to choose and act differently. A flexible intervener (as I have defined him) is by his very nature a *counterfactual* intervener. In contrast, a rigid intervener is only contingently a counterfactual intervener (as in the Frankfurt cases).

---

[11] Alfred R. Mele has presented a position he has called "Soft Libertarianism." See, for example, Alfred R. Mele, *Free Will and Luck* (Oxford: Oxford University Press, 2006), pp. 95–102. The soft libertarian argues that free action and moral responsibility may well be compatible with causal determinism, but he maintains "that the falsity of determinism is required for a more desirable species of free action and a more desirable brand of moral responsibility" (Mele, *Free Will and Luck*, p. 95). Note that nothing in my argument in the text would support Soft Libertarianism. That is, I have argued that, from the abstract perspective, regulative control (which involves freedom to do otherwise) is desirable. But the argument is neutral about the relationship between causal determinism and regulative control. If one combined the argument in the text for the *ex ante* rationality of a preference for regulative control with an argument (such as the Consequence Argument) for the incompatibility of causal determinism and such control, then one would indeed have an explanation of the appeal of Mele's Soft Libertarianism.

Note that the existence of *either* sort of intervener—a rigid or flexible intervener—equally rules out regulative control or freedom to do otherwise (and thus Scanlon's Value of Choice). But from the *ex ante* perspective I do not see any reason to object to a *flexible*, as opposed to a *rigid*, intervener. Thus it is not quite correct to say that from the more abstract perspective of evaluation it would be rational to prefer regulative control to the absence of regulative control. Rather, what would be problematic from that perspective is a rigid intervener—a certain way of eliminating regulative control. Of course, in the real world as we know it and in various relevant alternative worlds, the threats to regulative control would *not* be flexible in the way involved in flexible (counterfactual) intervention. Thus, although it is a simplification to suppose that we would prefer regulative control from the more abstract perspective (and thus that the Value of Choice emerges from the abstract perspective), it is not perhaps an objectionable or distorting simplification, given the nature of the sorts of threats to our freedom that are realistic.[12]

Scanlon points out that both judgment-sensitivity and the Value of Choice could be present in causally deterministic worlds (and also worlds in which there is universal causation that is not deterministic causation). Thus, he believes that his analysis can aid in the project of defending compatibilism. Scanlon states:

> The reasons I have listed for preferring principles that make what happens to us depend on the ways we respond when presented with alternatives are not undermined if it turns out that these responses have causes outside us. As long as these causes affect our responses only by affecting what we are like, it will remain true that these responses can be good predictors of what will bring us enjoyment or advance our aims. Similarly, in the case of representative value, it is quite plausible to suppose that many of the tastes and capacities for discernment that we want our choices to express have a basis in our causal makeup, but this fact does not make them less a part of us and hence does not diminish the value of choices that express them.[13]

Whereas I am sympathetic to the general project of defending compatibilism, I am not sure how far we can get with Scanlon's intriguing suggestion. I can concede

---

[12] In his essay, "The Interest in Liberty on the Scales," in Joel Feinberg, *Rights, Justice, and the Bounds of Liberty: Essays in Social Philosophy* (Princeton, NJ: Princeton University Press, 1980), pp. 30–44, Joel Feinberg helpfully explores the question of our interest in liberty (or, in my terminology, regulative control). He argues that a central interest we have in liberty is our interest in not being coerced or forced to do what we do; but the analysis in the text shows that this interest entails only an interest in securing guidance control, not regulative control. Additionally, when one considers the Scanlonian Value of Choice, this strictly speaking only entails the absence of a rigid intervener (and similar constraints), rather than the absence of a flexible (and thus merely counterfactual) intervener. Thus, *strictly speaking*, our interest in satisfying our preferences, whatever they turn out to be, as it emerges from the abstract evaluative perspective, does not *entail* an interest in regulative control. Of course, as I argue in the text, this point is compatible with the idea that it is plausible to prefer regulative control *ex ante*, given reasonable assumptions about the nature of threats to such control.

[13] Scanlon, *What We Owe to Each Other*, p. 255.

that nothing should force someone taking the more abstract perspective of evaluation to reject causation or causal determinism. But this still leaves it open what the precise notion of freedom is that plays a crucial role in PAP. Even the concrete mode of evaluation issues in the conclusion that judgment-sensitivity is not the sort of freedom that is linked to responsibility as attributability. More specifically, it issues in the conclusion that judgment-sensitivity is not *necessary* for such responsibility. And just as above (in our discussion of the conditional conception of freedom), it is quite implausible (or, at the very least, highly contentious) to suppose that judgment-sensitivity would be *sufficient* for the sort of freedom linked to moral responsibility.

Earlier it was pointed out that the truth of such conditionals as, "If I were to choose to do Y, I would do Y" cannot be sufficient for the freedom to do Y, since the conditional can be true compatibly with my having some pathological aversion to choosing Y. Presumably the same sort of analysis can be applied, *mutatis mutandis*, to the subjunctive conditionals that specify judgment-sensitivity. Thus, the reasons why the conditional conception of freedom is too weak to help significantly with the compatibilist project would apply, *mutatis mutandis*, to judgment-sensitivity. For example, it can be conceded that the truth of causal determinism does not render false subjunctive conditionals, such as, "If I were to choose to do Y, I would do Y." But this is not yet enough to show that causal determinism does not rule out the sort of freedom that is necessary and sufficient for moral responsibility. Similarly, it can be conceded that the truth of causal determinism does not render false the subjunctive conditionals that specify judgment-sensitivity. But this is not yet enough to show that causal determinism does not rule out moral responsibility. There is a crucial gap between showing that causation or causal determination does not threaten the pertinent conditionals—or sever the relevant *connections*—and showing that causation or causal determination does not threaten moral responsibility. So even if we agree with Scanlon that causation or causal determination doesn't threaten *much* of what we care about and value in moral responsibility, we still do not get all the way to the conclusion that (for example) causal determination is compatible with the kind of freedom linked with moral responsibility.

In a fascinating discussion of the "preconditions of moral appraisal," Scanlon argues that a careful analysis of the conditions in which we would withhold or modify moral appraisal does not issue in the conclusion that causal determinism (or causation that falls short of deterministic causation) rules out such appraisal (and thus moral responsibility).[14] Scanlon divides the conditions that can undermine moral appraisal into three categories: those in which the action is not, in the

---

[14] This is, roughly speaking, a "Strawsonian" strategy for defending compatibilism. See P. F. Strawson, "Freedom and Resentment," *Proceedings of the British Academy* 48 (1962), pp. 187–211; for a detailed development of such a strategy, see R. Jay Wallace, *Responsibility and the Moral Sentiments* (Cambridge: Harvard University Press, 1994).

proper sense, attributable to the agent; those which do not block attribution of an action to an agent but do change the character of what can be attributed (such as duress and coercion); and those that render it true that the individual lacks the capacity to understand and assess reasons or that his judgments have no effect on his actions. He concludes:

> These explanations of how various conditions can undermine moral blame do not lead to the conclusion that blame is always inapplicable if determinism, or the Causal Thesis, is true. The mere truth of those theses would not imply that our thoughts and actions lack the continuity and regularity required of rational creatures. It would not mean that we lack the capacity to respond to and assess reasons, nor would it entail the existence of conditions that always disrupt the connection between this process of assessment and our subsequent actions. So, even if one of these theses is true, it can still be correct to say that a particular action shows a person to have governed herself in a way that is morally deficient.[15]

It is interesting to note that Scanlon focuses on conditions that actually play a role in forming one's character, the production of judgments and choices, and the connection between those motivational states and actions. He argues that causal determination (or causation) in itself need not threaten the relevant capacities for assessment of reasons, the proper generation of judgments and choices, or the appropriate connections between such states and actions.

I am largely in agreement with Scanlon here. That is, I agree that there is nothing in causation or causal determination *per se* that would rule out the kind of capacities of reasons-assessment required for moral responsibility; nor do I believe that there is anything in causation or causal determination *per se* that would imply that the way that our judgments and choices are produced are inconsistent with moral responsibility, or that would etiolate the required connections between such motivational states and actions. I do, however, disagree with Scanlon's contention that the basis of moral responsibility is judgment-sensitivity. Clearly, judgment-sensitivity is not ruled out by causation or causal determination, but I have argued that it is *not* a necessary condition for moral responsibility.

Recall that judgment-sensitivity involves a certain sort of counterfactual dependence on judgment. So, the idea is that judgment-sensitivity (with respect to *Y*) would be present only if the following two kinds of subjunctive conditionals would be true: "If the individual were to judge *Y* best, he would choose and do *Y*," and "If the individual were to judge *not-Y* best, he would choose and do *not-Y*." It is important to note that the mere presence of Black—or any similar counterfactual intervener—will render the second subjunctive conditional false, and yet (as argued above) have no impact on the individual's moral responsibility. Notice that

---

[15] Scanlon, *What We Owe to Each Other*, p. 281.

the mere existence of a counterfactual intervener has absolutely no impact on the actual production of the pertinent motivational states, and, similarly, no impact on the actual connection of those motivational states with the relevant action. The existence of the counterfactual intervener simply has an impact on the "hypothetical" or "counterfactual" connection between the relevant motivational states and the action in question.

This shows that (somewhat ironically) it is (arguably) *more difficult* to reconcile judgment-sensitivity with causal determination than it is to reconcile causal determination (or causation) with moral responsibility. Thus the appeal to judgment-sensitivity in seeking to provide a basis for moral responsibility makes compatibilism *more difficult* to support—more difficult than it already is, and more difficult than it need be! Again, my complaint is not with Scanlon's compatibilist conclusion or his Strawsonian strategy of argumentation; indeed, I have expressed my basic agreement with the contentions that causal determination and causation do not threaten the relevant requirements for production of judgments and choices, or the required connections between these sorts of states and behavior. I have, however, pointed out that the invocation of judgment-sensitivity does not quite get the freedom-relevant condition on moral responsibility correct; and because it is too strong, it would make the reconciliation of causal determinism and moral responsibility needlessly difficult.[16]

Scanlon's invocation of judgment-sensitivity is thus, in the end, a distraction; he employs judgment-sensitivity as an explanation for why (say) causal determination is compatible with moral responsibility, but insofar as it can be absent even in the presence of moral responsibility, it cannot be an explanation of (or the "basis of") moral responsibility. It is not necessary to demand for moral responsibility a *hypothetical connection* between (say) judgment and action; and if one makes this sort of demand, one needlessly opens oneself up to devastating counterexamples.

Perhaps Scanlon overlooks (or fails to focus on) this point because (as far as I can see) he never addresses the Frankfurt cases. That is, as far as I can tell, although in his work Scanlon discusses some of Frankfurt's work on moral responsibility, in particular, Frankfurt's "hierarchical" model of moral responsibility, he never refers to or discusses Frankfurt examples.[17] This is in some ways understandable, but also a bit puzzling, and I wish to say a few words about why.

---

[16] Of course, this is precisely the claim I have made about the purported requirement of freedom to do otherwise (regulative control) for moral responsibility. In both the instances of regulative control and judgment-sensitivity, not only do the Frankfurt cases show that the requirements in question are implausible, but they render the compatibilist project much more challenging than it need be. See, for example, John Martin Fischer, "Frankfurt-type Compatibilism" in S. Buss and L. Overton (eds.), *Contours of Agency: Essays on Themes from Harry Frankfurt* (Cambridge: The MIT Press, 2002), pp. 1–26, reprinted in G. Watson (ed.), *Free Will*, 2nd ed., (Oxford: Oxford University Press, 2003), pp. 190–211.

[17] Frankfurt first presents the hierarchical approach in: Harry G. Frankfurt, "Freedom of the Will and the Concept of a Person," *The Journal of Philosophy* 68 (1971), pp. 5–20.

Some years ago I pointed out that Frankfurt examples are a special case of a wider phenomenon I called "Schizophrenic Situations."[18] That is, I argued that the analytical situation with respect to "passive powers," such as malleability, fragility, solubility, and so forth is the same as that with respect to the "active power," freedom. So, just as the Frankfurt cases show that a (simple) conditional analysis cannot give the correct account of freedom, so structurally similar examples show that simple conditionals cannot give the correct analyses of the various passive powers. Indeed, the fact that such conditionals cannot give adequate analyses of the passive powers has been widely noted and discussed.[19] In more recent years, there have been discussions of the relationship between "masks" and "finks" in the literature on passive powers, and the Frankfurt cases.[20]

Here I obviously cannot go into the details of the literatures on "masks" and "finks." Nor do I intend to chart the various isomorphisms between this literature and the discussions of the Frankfurt cases. I simply wish to note that, in seeking an adequate account of the passive powers, it would be deemed inappropriate simply to ignore, dismiss, or brush aside the examples of masks, finks, and related challenges to the simple conditional analyses. Given the structural similarity in the issues, I find it at least *prima facie* puzzling when philosophers fail to address the Frankfurt cases in giving their analyses of moral responsibility.[21]

II. Guidance Control versus Regulative Control

I presented the worry articulated by Gary Watson that the Consequence Argument is (in a problematic way) a "no-brainer." That is, it should be obvious to everyone that causal determinism (in virtue of its very definition) rules out a freedom to do

---

[18] John Martin Fischer, *The Metaphysics of Free Will: An Essay on Control* (Oxford: Blackwell Publishers, 1994), pp. 154–158.

[19] The relevant literature is enormous. For some important papers, see C. B. Martin, "Dispositions and Conditionals," *Philosophical Quarterly* 44 (1994), pp. 1–8; David Lewis, "Finkish Dispositions," *Philosophical Quarterly* 47 (1997), pp. 143–148; Rae Langton and David Lewis, "Defining 'Intrinsic'," *Philosophy and Phenomenological Research* 58 (1998), pp. 333–345; and Mark Johnston, "How to Speak of the Colours," *Philosophical Studies* 68 (1992), pp. 221–263.

[20] Here is just a sampling: Kadri Vihvelin, "Free Will Demystified: A Dispositional Account," *Philosophical Topics* 32 (2004), pp. 427–450; Daniel Cohen and T. Handfield, "Finking Frankfurt," *Philosophical Studies* 153 (2007), pp. 363–374; Randolph Clarke, "Intrinsic Finks" *Philosophical Quarterly* 58 (2008), pp. 512–518; Neil Levy, "Counterfactual Intervention and Agents' Capacities," *Journal of Philosophy* 105 (2008), pp. 223–239; and Jesse Steinberg, "Dispositions and Subjunctives," *Philosophical Studies* 148 (2010), pp. 323–341. I have benefited from conversations on these topics with Jesse Steinberg.

[21] It is interesting that most of the philosophers who take a "normative" approach to moral responsibility (discussed in a preliminary fashion in the previous chapter) tend to dismiss the Frankfurt cases. Perhaps one could defend such a dismissal if one could successfully argue that the Frankfurt cases and the parallel examples of masks, finks, and so forth in the passive powers are all somehow "skeptical challenges"; if one could distinguish skeptical worries from other considerations, maybe one could simply say that one is assuming *some* solution to the skeptical worries. But I am not sanguine about the project of sequestering the putatively skeptical worries in the requisite way.

otherwise that requires holding all elements of the past and all natural laws fixed. Who could deny this? Why would it be controversial at all? Watson suggested that we move from an absolute to a conditional conception of freedom in part to provide a notion of freedom that at least makes the debates about the Consequence Argument sensible; more specifically, it at least gives the compatibilist a chance. I have, however, argued that gaining this chance to rebut the Consequence Argument comes at a steep price: one opens oneself to *decisive* refutation by the Frankfurt cases.

What's a compatibilist to do? One approach would be to stick with an absolute conception of freedom to do otherwise, but construe it without the requirements of holding all elements of the past and all natural laws fixed. This would still be an absolute conception of freedom in that it would not be a conditional conception; it would not employ (simple) subjunctive conditionals to analyze freedom. But it would loosen the requirements that the past and laws be held fixed.[22] Here the compatibilist and the incompatibilist could be seen to be accepting an absolute (i.e., non-conditional) conception of freedom (in the sense that involves access to alternative possibilities), but simply disagreeing about the specific constraints on such freedom. Whereas this makes the debate about the Consequence Argument a real debate, it leads to what I have called a "Dialectical Stalemate."[23]

Because of the apparently intractable stalemates that issue from adopting an absolute conception of freedom together with the interpretation of such freedom as requiring genuine access to alternative possibilities (regulative control), I have suggested that we seek to "restructure" the debates by switching from an "alternative possibilities" notion of freedom (regulative control) to an "actual-sequence" notion of freedom (guidance control). I will be the first (well, maybe among the first!) to admit that the Frankfurt cases do not *decisively* establish that absolute freedom to do otherwise is not required for moral responsibility; I have conceded that there is considerable controversy about this point. Here I shall simply assert that I believe that the Frankfurt cases show that absolute freedom to do otherwise is not required for moral responsibility, even though I am well aware that the examples and ancillary argumentation fall short of being apodictic.[24] I have argued that the Frankfurt cases show that all the freedom that is required for moral responsibility is "acting freely" or, in my terminology, "guidance control."

---

[22] For such compatibilist approaches, see Keith Lehrer, "'Can' in Theory and Practice: A Possible-Worlds Approach," in M. Brand and K. Walton (eds.), *Action Theory* (Dordrecht: D. Reidel Publishers, 1976), pp. 241–270; and Terence Horgan, "'Could,' Possible Worlds, and Moral Responsibility," *The Southern Journal of Philosophy* 78 (1979), pp. 345–358. For critical discussions, see Terence Horgan, "Lehrer on 'Could'-Statements," *Philosophical Studies* 32 (1977), pp. 403–411; and John Martin Fischer, "Lehrer's New Move: 'Can' in Theory and Practice," *Theoria* 45 (1979), pp. 49–62.

[23] I define the term "Dialectical Stalemate" and argue that the debates about the Consequence Argument seem to end in such stalemates in Fischer, *The Metaphysics of Free Will: An Essay on Control*, pp. 83–85.

[24] I have attempted to argue for this point elsewhere, most recently in Fischer et al., *Four Views of Free Will* (Oxford: Blackwell Publishers, 2007), pp. 56–61 and pp. 188–190. See also chapter 2 of this book.

In previous work, I have contended that the best way to accommodate the insights of the Frankfurt cases is to distinguish between the "actual-sequence mechanism" that issues in the relevant choices and behavior and those mechanisms that play roles in the range of non-actual or hypothetical scenarios. I was careful to say that my use of "mechanism" did not presuppose or signify any kind of "reification;" I think of a mechanism as a process or, more abstractly, a "way"— in this case, a way of producing choices and behavior. In my view, an analysis of the Frankfurt cases should start by noting that the actual sequence flows in a different way from the salient alternative scenario: in the actual sequence, one finds (say) the unimpaired operation of the normal human deliberative mechanism, whereas in the salient alternative scenario one finds (say) direct electronic stimulation of the brain. Even if we do not have an elaborate theory of individuation of such processes, it is intuitively clear that the ordinary human deliberative mechanism is different from a range of "manipulation mechanisms."

So the first step in analyzing the Frankfurt cases is to distinguish the actual-sequence mechanism from the alternative-sequence mechanism(s). I then suggest that we "hold fixed" the actual mechanism—that is, the *kind* of mechanism that actually operates—and ask whether it is suitably reasons-responsive. The Frankfurt cases are examples in which the actual-sequence mechanism is appropriately reasons-responsive, but the *agent* is not. That is, the agent could not have responded to a good reason to do otherwise, since Black (or his representative!) would have stepped in; but there is no reason to deny the reasons-responsiveness of human practical reasoning *holding fixed the non-intervention of Black.*

Of course, this is the barest sketch of the approach I find most promising, and the details need to be filled in.[25] Some philosophers do not draw the same conclusions I draw from the Frankfurt cases, and there are certainly other ways of seeking to make sense of the conclusions, if one does agree with them. I am certainly aware that there are difficult problems with mechanism-individuation and also specifying the relevant sort of reasons-responsiveness, and I have sought to provide at least some preliminary work toward addressing them.

It is perhaps not entirely surprising that the approach I have suggested has not met with universal approval, even among theorists inclined toward my compatibilist conclusion. Consider, for example, this passage from R. Jay Wallace:

> The deeper problem, however, lies in the supposition that questions of moral accountability can be clarified by attending exclusively to the modal properties of the "mechanisms" involved in action. This approach brings an objectifying, third-personal vocabulary to bear on phenomena that have their natural place within the deliberative perspective of practical reason, with the result that the intuitive locus of responsibility, the person, seems to

---

[25] For at least some of the details, see Fischer and Ravizza, *Responsibility and Control: A Theory of Moral Responsibility* (New York: Cambridge University Press, 1998), and Fischer, *My Way.*

drop out of view. A better approach would focus not on the counterfactual behavior of the *mechanisms* that issue in action, but on the normative competence of the *agents* who performs those actions, and are morally responsible for them.[26]

The switch to guidance control and the accompanying switch from the dispositions of persons to the dispositions of mechanism was designed to accommodate the lessons of the Frankfurt cases. These moves also allow us to sidestep the Dialectical Stalemates produced by the Consequence Argument. Wallace's claim that this approach "brings an objectifying, third-personal vocabulary to bear on phenomena that have their natural place within the deliberative perspective of practical reason" is difficult to assess; it raises various issues that are beyond the scope of this paper. Perhaps it suffices here to note that it is not obvious that it is wrong-headed to seek a broadly "naturalistic" approach to the phenomena of deliberation and moral responsibility, or at least an approach that is *compatible* with naturalism. I am not sure, however, that Wallace would disagree here, or that my observation is indeed inconsistent with his claim; this is in part because I am not sure exactly what the claim amounts to.

I would also simply point out that, whatever Wallace's claim amounts to in the end, it does not have the "result that the intuitive locus of responsibility, the person, seems to drop out of view." After all, it is the *person* who is morally responsible (partly) *in virtue of* the operation of *his own* suitably reasons-responsive mechanism. I do not believe I have ever contended that we attend "exclusively" to the modal properties of the relevant mechanisms, if this entails (or suggests) that we do not thereby have a deep interest in the agents who own the mechanisms. Note an important parallel here with "reliabilist" accounts of justification or knowledge. In such an approach, an individual S has (say) justification for believing that p only if he believes that p as a result of a reliable belief-producing mechanism. Here it is evident that an analysis that adverts to the modal properties of the relevant mechanism does not in any way entail or lead to the disappearance of the knower; similarly, an analysis of moral responsibility that adverts to the modal properties of the actually operative action-producing mechanism need not lead to the agent's dropping out of view.

The sort of analysis of actual-sequence freedom ("acting freely" or "guidance control") that employs the distinction between the actual kind of process that issues in behavior and alternative kinds of processes could be invoked to defend a Scanlon-type approach. That is, one could in principle combine a demand for judgment-sensitivity with the requirement of holding fixed the actually operative

---

[26] R. Jay Wallace, "Review of *The Metaphysics of Free Will: An Essay on Control*, by John Martin Fischer," *The Journal of Philosophy* 94 (1997), p. 159.

kind of mechanism. Of course, Scanlon does not avail himself of this theoretical resource, and he might share some of Wallace's worries. But it seems to me that Scanlon in the end would need some similar sort of theoretical machinery—some way of distinguishing the properties (some of which are modal) of the *actual* process from properties of *other* processes (the kinds that would take place in salient alternative scenarios). If this is correct, then whatever worries there are about my specific approach to analyzing actual-sequence freedom would apply more broadly; indeed, I think they would apply to *any* account that sought to accommodate the insights of the Frankfurt cases.

I wish to pause to emphasize the point that Scanlon can make use of the sort of theoretical machinery I have introduced (involving a distinction between the actual-sequence kind of process and the kinds of processes in various alternative scenarios). So, even if I am correct that judgment-sensitivity cannot be spelled out in terms of "simple" or "straightforward" counterfactuals (because of the problems raised by the Frankfurt cases), this would *not* show that moral responsibility is not associated with judgment-sensitivity *suitably specified*. Perhaps Scanlon has *some* sort of actual-sequence specification in mind, even if he doesn't say so explicitly. The critique I have presented (based on the Frankfurt cases) seems to me to show that Scanlon *must* either have some further actual-sequence qualifications in mind or be inclined to accept this sort of modification to his theory; but my critique is not intended as showing that *no* version of a Scanlon-type approach (including judgment-sensitivity) is acceptable. Of course, Scanlon has not explicitly addressed these issues, and Wallace (with whom Scanlon might not agree on this point) has rejected the sort of actual-sequence machinery I introduced.

Wallace contends (in the passage quoted above) that we should not focus on the properties of the kinds of processes that issue in our choices and behavior, but rather, on the "normative competence" of agents.[27] If normative competence requires access to alternative possibilities, which is a very natural assumption, then the Frankfurt-case argumentation raises serious problems. As I have suggested previously with respect to a related set of issues, an appealing way to handle these problems would be to distinguish between displays of *this competence* and

---

[27] Similarly, Gary Watson says:

What is missing here [in someone who does not meet one of the conditions specified in Fischer and Ravizza, *Responsibility and Control: A Theory of Moral Responsibility* for "taking responsibility" and thus for guidance control], it seems to me, is a set of beliefs and (I would add) concerns and skills in virtue of which individuals are capable of reflective critical reason and are therefore capable of participating in the practices of critical evaluation. It is not relevant, as far as I can see, how, or even whether (if this supposition is coherent) they acquired them. What is crucial is not a kind of control but the competence required for meaningful response to the norms to which we hold one another responsible. Gary Watson, "Reasons and Responsibility: Review Essay on *Responsibility and Control: A Theory of Moral Responsibility*, by John Martin Fischer and Mark Ravizza," *Ethics* 111 (2001), p. 393.

behaviors that issue from some *different kind of capacity*. The approach would then hold fixed the capacity in question—the actually operative normative competence—when assessing moral responsibility. But this approach would seemingly run afoul of exactly the same sort of worries that Wallace adduces against my approach. Of course, I am not at all convinced that they are genuine or insuperable objections; I wish here simply to point out that they would apply to a "normative competence" view, construed so as not to require access to alternative possibilities.[28]

To summarize, Wallace suggests that we replace my notion of "guidance control" with "normative competence" (Watson evidently seconds the motion). Wallace objects to my specific analysis of guidance control insofar as it invokes the modal properties of mechanisms (or kinds of mechanisms). I have replied by addressing Wallace's worries about mechanisms; that is, I have emphasized that my use of "mechanism" is not intended to pick out something inappropriately reified, but rather a process or "way." Further, I have suggested that *any* plausible approach to accommodating the insights of the Frankfurt cases (and, in general, structures of preemptive overdetermination) will involve something like my distinction between how the actual sequence proceeds and how salient alternative sequences develop.

An appeal to normative competence might be part of an approach to moral responsibility that either embraces freedom to do otherwise (regulative control) as the freedom required for moral responsibility or acting freely (guidance control) as the freedom required for moral responsibility. In the first approach, both the Consequence Argument and the Frankfurt cases present significant challenges. I would thus argue for the second approach, insofar as one wishes to appeal to normative competence at all. Switching from regulative to guidance control not only avoids the Dialectical Stalemates deriving from the Consequence Argument, but allows one to accommodate the insights provided by the Frankfurt cases. But *any* such approach would seem to require *some* distinction between the relevant features of the actual sequence and the range of alternative (non-actual) sequences.

---

[28] In his monograph, *Responsibility and the Moral Sentiments*, Wallace appears to endorse the view that all that is required in the way of freedom or control is that an agent perform an action while possessing a general capacity to understand and respond to reasons. That is, Wallace seems to hold that the freedom-relevant condition on moral responsibility does not require viewing the action as issuing from the relevant general capacity or normative competence; it is enough that the agent possess that competence. Whereas this approach avoids the putative problems with my approach—including the vexed issue of mechanism-individuation—it faces significant problems of its own. For example, an agent who possesses the relevant general capacity might act as a result of "manipulation" of some sort; in Wallace's theory, it would appear that such an agent must be deemed morally responsible. Of course, one might seek to respond to such cases in various ways, and I do not contend that the possibility of direct clandestine manipulation straightforwardly provides a decisive refutation of Wallace's approach. For a more detailed discussion, see John Martin Fischer, "Review of R. Jay Wallace, *Responsibility and the Moral Sentiments*" *Ethics* 106 (1996), pp. 850–853.

III. Conclusion

Some philosophers—especially compatibilists—have wondered what the big fuss is over the Consequence Argument. They point out that it is just obvious that absolute freedom, holding the past and laws fixed, is incompatible with causal determinism—that is a "no-brainer." But the compatibilist might also point out that he never meant to deny the claim, so interpreted. In the previous chapter, I considered a suggestion—derived from comments by Gary Watson but not explicitly endorsed by Watson—that the compatibilist is really employing a conditional notion of freedom. I have argued that whereas this move provides an interpretation of compatibilism according to which it can respond to the Consequence Argument, it renders compatibilism hopelessly vulnerable to the Frankfurt cases. I have granted that there are many difficulties and controversies pertaining to the Frankfurt cases, but I have pointed out that these are largely if not entirely avoided, once a compatibilist makes it explicit that he is employing a conditional notion of freedom.

In this chapter I have explored some themes in Scanlon's work on moral responsibility. I have noted that the problems posed by the Frankfurt cases for conditional freedom are reinscribed within the context of an evaluation of Scanlon's association of moral responsibility with judgment-sensitivity (defined in terms of simple subjunctive or counterfactual conditionals). Thus Scanlon must offer a more nuanced account of the relevant sort of judgment-sensitivity; a natural and appealing approach, here, would be to introduce machinery that secures a restriction to actual-sequence phenomena. Such a restriction is part of my account of guidance control, but is not explicitly included in Scanlon's development of judgment-sensitivity.

In assessing Scanlon's view, it is important to distinguish a more concrete from a more abstract perspective. Strictly speaking, the Value of Choice—or the interest in regulative control—does not emerge unconditionally from either perspective. But from the more abstract evaluative perspective it is plausible to prefer regulative control, given natural assumptions about the threats to such control. The distinction between the different perspectives thus helps to explain why we all might care about having political institutions that safeguard certain liberties while some of us at least also accept that the Frankfurt cases show that we do not need regulative control in order to be morally responsible; that is, the distinction between perspectives shows how political liberalism (in a classical sense) is entirely consistent with the denial that regulative control (freedom to choose/do otherwise) is necessary for moral responsibility, dignity, and personhood.

My discussion in these two chapters has revealed (at least) three dimensions of variation among theorists who link freedom with moral responsibility. (Note that these dimensions of variation cut across the compatibilism/incompatibilism divide.) First, in accepting PAP, some theorists opt for absolute freedom, whereas others select conditional freedom. Second, among those who adopt absolute freedom, there are various different constraints on this freedom; some of these involve assumptions about the past and natural laws. Finally, some philosophers wish to reject PAP. They typically distinguish an actual-sequence notion of freedom (acting freely or guidance control) from a notion that involves metaphysical access to alternative possibilities (freedom to do otherwise or regulative control). One's philosophical challenges will depend importantly on the kind of freedom one selects as relevant to moral responsibility.[29]

---

[29] I am indebted to Joseph Campbell for insightful and helpful comments on a previous version of this chapter.

10

Sourcehood: Playing the Cards That Are Dealt You

The presiding judge gave a short cough, and asked me in a very low tone if I had anything to say. I rose, and as I felt in the mood to speak, I said the first thing that crossed my mind: that I'd had no intention of killing the Arab. The Judge replied that this statement would be taken into consideration by the court. Meanwhile he would be glad to hear, before my counsel addressed the court, what were the motives of my crime. So far, he must admit, he hadn't fully understood the grounds of my defense.

I tried to explain that it was because of the sun, but I spoke too quickly and ran my words into each other. I was only too conscious that it sounded nonsensical, and, in fact, I heard people tittering.

My lawyer shrugged his shoulders…

—ALBERT CAMUS, *THE STRANGER*

I. Introduction: Responsibility and Sourcehood

Various philosophers have put forward arguments according to which we must have a certain kind of "ultimate control" in order to be morally responsible for our behavior. In Galen Strawson's view, the very concept of moral responsibility involves the requirement of a kind of "self-creation" that is, upon reflection, incoherent; the incoherence putatively stems from our ordinary notion of moral responsibility

Part of this paper is based on "Playing the Cards That Are Dealt You," which appeared in an issue of *Journal of Ethics* in honor of Joel Feinberg. Joel Feinberg was a careful, systematic, and penetrating philosopher. He was also one of the "good guys" of our profession.

and not from any "special" assumption, such as causal determinism.[1] Others, including most notably Saul Smilansky and Robert Kane, have argued that moral responsibility requires that we be the "source" of our behavior in a way that would be ruled out by causal determinism. Smilansky argues for reasons similar to those of Strawson that causal determination would rule out sourcehood in the sense required for anything other than a "shallow" sort of moral responsibility. Kane argues that we must meet an "ultimacy" condition on responsibility—a condition that is incompatible with causal determinism.[2]

It is uncontentious that we want to be the "initiators" or "ultimate sources" of our behavior, in some suitable sense, and that a morally responsible agent must meet some conditions that capture these ideas appropriately. It is, however, controversial whether the relevant idea of sourcehood entails the strong sort of "self-creation" that seems to be envisaged by Strawson, Smilansky, and even Kane.

In this chapter I seek to understand the basic motivation for the views of Strawson and Smilansky, on the one hand, and philosophers such as Kane, on the other. I shall suggest that their views may depend on an inappropriate and unduly demanding picture, according to which the locus of control must be entirely "internal" to the agent, in order for there to be robust, genuine moral responsibility. I do not suppose that I will have offered decisive objections to the views under consideration; rather, my goal is to raise some questions and to propose some challenges for these views.

II. Feinberg on Self-Creation

Although he was explicitly addressing the notion of "autonomy," Joel Feinberg's remarks also apply to the closely related notions of metaphysical freedom and moral responsibility. Here, as always, Feinberg was notably and admirably sensible:

> The autonomous person is often thought of as a "self-made man." He cannot, of course, be literally and wholly self-made without contradiction. Even his character as authentic cannot be entirely the product of his own doing. To suppose otherwise is to conceive of authenticity in such an exalted way that its criteria can never be satisfied, or else to promote the ideal of authenticity in a self-defeating way. To reflect rationally, in the manner of the autonomous-authentic person, is to apply some already

---

[1] Galen Strawson, *Freedom and Belief* (Oxford: Oxford University Press, 1986). There is a recent articulation of the argument in Galen Strawson, "The Bounds of Freedom," in Robert Kane, ed., *The Oxford Handbook on Free Will* (New York: Oxford University Press, 2002), pp. 441–460.

[2] Robert Kane, *The Significance of Free Will* (Oxford: Oxford University Press, 1996).

accepted principles, in accordance with the rules of rational procedure, to the text of more tentative principles or candidates for principles, judgments, or decisions. Rational reflection thus presupposes some relatively settled convictions to reason from and with. If we take authenticity to require that *all* principles (beliefs, preferences, etc.) are together to be examined afresh in the light of reason on each occasion for decision, then nothing resembling rational reflection can ever get started.

The point is a modest one, but commonly overlooked by those whose conception of autonomy is unrealistically inflated. It is simply that a person must already possess at least a rudimentary character before he can hope to *choose* a new one ... There can be no magical *ex nihilo* creation of the habit of rational reflection. Some principles, and especially the commitment to reasonable self-criticism, must be "implanted" in a child if she is to have a reasonable opportunity of playing a part in the direction of her own growth.[3]

Feinberg goes on to point out that we find talk of "self-made persons" in philosophers as different as Aristotle and Sartre.[4] But he says:

A common-sense account of self-creation (the term "self-determination" has a less grating and paradoxical sound) can be given, provided we avoid the mistake of thinking that there can be no self-determination unless the self that does the determining is already fully formed ... The extent of the child's role in his own shaping is ... a process of continuous growth already begun at birth. From the very beginning that process is given its own distinctive slant by the influences of heredity and early environment. At a time so early that the questions of how to socialize and educate the child have not even arisen yet, the twig will be bent in a certain definite direction. From then on, the parents in promoting the child's eventual autonomy will have to respect that initial bias.[5]

Feinberg goes on to sketch a very sensible and plausible commonsense account of a child's development into an autonomous agent. He then concludes:

At least that is how growth proceeds when parents and other authorities raise a child with maximum regard for the autonomy of the adult he will one day be. That is the most sense that we can make of the ideal of the "self-made person," but it is an intelligible idea, I think, with no paradox in it.

[3] Joel Feinberg, *Harm to Self*. Volume Three: *The Moral Limits of the Criminal Law*. (New York: Oxford University Press, 1986), pp. 33–34.
[4] Joel Feinberg, *Harm to Self*, p. 34.
[5] Joel Feinberg, *Harm to Self*, p. 34.

Perhaps we are all self-made in the way just described, except those who have been severely manipulated, indoctrinated, or coerced throughout childhood. But the self we have created in this way for ourselves will not be an authentic self unless the habit of critical self-revision was implanted in us early by parents, educators, or peers, and strengthened by our own constant exercise of it. Self-creation in the authentic person must be a process of self-*re*-creation, rationally accommodating new experiences and old policies to make greater coherence and flexibility. Self-creation is possible but not *ex nihilo*.[6]

Here Feinberg approvingly cites Gerald Dworkin, who says that, at the dawn of rational self-awareness:

We simply find ourselves motivated in certain ways, and the notion of choosing, from ground zero, makes no sense. Sooner or later we find ourselves, as in Neurath's metaphor of the ship in mid-ocean, being reconstructed while sailing, in mid-history. But [insofar as we are autonomous] we always retain the possibility of stepping back and judging where we are and where we want to be.[7]

I find Joel Feinberg's observations to be right on the money. It seems to me that they apply to the kind of initiation or ultimate sourcehood that is involved in moral responsibility just as well as they apply to the parallel notions in regard to autonomy. It is eminently reasonable to suppose that we should not demand a self-contradictory sort of ultimacy in order to be morally responsible. Some might identify an idea of self-creation or initiation with some intuitive appeal, and, having noted that it is in the end self-contradictory, conclude that we cannot be morally responsible, in the ordinary sense. In contrast, Feinberg correctly concludes that such an idea, although perhaps initially attractive, is way too strong and not really part of common sense. Why, Feinberg might ask, is it more plausible to jettison moral responsibility and cling to a very demanding notion of self-creation ("an inflated conception of autonomy") than to scale down the demands of self-creation to something more reasonable?

III. Galen Strawson on Ultimate Sourcehood

III.1. STRAWSON'S VIEW

Galen Strawson has argued that our ordinary conception of moral responsibility requires a kind of ultimate self-creation that is incoherent. Strawson gives various

---

[6] Joel Feinberg, *Harm to Self*, pp. 34–35.
[7] Gerald Dworkin, "Autonomy and Behavior Control," *Hastings Center Report* 16 (1976), p. 25. Feinberg refers to the Dworkin's piece in *Harm to Self*, p. 35.

different formulations of the argument, but I find the versions presented in his article, "The Bounds of Freedom," particularly lucid.[8]

Strawson begins by describing a certain notion of being morally responsible: "ultimately, truly, and without qualification responsible and deserving of praise or blame or punishment or reward."[9] I find that it is easier, and perhaps avoids confusion, simply to employ the term, "morally responsible," where we keep in mind that this involves genuine, robust moral responsibility (and not a revised or watered down version of the ordinary concept).[10] As I present Strawson's argument, I will simply employ the term "morally responsible," construed in this way. I shall follow Strawson in sometimes using "ultimately" to qualify "morally responsible," but I am not exactly sure what Strawson means in employing "ultimately" in this way.

Here are a couple of versions of Strawson's argument.[11] The first version is as follows. When you act, you do what you do—in the situation in which you find yourself—because of the way you are. If you do what you do because of the way you are, then in order to be ultimately morally responsible for what you do, you must be ultimately morally responsible for the way you are. But you cannot be ultimately morally responsible for the way you are. Thus, you cannot be ultimately morally responsible for what you do.

The second version is this. One cannot be *causa sui*—one cannot be the cause of oneself. But one would have to be *causa sui*, at least in certain crucial mental respects, in order to be ultimately morally responsible for one's thoughts and actions. Thus one cannot be ultimately morally responsible for one's thoughts or actions.

Strawson holds that being morally responsible (in the genuine and robust sense) requires being ultimately morally responsible. Strawson thus concludes that we cannot be morally responsible for any of our thoughts or actions. This argument allegedly goes through, quite apart from whether causal determinism is true; it does not presuppose causal determinism. Strawson says:

> "*No one* is accountable for existing at all, or for being constituted as he is, or for living in the circumstances and surroundings in which he lives," as Nietzsche remarked:

> The *causa sui* is the best self-contradiction that has been conceived so far; it is a sort of rape and perversion of logic. But the extravagant pride of man has managed to entangle itself profoundly and frightfully with just this nonsense.

---

[8] Galen Strawson, "The Bounds of Freedom."

[9] Galen Strawson, "The Bounds of Freedom," p. 442.

[10] Note that terminology such as "ultimately, truly, and without qualification responsible" can have a rhetorical effect that influences one to insist on more rigorous requirements for moral responsibility than are perhaps warranted.

[11] These follow closely Strawson's presentation in "The Bounds of Freedom," especially pp. 443–444.

The desire for "freedom of the will" in the superlative metaphysical sense, which still holds sway, unfortunately, in the minds of the half-educated—the desire to bear the entire and ultimate responsibility for one's actions oneself, and to absolve God, the world, ancestors, chance, and society—involves nothing less than to be precisely this *causa sui* and, with more than Baron Munchhausen's audacity, to pull oneself up into existence by the hair, out of the swamps of nothingness.[12]

III.2. CRITIQUE OF STRAWSON

Strawson's argument is elaborated with great intelligence and sophistication, and I cannot possibly do justice to it here.[13] Instead, I shall first simply point out that Feinberg seems to be on the correct side of this debate. That is, if one is presented with an "inflated" notion of self-creation or autonomy, one ought to jettison it in favor of something more reasonable. Why suppose that we must be "ultimately morally responsible" for the way we are? Alternatively, why suppose that we must be "ultimately morally responsible" for the way we are in a way that is impossible? Similarly, why suppose (with Strawson and Nietzsche) that we must be *causa sui*, or *causa sui* in a way in which we cannot possibly be? It seems much more plausible to suppose that we must be the "ultimate sources" of our behavior in some genuine way, but a way that is at least possible to realize in the world (apart from any special assumption, such as that causal determinism obtains).

Rather than seeking to engage Strawson's subtle argumentation in its detail, I wish to defend Feinberg's position by raising some *prima facie* problems and challenges for Strawson's view.[14] Suppose my parents had beaten me mercilessly when I was very young, so that I had significant physical (neurological) and emotional damage. If the damage had been sufficiently bad, I would never have developed into an agent at all. And yet it is quite clear that I never had any control over whether my parents beat me in this way. Similarly for an infinitely large number of factors. For example, I had no control over whether I was born with a significant brain lesion that would impair or expunge my agency. Had I been born with such

---

[12] Galen Strawson, "The Bounds of Freedom," p. 444. The quotation from Nietzsche is from *Twilight of the Idols, or: How to Philosophize with a Hammer*, Section 8, "The Four Great Errors." (Leipzig: Naumann, 1889). For a discussion of Nietzsche's views on these matters, see Brian Leiter, "The Paradox of Fatalism and Self-Creation in Nietzsche," in C. Janaway, ed., *Willing and Nothingness: Schopenhauer as Nietzsche's Educator* (Oxford: Oxford University Press, 1998), pp. 217–257.

[13] Despite my disagreement with Strawson about ultimacy, I have considerable admiration for his work on free will and moral responsibility: John Martin Fischer, "Review of Galen Strawson's *Freedom and Belief*," *Times Literary Supplement* (August 1987), p. 852.

[14] For more careful and detailed engagement, see Randolph Clarke, *Libertarian Accounts of Free Will* (Oxford: Oxford University Press, 2003), pp. 170–176; and "On an Argument for the Impossibility of Moral Responsibility," *Midwest Studies in Philosophy* 29 (2009), pp. 13–24.; and Alfred Mele, *Autonomous Agents: From Self-Control to Autonomy* (New York: Oxford University Press, 1995), pp. 221–230.

a lesion, I would never have developed into an agent at all, or would have developed into an agent with a very different character and set of dispositions. Again: I had no control over the fact that I was not dropped on my head (accidentally or deliberately) by my parents when I was very young. But had I been dropped on my head in a certain way, I would not have developed into an agent at all, or might have developed into a very different sort of agent.[15]

When one begins to think about this sort of thing, one quickly realizes that we are incredibly lucky to be as we are. I had no control over the fact that I was not hit by a bolt of lightning when I was young (or, for that matter, yesterday), or that I was not hit by a meteorite, and so forth. But had any of these things occurred, I would not be the way I am today—and I certainly would not be typing this paper at my computer! Life is extraordinarily fragile, and (from a certain perspective) we are remarkably lucky to be agents at all, or the particular agents we are (with the particular dispositions, values, and psychological propensities we actually have). Intuitively speaking, I am not "ultimately responsible" for my particular psychological traits or even for my very agency. We are not "ultimately responsible" for "the way we are," and yet it just seems crazy to suppose that we are thereby relieved of moral responsibility for our behavior. Does it not seem highly counterintuitive to suppose that I am not a morally responsible agent in virtue of the fact that I had no control over whether the earth was hit by a meteorite or the sun flickered out when I was young (or yesterday, for that matter)? How could my moral responsibility hinge on whether or not I can prevent the sun from rising or flickering out?[16] We do not have "ultimate responsibility," but it would seem much more plausible to suppose (with Feinberg) that such responsibility is not required for genuine, legitimate moral responsibility than to conclude that we are thereby rendered incapable of being held morally responsible.

Note that all of the considerations above involve the existence of conditions "entirely external" to the relevant individual in some very natural, intuitive sense, over which the relevant individual has absolutely no control, and which is a causal contributor to his psychological constitution (to his being the way he is, in the pertinent sense) and to his behavior.[17] Indeed, the conditions are causal sustainers in

---

[15] Note that I have described the factor in question "negatively": my not having been dropped on my head. But one could equally describe the relevant causal background condition "positively": my having been handled carefully and treated well by my parents, and so forth. Nothing in my argument depends on any sort of assumption that "negative" facts can be causal.

[16] In Molly Bloom's soliloquy, she says: "...who was the first person in the universe before there was anybody that made it all who ah that they don't know neither do I so there you are they might as well try to stop the sun from rising tomorrow the sun shines for you he said..." James Joyce, *Ulysses* (New York: Random House, 1961), p. 782.

[17] We would typically *select* from among the various causal contributors to an event and thus highlight some factor or factors in making causal attributions and offering causal explanations. Joel Feinberg's treatment of the considerations that guide such selection is highly illuminating: "Action and Responsibility," in Joel Feinberg, *Doing and Deserving* (Princeton, NJ: Princeton University Press, 1970), pp. 119–151. Here Feinberg emphasizes the pragmatic dimensions of causal attributions—their

that they contribute to the causally necessary conditions for the individual's being the way he is and behaving as he does. After all, the sun's continuing to shine is a necessary condition of the existence of human beings. The sun's continuing to shine is a causal "background condition" that *enables* me to be the way I am and to act as I do. Similarly, my parents' treating me in certain ways when I was young—feeding and clothing me when I was young, taking care of me gently, and so forth—were causal contributors in exactly the same way to my becoming the sort of agent I became, and, indeed, to my becoming an agent at all.

---

purpose-relativity, and so forth. He identifies various features in virtue of which we pick out or select certain of the causal contributors as "the cause," relative to certain purposes. (See, especially, "Action and Responsibility," pp. 143–147). This is, in my view, a brilliant discussion. I should point out that everything Feinberg says about our practices of making causal attributions and offering (and accepting) causal explanations is compatible with there being an indefinitely large number of causal background conditions or causal contributors to an event, on which the occurrence of the event depends, and which are "external" to the relevant agent. These are the factors from which the pragmatically informed selection is made in the context of causal explanation.

When Meursault says that he killed the Arab "because of the sun," this may have evoked the "tittering" of the jury simply because it was an inappropriate selection of a causal background condition as "the cause." Feinberg's discussion can help to explain why, in a typical context, such a selection would be inappropriate. Camus appears to present "the sun" as more than merely a causal background condition in the following famous and beautiful, but puzzling, passage:

> I waited. The heat was beginning to scorch my cheeks; beads of sweat were gathering in my eyebrows. It was just the same sort of heat as at my mother's funeral, and I had the same disagreeable sensations—especially in my forehead, where all the veins seemed to be bursting through the skin. I couldn't stand it any longer, and took another step forward. I knew it was a fool thing to do; I wouldn't get out of the sun by moving on a yard or so. But I took that step, just one step, forward. And then the Arab drew his knife and held it up toward me, athwart the sunlight.
>
> A shaft of light shot upward from the steel, and I felt as if a long, thin blade transfixed my forehead. At the same moment all the sweat that had accumulated in my eyebrows splashed down on my eye-lids, covering them with a warm film of moisture. Beneath a veil of brine and tears my eyes were blinded; I was conscious only of the cymbals of the sun clashing on my skull, and, less distinctly, of the keen blade of light flashing up from the knife, scarring my eyelashes, and gouging into my eyeballs.
>
> Then everything began to reel before my eyes, a fiery gust came from the sea, while the sky cracked in two, from end to end, and a great sheet of flame poured down through the rift. Every nerve in my body was a steel spring, and my grip closed on the revolver. The trigger gave, and the smooth underbelly of the butt jogged by palm. And so, with that crisp, whipcrack sound, it all began. I shook off my sweat and the clinging veil of light. I knew I'd shattered the balance of the day, the spacious calm of this beach on which I had been happy. But I fired four shots more into the inert body, on which they left no visible trace. And each successive shot was another loud, fateful rap on the door of my undoing. Camus, *The Stranger*, translated by Stuart Gilbert. (New York: Random House, 1942), pp. 75–76.

This passage is puzzling for many reasons. Camus appears to be describing Meursault as experiencing the sun as a "triggering cause," and not a mere background enabling causal factor. And yet this is implausible. Why doesn't Meursault subject his impressions to critical scrutiny? Does he really suppose that the Arab is attacking him? If the light is "transfixing [his] forehead" and "scarring [his] eyelashes, and gouging into [his] eyeballs," why doesn't he feel the pain, or notice any blood? Why doesn't he seek to run away from the Arab, rather than attacking him? Doesn't anyone have the duty to monitor his perceptions and check for illusions? Of course, these are just a few obvious and perhaps flat-footed questions.

So there are infinitely many factors over which I had no control, which are such that, if they had occurred, I would not be as I am. Similarly, there are infinitely many factors over which I currently have no control, which are such that, if they were to occur, I would cease being as I am (and behaving as I do). I currently have no control over whether there is a huge earthquake that hits Southern California; if there were such an earthquake, I might well not continue to be the way I currently am (for various reasons). The earth's continuing to sustain me, the air's continuing to be (barely!) breathable, and so forth are causally sustaining conditions for my agency, over which I have absolutely no control. I am thus not "ultimately morally responsible." And yet this does not in itself seem to expunge or etiolate my agency and my moral responsibility. To suppose that we must be ultimately morally responsible, in the way imagined by Strawson, seems to me to be a wild extrapolation from the quite legitimate desire to be the initiator or source of one's behavior, in some genuine and reasonable sense. It seems to be a kind of metaphysical megalomania.

Perhaps the requirement of ultimate responsibility (construed in the "inflated" way) comes from, or is suggested by, a certain "picture." In this picture, the locus of control must be *within* us, if we are to be "genuinely" or "unqualifiedly" morally responsible. But when there is some factor that is external to us, over which we have no control, and upon which our behavior and "the way we are" is counterfactually dependent, the locus of control is not within us (in the relevant way). I have sought to show that this picture misleads us; it suggests that we can plausibly want a kind of control that is in reality unreasonable and, indeed, a mere chimera (tantalizing as it might be). After all, to be ultimately responsible, we would have to be morally responsible for the sun's continuing to shine!

It is as if Strawson thinks of free and morally responsible agents as having "total control." An agent has total control over X only if for any factor f which is a causal contributor to X and which is such that f were not to occur, then X would not occur, the agent has control over f. But we have seen that total control is a fantasy. To have total control would be to have control over the sun's continuing to shine, the earth's not being hit by a meteorite, and so forth. The desire for total control is a reflection of a kind of metaphysical "over-reaching," if anything is.

When one has total control, the locus of control is entirely within the agent; there is no factor external to the agent (and out of the agent's control) that is a causal contributor to the outcome in question and which is such that if it were not to occur, the outcome would not occur. In this view, it is as if we (*qua* moral agents) have a protective bubble around us, or perhaps we are in our armored vehicles. Alternatively, we are circumscribed by a fortress, and the Inner Citadel is a protected domain of control.[18] But I have shown that this is an illusory picture of

---

[18] Isaiah Berlin says:

I wish my life and decisions to depend on myself, not on external forces of whatever kind. I wish to be the instrument of my own, not other[s'] acts of will. I wish to be a subject, not an

agency and autonomy. We are at every point thoroughly subject to factors entirely outside our control. We are not even in a tiny bubble of control, but we are, in a sense, naked, swimming in a vast ocean of chance and luck.[19]

Now Strawson might reply that this is precisely his point, and that this is exactly the problem. That is, Strawson might say that our intuitions about agency imply an implausible notion of autonomy, and this notion of autonomy renders moral responsibility indefensible. Simply showing that the autonomy condition is bizarre or inflated does not imply that our intuitions about moral responsibility do not require it; rather, it would mean that our intuitions (and responsibility practices based on those intuitions) are misguided.[20]

In my view, however, it is much more sensible simply to recognize and accept that our lives are thoroughly subject to factors entirely outside our control and to scale back our demands for the sort of autonomy and "sourcehood" required for moral responsibility. (Note that this does not involve etiolating or watering down moral responsibility; rather, it encapsulates a recognition that we must be more sensible in articulating our inchoate notion of sourcehood, insofar as it is required for robust responsibility.) Of course, a full response to Strawson would need to explain how our intuitions about blame and fairness do not really lead us to such an excessively demanding and "exalted" autonomy condition, and how our practices are justifiable in the face of the failure to fulfill this condition. I do not attempt such a response here. Rather, I am highlighting a dialectical move evidently not considered (or not given sufficient attention) by Strawson: that the sort of autonomy we might initially find attractive does not survive critical scrutiny—it is unduly demanding.

In light of the implications of Strawson's picture of autonomy, one could go in either of two directions. One could say that such a picture is endorsed by commonsense but utterly impossible to fulfill. Or one could say that such a picture, being obviously and straightforwardly impossible to fulfill, cannot be the picture endorsed, upon reflection, by commonsense. The latter possibility seems to be

---

object... I wish to be somebody, not nobody. "Two Concepts of Liberty," in *Four Essays on Liberty* (Oxford: Oxford University Press, 1969), pp. 118–172, esp. p. 131.

It is as if I had performed a strategic retreat into an inner citadel—my reason, my soul, my 'noumenal' self—which, do what they may, neither external blind force, nor human malice, can touch. I have withdrawn into myself; there, and there alone, I am secure. "Two Concepts of Liberty," p. 135.

Berlin was not endorsing the Inner Citadel model, but it captures nicely a certain picture of autonomy. As regards the wish to "be somebody," Lily Tomlin says, in her one-person play, *The Search for Intelligent Life in the Universe*, "I always wanted to be somebody when I grew up. I should have been more specific!"

[19] We are thus even worse off than in Neurath's famous ship, which we must rebuild plank by plank while occupying it; in my view, we are, if I may be allowed to put it this way, in a body of water without (even) a paddle!

[20] I am indebted to Matt Talbert for this point.

the approach suggested by Feinberg, and it seems to me to be the path recommended by a certain sort of philosophical maturity and wisdom. Be that as it may, my more minimal point (to which I would retreat if pressed) is simply that the latter approach is no less plausible than the former, given the considerations adduced by Strawson. His argument is, at best, incomplete at this critical juncture.

Kant famously argued that we are at least in control of our will, even if we cannot legitimately be held morally responsible for certain unforeseeable consequences of our exercise of free will, and our actions. In this view, a certain sort of moral luck is ruled out: luck in consequences. So two individuals who will the same things in similar circumstances are to be evaluated as equally praiseworthy or blameworthy, apart from differences in consequences (that could not reasonably be foreseen). I am inclined to find this view attractive. But it is entirely compatible with the point I would insist upon: that our exercising our free will, in any given circumstance, or even our being free agents at all, depends on factors entirely out of our control. If the sun were to flicker out, I would no longer be a free agent at all, and I would certainly not be able to exercise my free will; and, obviously, I have no control over whether the sun flickers out (or whether the earth is hit by a meteorite, or whether I am struck by an unexpected bolt of lightning, etc.).

IV. Source Incompatibilism: The Sun Shines for You

IV.1. SMILANSKY'S VIEW

Strawson's argument does not depend on any "special" assumption, such as that causal determinism obtains. I now turn to a similar but importantly different view, according to which causal determinism would entail that we cannot be the "source" of our behavior, in the sense required for (robust and genuine) moral responsibility. This sort of view is defended by such philosophers as Saul Smilansky, Robert Kane, and Derk Pereboom (among others).[21]

I shall begin by discussing Smilansky's argument for the contention that causal determination would rule out the relevant sort of "sourcehood."[22] Smilansky argues that whereas a "compatibilist" notion of control is coherent and can be invoked to make important distinctions among agents who are ordinarily thought to differ in their moral accountability (and "desert"), it is nevertheless problematic. The

---

[21] Saul Smilansky, *Free Will and Illusion* (Oxford: Clarendon Press, 2000); Robert Kane, *The Significance of Free Will*; and Derk Pereboom. *Living Without Free Will* (Cambridge: Cambridge University Press, 2001).

[22] For a preliminary development of some of the ideas presented here, see: John Martin Fischer, "Review of Saul Smilansky's *Free Will and Illusion*," *Times Literary Supplement* (October 26, 2001), p. 28. As with Strawson, despite my disagreement about the sourcehood condition, I admire Smilansky's book.

compatibilist argues that causal determinism is compatible with the sort of control that grounds ascriptions of moral responsibility. Smilansky contends that the sort of control that we could have in a causally deterministic world is insufficient to ground moral responsibility in an ultimate or deep sense; he says that compatibilist responsibility is "shallow" and "superficial."

In simple form, Smilansky's argument here is as follows. If causal determinism is true, then all our deliberations, choices, and behavior are the result of causally deterministic sequences that began well before we were even born (or had any sense of the relevant options and the values that might be brought to bear on them, etc.). Since we are not responsible for initiating these sequences, and since our decisions and behavior are the necessary results of them, we are not "ultimately" in control of our deliberations and actions in the sense relevant to robust moral responsibility and ethical desert. If causal determinism is true, then it can be seen from a more objective or expansive perspective that what we choose to do, and in fact do, are purely a matter of "luck": what we choose may be "up to us" in a superficial sense, but what we choose is causally determined by our values and background dispositions, which are causally determined by our previous experiences, and so forth.

Smilansky refers to the responsibility-undermining characteristic of causal determination as the "unfolding of the given."[23] He says that causal determinism would entail that "people cannot ultimately create themselves, and their choices, including their choices to change themselves, and anything they do, can only follow from factors ultimately beyond their control."[24] He goes on to conclude, "We cannot shirk the perspective from which all that happens is ultimately a matter of *luck*, and hence in one way morally arbitrary and an unfit basis for fair differentiation among people...Compatibilism is, in itself, *morally shallow*..."[25]

I wish to focus my critical remarks on Smilansky's provocative claim that compatibilism is morally shallow. The crucial contention here is that the fact that our choices and behavior would merely reflect (on the assumption of causal determinism) the "unfolding of the given" renders it true that such choices and behavior are morally arbitrary—a matter of mere luck. After all, we have no control over the beginnings of the causal sequences that causally necessitate our choices and behavior; from the perspective of our control, there might just as easily have been *different* beginnings of those sequences, and thus different choices and actions.

In my view, Smilansky's argument is open to exactly the same sort of objections to which Strawson's view is vulnerable. As I argued above, it cannot be the *mere existence* of some causally contributing factor entirely outside the agent

[23] Saul Smilansky, *Free Will and Illusion*, p. 284.
[24] Saul Smilansky, *Free Will and Illusion*, p. 284.
[25] Saul Smilansky, *Free Will and Illusion*, pp. 284–285.

(and over which the agent has no control) which is such that if it were not to occur, the outcome in question would not occur, that makes it the case that the agent is not morally responsible. After all, the sun's continuing to shine is precisely such a factor, and, quite apart from a special assumption (such as that causal determinism obtains), there are an indefinitely large number of such factors. And, intuitively, many (if not all) of these factors are *irrelevant* to one's moral responsibility. It is a wild fantasy to suppose that one could have control over *all* of the factors which affect an outcome (in the relevant way); total control is, in Feinberg's term an "inflated" idea of autonomy. (One must guard against inflation in autonomy, as well as the economy!)

In recent work, Smilansky has sought to defend his approach against the sorts of criticisms I have just sketched.[26] He approvingly quotes Thomas Nagel, who says: "We can always undermine the sense of our own autonomy by reflecting that the chain of explanation or absence of explanation...can be pursued till it leads outside our lives."[27] Smilansky says:

> While compatibilists like Dennett have tried to convince us that luck is not meaningfully present in pertinent cases, Fischer takes the opposite approach, in the attempt to neutralize the sting of luck. Matters could easily have been different in our lives, he points out, and the fact that they are not different is, in the end, a matter of luck. Since skeptics must agree, then their own luck-based argument is put in jeopardy. If we do not mind the necessary presence of luck in our lives, then why should we be worried about the threat of "ultimate luck"?[28]

Smilansky goes on to offer a "direct" reply and also an analogy to bolster his point. His reply is that it is not the "presence of luck in itself" that is the problem. He says:

> After all, we are also all fortunate that the earth was not hit yesterday by a huge meteorite, but that seems scarcely relevant to the free will issue. Luck is undoubtedly present in our lives, but the central question is how its presence is manifested...[T]he difficulty is that compatibilist control is set by the way we are constituted so that every choice we make and every action we undertake is an unfolding of the arbitrarily given—the luck is not located in some corner but, when we look deeply, we see that it *goes all the way through*.[29]

[26] Saul Smilansky, "Compatibilism: The Argument from Shallowness," *Philosophical Studies* 115 (2003), pp. 257–282; "Fischer on Free Will and Luck," presented at the American Philosophical Association Central Division Meetings, April 2004.

[27] Saul Simlansky, "Fischer on Free Will and Luck," ms. p. 1; the quote is from Thomas Nagel, *The View from Nowhere* (New York: Oxford University Press, 1986), p. 136.

[28] Saul Smilansky, "Fischer on Free Will and Luck," ms. p. 2.

[29] Saul Smilansky, "Fischer on Free Will and Luck," ms. p. 3; this passage is also found in "Compatibilism: The Argument from Shallowness," p. 275.

He then presents his analogy:

> Assume that you begin to suspect that your love of some years does not in fact love you, but merely lives with you out of economic calculation. Indeed, you begin to suspect that she is not capable of deep personal love at all, that all the apparent manifestations of caring for other people are, ultimately, no more than sophisticated expressions of basic egoism. Now, you always knew that she viewed her boring but lucrative job as no more than a way of earning money; you believed, however, that in close personal relationships, and particularly in her life with you, things are different. When you begin to suspect that perhaps all there is with this person is all-encompassing egoism, you would hardly be comforted by a Fischer-like argument to the effect that egoism as such should not bother you, for, after all, her work-place egoism has never disturbed you.[30]

IV.2. RESPONSE TO SMILANSKY

I certainly did not think my argument should incline one to conclude that "luck is located in some corner." In fact, the argument is that luck is thoroughly pervasive. And it manifests itself, not just in a range of alternative scenarios or non-actual possible worlds, but in the actual world. So, as I emphasized previously, I am not in control of whether the sun continues to shine; clearly, the sun's continuing to shine is a contributing, and, indeed, a sustaining cause of my continuing to be an agent (and continuing to exist!). This is a causal factor entirely outside of my control, on which the outcome in question (my agency and its consequences) depends (in the relevant way), and it manifests itself in the actual sequence issuing in my behavior. Of course, this is just one example of an indefinitely large number of such factors—all of which play an *actual causal role*, even in a causally indeterministic world. So I would hardly say that luck is in a corner. Rather, it is everywhere.

But what exactly does Smilansky mean by "luck...*goes all the way through*," if causal determinism is true? One thing he could mean is that the external factors in question (together with relevant background conditions) are not just causal contributors or even sustainers of the outcome: they are causally *sufficient* conditions. As I pointed out, Smilansky's argument is that causal determinism poses a *special* challenge for our sourcehood and moral responsibility; in this way his argument differs from that of Galen Strawson.

In the case of causal determination of a choice (and subsequent behavior), the relevant agent lacks control of a *sufficient* condition that flows through the actual sequence to the choice and behavior. In contrast, in the cases I presented above, the agent lacks control over a *necessary* condition of the behavior; this necessary

---

[30] Saul Smilansky, "Fischer on Free Will and Luck," ms. p. 4.

condition posits the *failure to occur* of some event that, if it did occur, would prevent the possibility of the behavior in question (the sun's continuing to shine, the earth's not being hit by a meteorite, one's not having been beaten by one's parents as a child, etc.). Whereas I grant this distinction, I contend that it is unclear why exactly this distinction should make a difference. That is, Smilansky appears to argue that the reason compatibilism is ultimately shallow is that it is unavoidably committed to a certain sort of moral arbitrariness and luck. But I have shown that this sort of luck is present in a wide array of cases—cases which do not presuppose determinism—in which we would *not* think that robust evaluations (of the relevant sorts) are challenged in any way. So it cannot be this distinctive sort of luck or arbitrariness per se that renders compatibilism problematic, if it is indeed problematic.

Smilansky might then say that compatibilism is unattractive insofar as it entails that we can be morally responsible, even though our choices and behavior are (under the assumption of causal determinism) the *mere unfolding of the given*. (Above I interpreted Smilansky as arguing that the *reason* why choices that are the mere unfolding of the given are problematic is that they embody objectionable arbitrariness and luck; here it is supposed that Smilansky is simply claiming that when choices result from the mere unfolding of the given, then it follows that the agents who make those choices cannot be held deeply or robustly morally responsible.) This is the claim that what is problematic is that, given causal determinism, I lack control of a *sufficient* causal condition of my behavior.

But now the dialectic becomes delicate. If one is a compatibilist, one contends that causal determination of choice is compatible with robust moral responsibility for that choice. In a context in which we are seeking to evaluate this compatibilist thesis, it does not seem to advance the debate to contend that choices which are the unfolding of the given (interpreted simply as the results of a causally deterministic sequences) cannot be choices of a responsible agent; for this does not appear to amount to more than simply denying the compatibilist view (and thus begging the question against the compatibilist).

In a typical case in which an agent lacks control of a necessary condition of the relevant behavior and yet is subject to robust assessments based on the behavior, it is tempting to say that the condition in question—the non-occurrence of some "prevention-event"—does not get in the way of or "crowd out" the features of the agent in virtue of which he is morally responsible for his behavior. I am inclined to say that the presence of causally sufficient conditions in the actual sequence similarly need not get in the way of or crowd out the features in virtue of which an agent can be (robustly) morally responsible for his behavior.[31] I believe, then, that

---

[31] For an argument for this contention, see John Martin Fischer, "The Transfer of Non-Responsibility," in J. Campbell, M. O'Rourke, and D. Shier (eds.), *Freedom and Determinism: Topics in Contemporary Philosophy Series*, vol. 2 (MIT Press, 2004), pp. 189–209; reprinted in John Martin Fischer, *My Way: Essays on Moral Responsibility* (New York: Oxford University Press, 2006), pp. 159–174.

there is a symmetry in the way these two sorts of conditions—necessary and sufficient—function in this context. To establish this would require more argumentation than I can give here, although I will offer some considerations in section IV.3.[32] Here I would simply point out that Smilansky has not established the superficiality of compatibilism by invocation of luck, moral arbitrariness, or the unfolding of the given. If causal determinism is in fact compatible with the sort of control that grounds ascriptions of robust moral responsibility, then the unfolding of the given need not be the "mere" unfolding of the given.

In more recent work, Smilansky has suggested another interpretation of his worry that if causal determinism were true, then all our choices and behavior would be the "mere unfolding of the given."[33] This interpretation stems from considerations developed by Thomas Nagel and Richard Taylor. The worry seems to be that once one takes the ultimate perspective, one can see that everything is the "mere unfolding of the given" and thus without deep meaning.[34] I am not exactly sure what the worry is and how to articulate it in a non-question-begging way, but it may be helpful to focus first on the worry as it applies to the meaning of life, and then move to the worry about moral responsibility.

As Smilansky notes, one finds the "zoom-out" argument in the discussions of the meaning of life. Most notably, one frequently finds this strategy in the work of Richard Taylor.[35] Taylor points out that Sisyphus' existence (as portrayed in the original myth) is tedious, cyclical, and pointless—and thus essentially meaningless. Taylor points out that the lives of non-human animals, such as migratory birds, spawning fish, and even the glow worms in the caves in New Zealand, are fundamentally the same: cyclical, pointless, and without objective meaning. And now comes a crucial move: Taylor contends that, if we take a certain perspective—the perspective "from a distance"—we will see that ordinary human lives are really no different from the lives of Sisyphus and the non-human animals.

Taylor says:

> We toil after goals, most of them—indeed every single one of them—of transitory significance and, having gained one of them, we immediately set forth for the next, as if that one had never been, with the next one being essentially more of the same. Look at a busy street any day, and observe the throng going hither and thither. To what? Some office or shop, where the same things will

---

[32] I give a bit more of the required argumentation in "Compatibilism," in John Martin Fischer, et al., *Four Views on Free Will*, pp. 44–84, esp. pp. 61–71.

[33] Saul Smilansky, "Fischer's Way: The Next Level," *Journal of Ethics* 12 (2008), pp. 147–155.

[34] Smilansky, "Fischer's Way: The Next Level."

[35] For example, see Richard Taylor, "The Meaning of Life," in his *Good and Evil* (Amherst, N.Y.: Prometheus Books, 2000), pp. 319–334; reprinted in David Benatar, ed., *Life, Death, and Meaning* (Lanham, MD: Rowman & Littlefield, 2004), pp. 19–18.

be done today as were done yesterday, and are done now so they may be repeated tomorrow.[36]

He concludes, "The two pictures—of Sisyphus and of our own lives, if we look at them from a distance—are in outline the same and convey to the mind the same image."[37]

Now it is indisputable that, looked at from a more detached perspective—from a distance, as it were—we can discern certain patterns (even cycles) in our lives. But surely this does not entail that our lives—even from a distance—will look relevantly similar to those of Sisyphus, salmon, or the glow worms! Even from a distance, our lives can be seen to be significantly more complex and richer than those of Sisyphus and the non-human animals, and it is plausible that this rich complexity can underwrite substantial meaning. Our composition and functional complexity can, after all, support not just consciousness, but advanced cognition and sophisticated affective and executive capacities. Creatures with such capacities can presumably have lives that are significantly different from those of Sisyphus (in the original myth), migratory birds, salmon, and (most certainly) the New Zealand glow worms; these lives may contain friendship, love, pursuit of scientific, scholarly, and artistic projects, and so forth. Why would the relevant capacities and activities disappear from view from the zoomed-out perspective? And, if they would, why would such a perspective be at all relevant?

I suppose that if you take a perspective that is sufficiently distant, then all relevant distinctions will disappear. So, for example, from a mile away I certainly couldn't distinguish—nor could anyone, I take it—a fine diamond from something that came out of a Cracker Jacks box. But this is of no interest whatsoever; it simply shows that distance obliterates distinctions (or, more carefully, the ability to discern the distinctions); but they are still there. So we can construct a rather obvious dilemma. On the one hand, we could take the perspective from afar. From this perspective, any relevant distinctions between our lives and those of Sisyphus and the non-human animals appear to disappear. But so what? Why take this perspective? On the other hand, we could take a detached perspective from which we can nevertheless see the phenomena that are there to be seen; from this perspective, there are clear differences between our capacities—and lives—and those of Sisyphus and the birds, salmon, and glow worms.

In general, I believe that we should ask various questions when we are invited to take up a perspective "from a distance" for the purposes of evaluation of something (the meaning of life, the nature of moral responsibility, etc.). The first question is about what can in fact be seen from the commended perspective. The second question is why this perspective should be taken at all—and why it should be deemed hegemonic, if indeed it is putatively so. Applying this schema to

---

[36] Taylor, in Benatar, ed., *Life, Death, and Meaning*, p. 24.
[37] Taylor, in Benatar, ed., *Life, Death, and Meaning*, p. 25.

Taylor's invitation to take the perspective "from a distance," it should be evident first that if the distance is not too great, there are many important differences that should be visible between us and (say) salmon. Of course, if the distance is too great, the differences will disappear. Then the question will arise as to why we ought to take this perspective (and thus whether its deliverances are dispositive).

Note that the considerations relevant to spatial distance should apply, *mutatis mutandis*, to other sorts of distance. It is often suggested that we take a temporally distant perspective in order properly to see that our current lives are meaningless. But consider Thomas Nagel's insightful critique:

> It is often remarked that nothing we do now will matter in a million years. But if that is true, then by the same token, nothing that will be the case in a million years matters now. In particular, it does not matter now that in a million years nothing we do now will matter.[38]

Nagel's point is that the fact that nothing will matter in a million years does not decide the issue; why take the perspective of a million years in the future as hegemonic?

One can bring forward considerably more mundane examples that appear to show that even a less drastic projection into the future may not be fruitful. Consider how absurd it would be to say that, because the pleasures of going to a concert will after all be over at some point in the future, we shouldn't go to the concert at all! Similarly, one might argue that, because the pleasures of sex will be over at some point after the activities are finished, there is no point in engaging in the sexual activities. (This would be a new excuse, kind of a philosophically sophisticated version of, "I have a headache.") But surely the argument would be ludicrous. In such contexts one wants to say that the temporally distant perspective is not decisive; what matters surely at least includes the "current" temporal perspective (or the perspective simultaneous with the relevant activities). Of course, the overall or all-things-considered desirability of engaging in certain activities might be fruitfully assessed from a temporally distant perspective; but the argument that, simply because the pleasure will end, it would be pointless to engage in it is a manifestly bad argument.

Again, I do not wish to suppose that it can never be illuminating or helpful to take a more detached perspective—either temporal or spatial. I just think we have to be very careful about such moves. It is certainly not the case that as we get more and more distant temporally or spatially, we always get closer to the truth, no matter what the domain. Frequently it is quite the opposite.

Return to Smilansky's invocation of the "ultimate" perspective: "If one puts things, in retrospect, under the ultimate perspective, the greatest personal struggles, and the most amazing achievements, or triumphs over the odds, or overcoming of temptations, begin to appear as no more than the way things developed, inevitably...the mere

---

[38] Thomas Nagel, "The Absurd," *Journal of Philosophy* 68, no. 20 (October 21, 2003), pp. 716–727; reprinted in David Benatar, ed., *Life, Death, and Meaning*, pp. 29–40; the quotation is from p. 30.

unfolding of the given. For people who understand and internalize the ultimate-level insight, and are not insensitive, this should be emotionally deflating." But now I have a dilemma for Smilansky (based on the considerations sketched previously).

Let us consider the first horn, according to which one takes either a temporally or spatially distant perspective that allows for some detachment but does not render invisible the real characteristics and properties that are there to be seen in the domain of human action. Then, just as in the case of the distinction between human beings and (say) birds, salmon, and glow worms, I would insist that there is a rich complexity that can underwrite moral responsibility. That is, from this perspective, one can see that individuals sometimes exhibit guidance control—they sometimes act from their own, moderately reasons-responsive mechanisms. The structures that permit this signature kind of control can surely be visible from a suitably detached perspective; indeed, they presumably cannot be seen from the subjective perspective of an agent—some detachment is required.

Now we might consider adopting a perspective from afar—so far that one cannot see that there are features in some creatures in virtue of which they exhibit guidance control, whereas other creatures and entities lack the relevant characteristics. From such a distance, the view would be deflating. But why take this perspective? Why take it here, any more than taking it when we are trying to distinguish a fine diamond from the prize in a Cracker Jacks box? Why should it be thought that the perspective from afar has hegemony? Thus, Smilansky's invocation of "zooming" arguments simply does not establish that compatibilism is in any interesting way "morally shallow."

Finally, let us return to Smilansky's interesting analogy about the "love of your life." He says that one would not be comforted by a "Fischer-type" argument upon discovering that the woman you have loved for many years is just as selfish at home as at the office. I grant this point, but deny the relevance of the story to my views about the pervasiveness of a certain sort of luck in the context of human agency. One natural way of understanding the story is to suppose that we accept as justified the egoism manifested at work. We now discover that a person we have loved for many years is *inappropriately* manifesting egoism in a context in which it does not belong. To say that this discovery should not disturb us because egoism in an *appropriate context* does not bother us is patently fallacious—and not analogous to my argument. Here one is invited to say that it somehow follows from a certain sort of behavior being acceptable in a certain context that it should be considered acceptable in a *different* context. In contrast, in my argument I seek to call attention to the fact that luck (of the relevant sort) is pervasive and, upon reflection, not problematic (in *any* context). I do not suppose that something that is clearly and indisputably problematic becomes less so in virtue of its ubiquity; rather, my point is that we should recognize that our initial view that a certain sort of luck is problematic and should be reevaluated in light of a broader understanding of the pertinent phenomena.

Exhibiting his allegiance to the Inner Citadel model of control, Smilansky says:

[C]ompatibilism is attractive as establishing an "Island of Control" countering random arbitrariness; a space where, as it were, arbitrariness has no entry. The sense of compatibilist control is not without some basis, but nevertheless it becomes incorporated in the deeper picture, where all is arbitrary.[39]

The mistake is to suppose that compatibilism seeks to identify an "Island of Control"—an Inner Citadel. It is better to think of compatibilism as conceding from the beginning that we are thoroughly subject to factors entirely outside our control. Nevertheless, according to the compatibilist, we can still exhibit a meaningful and robust sort of control. It is not as if the compatibilist seeks to carve out a sphere of pure "internality" and immunity to arbitrariness, and then must be embarrassed to discover that the inner sanctum is not secure. He never thought that we needed such a place.

IV.3. OTHER VERSIONS OF SOURCE INCOMPATIBILISM

Philosophers such as Robert Kane and Derk Pereboom have also argued for Source Incompatibilism.[40] Whereas Smilansky's argument for some sort of incompatibilistic ultimacy requirement follows Galen Strawson in emphasizing considerations pertaining to luck, the other philosophers do not explicitly base their acceptance of Source Incompatibilism on such considerations. Elsewhere I have sought to address some of the arguments for Source Incompatibilism.[41] I certainly do not suppose that I have adequately addressed all of the arguments. I would simply add the following reflections; I admit that these are merely suggestive (at best), and that they are hardly decisive.

According to my argument addressed to Strawson and Smilansky, one cannot motivate an incompatibilistic Ultimate Source requirement by reference to luck, at least as Strawson and Smilansky seek to defend the requirement (or in related ways). I suggested that an insistence on an incompatibilistic Ultimate Source requirement might come from holding an inflated picture of autonomy or human agency, according to which we must be the sole locus of control of our behavior and we must have what I called Total Control (in order to be morally responsible). If we have Total Control, the locus of control is entirely in us insofar we have control over all factors that can affect the relevant outcome. But I have argued that the

---

[39] Saul Smilansky, "Compatibilism: The Argument from Shallowness," p. 275.

[40] Robert Kane, *The Significance of Free Will*; and Derk Pereboom, *Living Without Free Will*.

[41] John Martin Fischer, *The Metaphysics of Free Will: An Essay on Control*, pp. 147–154; "Frankfurt-Style Compatibilism," in S. Buss and L. Overton (eds), *Contours of Agency: Essays on Themes from Harry Frankfurt* (MIT Press, 2002), pp. 1–26, reprinted in G. Watson (ed.), *Free Will: Oxford Readings in Philosophy*, 2nd ed., (Oxford: Oxford University Press, 2003), pp. 190–211; and "Introduction: A Framework for Moral Responsibility," in *My Way: Essays on Moral Responsibility* (New York: Oxford University Press, 2006).

desire for Total Control is out of proportion with what can reasonably be expected, when one reflects on the pervasiveness of luck (as it relates to human agency).

Now of course the specific Ultimate Source requirements of Strawson and Smilansky are different, and their common motivating idea is quite different from those of such philosophers as Kane and Pereboom. But my suggestion is that, once one sees that the picture that favors Total Control is seen to be inflated and illusory, one might have less inclination to accept an incompatibilistic ultimate source requirement of *any* sort for *any* reason. That is, once one sees that there are a huge (presumably infinite) number of factors which are entirely out of my control (like the sun's continuing to shine) that are such that, if they were not present, my agency would be very different or not even nonexistent, one might be less inclined to object to (or find problematic) the fact that, if causal determinism obtains, there will be a condition entirely "external" to the agent and over which he has no control which is causally sufficient for one's behavior.

As I pointed out above, there is admittedly an important difference between our lack of control of external necessary or enabling conditions, and our lack of control of external causally sufficient conditions. I grant this point. But my suggestion is that, once one scales back one's metaphysical aspirations (as Feinberg encouraged us to do so sensibly), an incompatibilistic source condition becomes less attractive. After all, one must admit that there are causally enabling conditions—conditions that, as it were, "set the stage" for our exercises of agency, and without which our agency would be different in central aspects or would not even exist—which are entirely out of our control. One might then wonder why precisely it is problematic that there are (or might be) causally sufficient conditions for our behavior that are external and entirely out of our control.

Imagine, quite fancifully, that our agency is a connected set of dots—a horizontal line-segment from point b to point c. Now imagine a vertical line coming from below, with an arrow pointing toward the Agency Line. This line represents a causally necessary condition, such as the sun's shining; the sun's shining causally sustains and "sets the stage" for the exercise of agency. Now add a line that is (like the Agency Line) horizontal, starting to the left of point b and with an arrow pointing toward b. This arrow represents a causally deterministic sequence issuing in b (the beginning of the exercise of agency). Suppose that the relevant agent is not in control of this antecedent causal sequence "pointing horizontally toward b," just as he is not in control of the sun's shining. My question is this: if one is not troubled by the existence of the vertical line, why be troubled by the horizontal line? They are both the same in the sense that they represent "external" factors that are entirely outside the relevant agent's control; in virtue of what is the horizontal line troubling in a way in which the vertical line isn't? A *mere* appeal to "externality" will not distinguish the two lines—they are equally "external" to the Agency Line. Similarly, the sun is "external" to the agent in just the same way as the antecedent causal sequence—each equally impugns Total Control, and both introduce just the same sort of luck. Of course, this is not to say that there

are no potentially relevant differences between causally sufficient and necessary conditions; but it is to issue a challenge to say what those differences consist in.

Let's imagine that our agency is a rocket ship. Suppose that the rocket cannot
take off unless it has a platform of a certain sort—the platform is a causally
necessary condition that enables the rocket to take off. The platform's features
causally contribute to the rocket's taking off, in the same way that the sun's
continuing to shine causally contributes to human agency. It seems to me that the
astronauts can be said to control the launching of the rocket ship, even if we stipulate that they had nothing to do with the building of the platform and cannot in
any way affect the platform's continued existence or features. We can have a robust
sort of control of our behavior, without controlling all the necessary features of our
exhibiting precisely this control.

Note that *any incompatibilist* who believes that we do in fact exercise the sort of
control that can ground moral responsibility *must* admit that there are factors that
are entirely "external" to us and "out of our control," and which make a difference as
to how we behave. This simply follows from indeterminism, and it is brought out by
the well-known Rollback Argument. For any given (say) choice, if we hold fixed
everything about the relevant agent and roll back the universe to a prior time, then
(given the truth of indeterminism) on subsequent "replays" there will be some
instances in which the agent makes a *different* choice. That is, the difference between
replays in which the agent chooses as he actually does and those in which he chooses
differently is *not traceable to anything in the agent's control*. As Robert Kane concedes,
it follows from the truth of causal indeterminism that agents lack "antecedent determining control."[42] This is in part to concede (what, no doubt, Kane would admit for
the sorts of reasons I adduce in this paper), that when we act, the locus of control is
not entirely within us (in the relevant sense)—and that we lack Total Control. To
suppose that we have control over every factor that plays a causal role in our behavior
can be seen to be problematic, even in a quite ordinary cause of indeterministic
event-causation (of the sort Kane believes exhibits a paradigmatic sort of control).

V. Conclusion: Playing the Cards That Are Dealt You

Human agency and moral responsibility do indeed require that we be the authors and
the sources of our behavior in a suitable sense. Galen Strawson has argued that this sort
of requirement involves a literally self-contradictory demand of self-creation. I have
followed Joel Feinberg in plumping for a more reasonable, less "exalted" conception of
the requirement of "initiation" or ultimate sourcehood. Also, I have contended that the
sorts of considerations that appear to show that Strawson's demand is unreasonable
also apply to Smilansky's defense of the contention that compatibilism is "morally shallow." I have further suggested that these considerations provide at least a plausibility

---

[42] Robert Kane, *The Significance of Free Will*, p. 144.

argument against *any* incompatibilistic version of the ultimate source requirement; an incompatibilistic requirement of ultimate sourcehood may issue from an illusory picture according to which it is plausible that we could have Total Control.

Robert Kane has argued that in order to be morally responsible, we have to meet a condition of "ultimacy," according to which the "causal buck must stop here."[43] Additionally, although Derk Pereboom believes that versions of the Frankfurt-type examples successfully show that PAP is false, he nevertheless defends the following principle:

> An action is free in the sense required for moral responsibility only if it is not produced by a deterministic process that traces back to causal factors beyond the agent's control.[44]

Pereboom says:

> [I]f all our behavior were "in the cards" before we were born—in the sense that things happened before we came to exist that, by way of a deterministic causal process, inevitably result in our behavior—then we cannot legitimately be blamed for [our] actions. If all of our actions had this type of causal history, then it would seem that we lack the kind of control over our actions that moral responsibility requires.[45]

Clearly, the demands that "the buck stops here" and that our behavior not be "in the cards before we were born" rely on suggestive metaphors. But I would argue that these metaphors can be misleading, and are, at best, of limited significance.[46]

We can, however, borrow—and transform—Pereboom's metaphor. Our behavior may well be "in the cards" in the sense that we simply have to play the cards that are dealt us. Further, just as an astronaut may still control the lift-off of the rocket, even though she did not build the platform that makes the launch possible (or ever have any control over the platform), we can be accountable for playing the cards that are dealt us, even if we did not manufacture the cards, write the rules of the game, and so forth. We can exercise precisely that sort of control of our behavior that moral responsibility requires, without having an inflated or exalted power of self-creation. It is a kind of wisdom—a wisdom found in Feinberg—to recognize that, when you play the cards that are dealt you (in a certain distinctive way), you can exercise a robust sort of control, even in the absence of the power to make the cards, to own the factory that makes the cards, to make up the rules of the game, and so forth (to infinity)...[47]

---

[43] Robert Kane, *The Significance of Free Will*, esp. pp. 33–37, and 60–78.

[44] Pereboom, *Living Without Free Will*, p. 3.

[45] Derk Pereboom, *Living Without Free Will*, p. 6.

[46] John Martin Fischer, "Frankfurt-Style Compatibilism."

[47] I am very grateful to the thorough, thoughtful, and insightful comments by Matt Talbert. Molly Bloom said (attributing the remark to Leopold Bloom), "...the sun shines for you..." Joel Feinberg's sun shone for all of us in philosophy. The light will continue to provide illumination, and the warmth of his personality will not be forgotten.

11

Guidance Control

I. Introduction

I have sought to sketch an overall framework for moral responsibility. (Much of this work has been done with my coauthor, Mark Ravizza.) Part of this framework involves the presentation of an account of a distinctive sort of control, guidance control; in our view, guidance control is the freedom-relevant condition necessary and sufficient for moral responsibility. (I distinguish guidance control from regulative control, according to which an agent must have genuine metaphysical access to alternative possibilities, and I contend that guidance control, and not regulative control, is properly associated with moral responsibility.)[1]

An insight from the Frankfurt cases helps to shape the account of guidance control: moral responsibility is a matter of the history of an action (or behavior)— of how the actual sequence unfolds—rather than the genuine metaphysical availability of alternative possibilities. In this view, alternative scenarios or non-actual possible worlds might be relevant to moral responsibility in virtue of helping to specify or analyze modal properties of the actual sequence, but not in virtue of indicating or providing an analysis of genuine access to alternative possibilities.

Note that, in a Frankfurt-type case, the actual sequence proceeds "in the normal way" or via the "normal" process of practical reasoning. In contrast, in the alternative scenario (which never actually gets triggered and thus never becomes part of the actual sequence of events in our world), there is (say) direct electronic stimulation of the brain—intuitively, a different way or a different kind of mechanism. (By "mechanism" I simply mean, roughly speaking, "way"—I do not mean to reify anything.) I assume that we have intuitions at least about clear cases of "same mechanism," and "different mechanism." The actually operating mechanism (in a Frankfurt-type

---

[1] John Martin Fischer and Mark Ravizza, *Responsibility and Control: A Theory of Moral Responsibility* (Cambridge, UK: Cambridge University Press, 1998).

case)—ordinary human practical reasoning, unimpaired by direct stimulation by neurosurgeons, and so forth—is in a salient sense responsive to reasons. That is, holding fixed that mechanism, the agent would presumably choose and act differently in a range of scenarios in which he is presented with good reasons to do so.

The above discussion suggests the rudiments of an account of guidance control of action. In this account, we hold fixed the kind of mechanism that actually issues in the choice and action, and we see whether the agent responds suitably to reasons (some of which are moral reasons). My account presupposes that the agent can recognize reasons, and, in particular, recognize certain reasons as moral reasons. The account distinguishes between reasons-recognition (the ability to recognize the reasons that exist) and reasons-reactivity (choice in accordance with reasons that are recognized as good and sufficient), and it makes different demands on reasons-recognition and reasons-reactivity. The sort of reasons-responsiveness linked to moral responsibility, in my view, is "moderate reasons-responsiveness."

But one could exhibit the right sort of reasons-responsiveness as a result (say) of clandestine, unconsented-to electronic stimulation of the brain (or hypnosis, brainwashing, etc.). So moderate reasons-responsiveness of the actual-sequence mechanism is necessary but insufficient for moral responsibility. I contend that there are two elements of guidance control: reasons-sensitivity of the appropriate sort and mechanism ownership. That is, the mechanism that issues in the behavior must (in an appropriate sense) be the *agent's own* mechanism. (When one is secretly manipulated through clandestine mind control as in *The Manchurian Candidate*, one's practical reasoning is not *one's own*.)

I argue for a subjective approach to mechanism ownership. In this approach, one's mechanism becomes one's own in virtue of one having certain beliefs about one's own agency and its effects in the world, that is, in virtue of *seeing oneself in a certain way*. (Of course, it is *not* simply a matter of saying certain things—one actually has to have the relevant constellation of beliefs.) In my view, an individual becomes morally responsible in part at least by taking responsibility; he makes his mechanism his own by taking responsibility for acting from that kind of mechanism. In a sense, then, one acquires control by *taking control*.

II. Reply to Mele

In a thoughtful critical paper, Alfred Mele presents examples that challenge my subjective account of mechanism ownership and also features of my account of moderate reasons-responsiveness.[2] It will be illuminating to consider Mele's

---

[2] Alfred R. Mele, "Reactive Attitudes, Reactivity, and Omissions," *Philosophy and Phenomenological Research* 61 (2000), pp. 447–452; and "Fischer and Ravizza on Moral Responsibility," *Journal of Ethics* 10 (2006), pp. 283–294. My discussion in the text is based on John Martin Fischer, "The Free Will Revolution (Continued)," *Journal of Ethics* 10 (2006), pp. 315–345; see also "Replies to Mele, Bratman, and Stump," *Philosophy and Phenomenological Research* 61 (2000), pp. 467–480.

examples. Mele's first example explores the issue of whether the condition of moderate reasons-responsiveness is too weak. Moderate reasons-responsiveness consists in regular reasons-receptivity, and at least weak reasons-reactivity, of the actual-sequence mechanism that leads to the action.[3] Reasons-reactivity is the capacity to translate reasons into choices (and then subsequent behavior). A mechanism of an agent is at least *weakly* reasons-reactive provided that although it issues in the agent's doing A in the actual world, there is some possible world with the same laws of nature in which a mechanism of this kind is operative in this agent, there is a sufficient reason to do otherwise, the agent recognizes this reason, and the agent does otherwise for this reason.[4]

Mele worries that there can be extreme cases of phobia or addiction in which we can imagine *some* reasons such that "if a troubled agent who A-ed had had that reason for B-ing, he would have B-ed for that reason rather than A-ing."[5] Here is Mele's story of Fred:

> Fred's agoraphobia is so powerful that he has not ventured out of his house in ten years, despite his family's many attempts to persuade him to do so and the many incentives they have offered him. Owing to his fear, he often has decided not to do things that he believed he had good reason to do (and then behaved accordingly), including some things that he believed he morally ought to do. For example, he recently decided to stay at home (and stayed there) rather than attend his beloved daughter's wedding in the church next door. Now, in some possible world with the same laws, there was a raging fire in Fred's house on his daughter's wedding day. Fred, it turns out, is even more afraid of raging fires than of leaving his house. Judging that he had a good reason to leave his house, he decided to do so, for that reason; and then, making a heroic effort, he walked next door to the church.[6]

Mele contends that Fred's relevant mechanism is weakly reasons-reactive. Indeed, nothing in Mele's story seems to rule out Fred's meeting the conditions I (and my coauthor) have presented as sufficient for guidance control (and thus, the freedom-component of moral responsibility); and yet Mele also believes that Fred is not morally responsible for missing the wedding because of his debilitating agoraphobia.

Now consider Mele's example of Phil:

---

[3] Fischer and Ravizza, *Responsibility and Control: A Theory of Moral Responsibility*, p. 86.

[4] Fischer and Ravizza *Responsibility and Control: A Theory of Moral Responsibility*, p. 63.

[5] Mele, "Fischer and Ravizza on Moral Responsibility," p. 288; see also "Reactive Attitudes, Reactivity, and Omissions," p. 450.

[6] Mele, "Reactive Attitudes, Reactivity, and Omissions," p. 450; and "Fischer and Ravizza on Moral Responsibility, p. 288.

Phil...is converted from a compatibilist believer that he and most people are morally responsible agents to a hard determinist during his visit to London in which, over the course of several months, Ted Honderich persuades him that determinism is true and Galen Strawson convinces him that determinism is incompatible with moral responsibility. Phil is intellectually committed to hard determinism—he is no less committed to it than, for example, most philosophical atheists are to atheism—and he is convinced that indignation, gratitude, and the like are unjustified and that there are no fair targets of the reactive attitudes. By hypothesis, Phil is mistaken and the world abounds with morally responsible agents who are fair targets of the reactive attitudes.

Phil's conversion does not drastically change his life. Among other things, he continues to care about pleasure, pain, well-being, and the like—both his own and others'; he does not believe that the changes in his philosophical convictions have rendered these things unimportant. Phil continues to be a good husband and father, to donate money to various charities, to spend time building Habitat for Humanity houses, and, in general, to treat people well. Also, occasionally, but no more frequently than in his compatibilist days, Phil indulges in repeating unfavorable rumors about people, tells small lies to make things easier for himself, and so on.[7]

Phil, who has come under the baleful but persuasive influence of Ted Honderich and Galen Strawson in his trip to the lovely city of London, meets all intuitive criteria for being a fully and robustly morally responsible agent, but he fails to meet one of the three criteria I (and Mark Ravizza) have set out for "taking responsibility," and thus he fails to meet the "subjective" criteria for moral responsibility (in our approach). This, I suppose, is the consequence of paling around with philosophical terrorists (in London)! More specifically, since Phil does not see himself as an apt target of the reactive attitudes, he does not count as morally responsible, on our approach. In contrast, the agoraphobe Fred *does* count as morally responsible, in our approach, despite the fact that Fred's agoraphobia is "so powerful that he has not ventured out of his house in ten years ..." He counts as morally responsible, in our view, because (roughly speaking) he would leave his house (holding the relevant things fixed) if there were a raging fire. His psychological compulsion (issuing from the agoraphobia) is strong but not literally irresistible. Mele thinks we have got it backward here, and that we should reevaluate our views of the moral responsibility of such agents as Phil and Fred.

I agree with Mele that such agents as Phil and Fred present good challenges to the view of moral responsibility presented (and subsequently defended) by Mark

---

[7] Mele, "Fischer and Ravizza on Moral Responsibility," pp. 284–285; see also "Reactive Attitudes, Reactivity, and Omissions," pp. 447–449.

Ravizza and me. My general methodological disposition is to seek to capture the *clear* cases by appealing to intuitively natural principles, but to admit that these principles may well have jarring consequences in certain cases. Of course, in the sort of methodology I favor, there must be some sort of "reflective equilibrium" (to use Rawls's phrase) in which one adjusts one's principles and "considered judgments" to seek harmony. Given the distinction between moral responsibility and blameworthiness/praiseworthiness, I frankly do not think it is *evident* that the Fischer-Ravizza approach to such agents as Phil and Fred counts decisively against our general theory. After all, the phenomena of moral responsibility are themselves messy around the edges, and it would be unreasonable to suppose that a largely successful and plausible approach would yield entirely comfortable results along all its perimeters.

But in the constructive spirit in which Mele's reflections are offered, I would also say that I believe that I could accept Mele's views without in any way jeopardizing the main features of the Fischer-Ravizza approach: that moral responsibility is compatible with causal determinism, and even that moral responsibility is historical and subjective in the relevant sense, and a matter of the appropriate reasons-responsiveness of the agent's own behavior-producing mechanism.

To consider Phil first. The various individuals discussed by Mele—the addict who believes he is an addict and thus cannot in the end successfully resist the urge for the drug, the sailor who knows that his rudder is broken [and thus does not try to steer the boat], and Phil—all lack a kind of "self-engagement." But Mele is right to want a finer-grained articulation of the self-engagement in question, and he is correct to note that Phil's situation is distinctive. Here are the three conditions Mark Ravizza and I have proposed for an agent's "taking responsibility" for the kind of mechanism issuing in the relevant behavior:

> First, an individual must see himself as the source of his behavior...in the sense that he must see that his choices and actions are efficacious in the world...Second, the individual must accept that he is a fair target of the reactive attitudes as a result of how he exercises this agency in certain contexts...The third condition on taking responsibility requires that the individual's view of himself specified in the first two conditions be based, in an appropriate way, on the evidence.[8]

These three conditions, suitably qualified and refined, are supposed to define a kind of "self-engagement" characteristic of a morally responsible agent. In the Fischer-Ravizza approach, they help to define "taking responsibility" and thus mechanism-ownership, one of the two chief elements of guidance control. It is notable that whereas the addict who knows he is an addict and the sailor who

---

[8] Fischer and Ravizza, *Responsibility and Control: A Theory of Moral Responsibility*, pp. 210, 211, and 213.

knows his rudder is broken (and other, similar individuals) fail to meet the first condition, Phil fails to meet the second condition. Thus, it may be that there is an important difference between Phil and the other agents, in virtue of which Phil is morally responsible whereas the others are not.

As I said, I am not confident about what to say about this case, but I am willing to entertain dropping the second condition. In this approach, one would keep the first and third conditions as defining some subjective notion of self-engagement related to the intuitive idea of "taking responsibility;" without the second condition, this notion could not plausibly be thought to capture the commonsense notion of taking responsibility, but this should not pose a problem, as long as we are clear that the characterization does not purport to analyze the pre-theoretic notion of "taking responsibility." In this approach, an individual "takes responsibility" (in the special, theoretical sense) insofar as he sees himself as an agent in a distinctive way, that is, sees that his choices and actions are efficacious in the world—and this conception of himself is based on the evidence in the appropriate way. It should be clear that this emendation preserves all the basic features of the Fischer-Ravizza approach, while allowing us to accommodate Mele's intuition about Phil.[9]

Some philosophers (and I'm not including Alfred Mele in this group) have dismissed the Fischer-Ravizza Semicompatibilism out of hand because of its implications for individuals such as Phil. I hope that the above discussion shows that all of the major components of our theory can be maintained compatibly with an adjustment that shows that we need *not* be committed to these implications.

Similarly, I would be open to an adjustment of the sort Mele suggests with respect to Fred. That is, I believe that Ravizza and I could accept Mele's generous suggestion that "an attractive strategy for avoiding the (apparent) problem that I have been developing is to beef up the reasons-reactivity condition in such a way that Fred and agents with equally severe psychological maladies of the pertinent kind do not count as reasons-responsive enough to be morally responsible for the relevant behavior."[10] This posits a more refined notion of moderate reasons-responsiveness, with what might be called "spheres of responsiveness;" the "outer spheres" wouldn't necessarily indicate sufficient responsiveness for moral responsibility.[11] Of course, it may not be straightforward to characterize precisely the "borders" of the spheres; that is, it might not be easy to say exactly what degree of

---

[9] Similarly, this adjustment in the theory would successfully respond to the thoughtful criticisms developed by Andrew Eshleman in "Being Is Not Believing," *Australasian Journal of Philosophy* 79(4) (2001), pp. 479–490. I have toyed with this adjustment for a while, and Carl Ginet also independently suggests it in "Working with Fischer and Ravizza's Account of Moral Responsibility," *Journal of Ethics* 10 (2006), pp. 229–253.

[10] Alfred Mele, "Fischer and Ravizza on Moral Responsibility," p. 290.

[11] Note that this is consistent with the not entirely uncontentious Fischer-Ravizza claim that reactivity is all of a piece; an agent who can react to any reason may have great difficulty in doing so in any particular context.

strength of the relevant sort of urge renders the agent in question immune to moral responsibility. But this need not be my task here.

Ultimately, I am not sure what to say about the difficult cases Mele presents. My main reply is to point out that these *are* difficult cases, and, further, that the major components of my overall theory can be maintained, even with adjustments to accommodate different views about these cases. That is, one can accommodate Mele's views while continuing to maintain a guidance control–based, compatibilistic theory, according to which moral responsibility is an essentially historical (and even suitably subjective) phenomenon.

III. Long's Critique

There is a set or range of scenarios that is puzzling and difficult for *any* account of moral responsibility; these scenarios involve various kinds of "manipulation" or "induction" of mental states. The scenarios are diverse, multifaceted, and perplexing. It is evident that one must be judicious with respect to one's considered judgments about the cases in these sorts of scenarios and also the application of one's theory to such cases. It should not be surprising that a fairly reasonable and plausible general theory of moral responsibility might not apply straightforwardly to all such scenarios, or might give indeterminate or even somewhat unexpected results in some cases. Also, it would not be a good idea to suppose that all manipulation examples should be treated in the same way by a theory of moral responsibility (or that, upon careful consideration, one would have the same view about the moral responsibility of the individuals in such scenarios).

It is nevertheless entirely fair to press worries about how my account of guidance control (and moral responsibility) would handle certain conceivable kinds of manipulation or artificial induction of mental states. Various philosophers have explored these issues helpfully and have pressed legitimate concerns.[12] Here, I wish to focus primarily on a thoughtful and probing challenge presented by Todd R. Long.[13] (Later I shall address a similar scenario and a related challenge presented by Neal Judisch.) Here is Long's story:

---

[12] See, for example, Eleonore Stump, "Control and Causal Determinism," in Sarah Buss and Lee Overton, eds., *Contours of Agency: Essays on Themes from Harry Frankfurt* (Cambridge, MA: MIT Press, 2002), pp. 33–60; Derk Pereboom, *Living Without Free Will* (Cambridge, UK: Cambridge University Press, 2001), pp. 110–126; Seth Shabo, "Fischer and Ravizza on History and Ownership," *Philosophical Explorations* 8 (2005), pp. 103–114; and Neal Judisch, "Responsibility, Manipulation and Ownership: Reflections on the Fischer/Ravizza Program," *Philosophical Explorations* 8 (2005), pp. 115–130. There are preliminary responses in John Martin Fischer, "Responsibility and Manipulation," *The Journal of Ethics* 8 (2004), pp. 145–177 and "Reply: The Free Will Revolution," *Philosophical Explorations* 8 (2005), pp. 145–156.

[13] "Moderate Reasons-Responsiveness, Moral Responsibility, and Manipulation," in Joseph Keim Campbell, Michael O'Rourke, and David Shier, eds., *Freedom and Determinism* (Cambridge, MA: MIT Press, 2004), pp. 151–172,

Schmidt is a high-ranking official in the German government just prior to Hitler's rise to dictatorial power. Having been raised by parents with a deep inner moral sense and resolve, Schmidt learned from an early age the difference between right and wrong. As he developed, so did his moral wisdom. Suffice it to say that Schmidt developed into a man of impeccable moral judgment.

Owing to Schmidt's high rank in the German government, he is a member of a secret group that will decide by vote whether or not Hitler is to be given supreme power. Schmidt has known Hitler for many years. The two became friends when each was a budding young politician. During those early years, they shared with each other their dreams and ideas about how to build a better Germany. Schmidt was impressed with both the ingenuity of Hitler's ideas and the deep moral sense that those ideas displayed. From the things that Hitler said to Schmidt during those early years, Schmidt had very good reasons to think that Hitler would be an honest, forthright, and morally upstanding asset to Germany's future. However, several years before the vote is to take place, Schmidt begins to hear disturbing stories about Hitler. From reliable sources, he hears that Hitler has intentions of building up a master race of pure-blooded Aryans, driving non-Aryans out of the country, and perhaps killing those who do not leave. Schmidt develops deep doubts about Hitler's moral character.

Schmidt's role in the decision is to cast the deciding vote, should the voting members reach a deadlock. The members do reach a deadlock, so Schmidt is called upon to cast the deciding vote. Schmidt deliberates. Waiting in the wings is Block, a malevolent being with extraordinary causal and predictive powers. Should it become clear to him that Schmidt is going to vote against Hitler, Block will take effective steps to ensure that Schmidt votes *for* Hitler. Otherwise, Block will do nothing. So, whatever Schmidt's initial preferences and inclinations, Block will have his way.[14]

Now Long considers two possibilities. In the first, Schmidt would deliberate and vote for Hitler on his own. This would involve Schmidt's freely acting out of character, and Long points out that it is plausible that here Schmidt would be both morally responsible and blameworthy for his choice and behavior. Long also notes that the Fischer-Ravizza approach can accommodate these views.

Long goes on to consider the second basic possibility, characterized by Schmidt's having a certain disposition: it is here true that Schmidt is such that, were Block not to intervene, Schmidt would vote against Hitler. Long divides the second basic possibility into three scenarios. In the first, a minute before Schmidt casts his vote, Block realizes that Schmidt is about to vote against Hitler (in the

---

[14] "Moderate Reasons-Responsiveness, Moral Responsibility, and Manipulation," pp. 157–158.

absence of Block's intervention), and Block manipulates Schmidt in such a way as to ensure that Schmidt votes for Hitler. We can here imagine that Block does something directly to Schmidt's central nervous system; the intervention "bypasses" Schmidt's normal deliberative voting mechanism.[15] Long observes that the Fischer-Ravizza approach would correctly imply that Schmidt is not morally responsible for his choice and behavior here insofar as Schmidt's behavior does not issue from his own, moderately reasons-responsive mechanism. Presumably, the mechanism in question would neither be Schmidt's own nor would it be suitably reasons-responsive.

Here is Long's description of the second scenario:

> A minute before Schmidt casts his vote, Block becomes convinced that Schmidt is going to vote against Hitler. Block goes into action: he *adds* new inputs into the *very same mechanism* that is operant in the actual sequence. Suppose that these new inputs come in the form of *reasons* for voting for Hitler. Block directly feeds into Schmidt's deliberative voting mechanism enough reasons, or reasons powerful enough, to ensure that Schmidt will vote for Hitler.[16]

Long contends that simply adding inputs to a deliberative mechanism should not "change the mechanism." So he initially says that this case "appears" to be a counterexample to the Fischer-Ravizza contention that guidance control is the freedom-relevant condition sufficient for moral responsibility.[17] Long gives a similar analysis of his third scenario, which is like the second except that instead of adding an input Block *removes* inputs from what is putatively *the very same mechanism*; these inputs are Schmidt's own reasons for voting against Hitler.[18] Since I believe the issues raised by scenarios two and three under the second "basic possibility" are the same, I shall, for simplicity's sake, focus on scenario two.

As I said before, Long initially says that this case appears to be a counterexample to the Fischer-Ravizza theory. Later in the paper, however, Long returns to the second scenario, and this time he argues that the initial appearance that such a case provides a counterexample to the Fischer-Ravizza approach is mistaken. He says:

> [In the second scenario] not only did Schmidt meet the conditions of [moderate reasons-responsiveness], but he also intuitively did the morally responsible thing, given the evidence he had to go on. And if we knew the relevant facts about each case, we might even praise him for his action, even as we deeply regret or deplore the trick Block played on him and the

---

[15] "Moderate Reasons-Responsiveness, Moral Responsibility, and Manipulation," p. 158.
[16] "Moderate Reasons-Responsiveness, Moral Responsibility, and Manipulation," p. 159.
[17] "Moderate Reasons-Responsiveness, Moral Responsibility, and Manipulation," p. 160.
[18] "Moderate Reasons-Responsiveness, Moral Responsibility, and Manipulation," pp. 160–161.

consequences that followed…The moral is that we are morally responsible for our actions when they are consonant with our reasons in an appropriate way…but whether we are praiseworthy or blameworthy for our actions depends on additional facts about the cases.[19]

Given the distinction between moral responsibility and praiseworthiness/blameworthiness, then, Long is willing to accept that Schmidt is morally responsible for his choice in scenario two. He says, "After doing this ground clearing, we are in a position to see that [Fischer and Ravizza's] theory *does* get the cases right."[20]

On the occasion of Long's presentation of the main criticism contained in his paper at the Inland Northwest Philosophy Conference, I said that it was my intuition that Schmidt is not responsible in case two. I further suggested that the Fischer-Ravizza account would have this result, since the installation of inputs by Block would seem to render the mechanism a different one—not Schmidt's own deliberative mechanism. Long says:

> Fischer himself has responded to my examples by saying that intuitively Schmidt is not morally responsible in [scenario two]. Fischer infers from this intuition that the manipulation of the inputs makes the mechanism in those cases a different mechanism from the one operant in the actual-sequence [the first basic possibility]. I find this response disappointing, for Fischer concedes that he has no principled way to distinguish the mechanisms in question.[21]

I wish to note that I did not intend to infer straightforwardly from my intuitive judgment about the case to the conclusion that the mechanism is different from the one operant in the actual-sequence. That would be circular in a troubling way. I do, however, grant that the methodological issues here are complex; I have sought to address them elsewhere.[22] Additionally, I have sought to explain the role of mechanism-individuation in my overall approach. Like Long and others, I also find it somewhat disappointing that I do not have a general and completely reductive account of mechanism-individuation; but I do not judge this to be a decisive reason to reject my overall approach.

In defending his judgment that Schmidt is morally responsible in cases two and three, Long says:

> Nothing about Block's manipulation prevents Schmidt from meeting [the conditions for "taking responsibility" posited by Fischer and Ravizza]. To think that Schmidt fails to satisfy those conditions is to suppose that Schmidt

---

[19] "Moderate Reasons-Responsiveness, Moral Responsibility, and Manipulation," p. 164.

[20] "Moderate Reasons-Responsiveness, Moral Responsibility, and Manipulation," p. 164.

[21] "Moderate Reasons-Responsiveness, Moral Responsibility, and Manipulation," p. 164.

[22] John Martin Fischer, "Responsibility and Manipulation," *The Journal of Ethics* Vol. 8, No. 2 (2004): 145–177.

would have to be responsible both for his prior evidence (or beliefs) and for the way in which he acquired that evidence (or those beliefs). But, surely this is to add too much to the notion of taking responsibility. Evidence (and reasons) supporting beliefs come to us from various directions and in many different ways. Some of it we are quite aware of, and some of it were are less aware of. Earlier I mentioned that nobody would balk at the suggestion that Schmidt could have been convinced to vote for Hitler by more ordinary external means (news reports, personal testimony, etc.). What is the relevant difference between manipulating the inputs in those ways and manipulating the inputs directly?

Consider a case in which a group of conniving folk manipulate the inputs of someone's deliberative mechanism by affecting the information that person gets. Suppose a group of Young Republicans who work at a news press manipulate the inputs that Karen's deliberative voting mechanism receives by changing the text of Karen's newspaper every time something good is said in print about being a Democratic candidate. Would this prevent Karen from being morally responsible for her voting? If you are inclined to answer "yes," then you owe us an explanation of why *any* of us are morally responsible for our acts of voting. After all, very few of us control the political reports or the political opinions that are propounded in our newspapers and other media; thus, most of us do not control the inputs our deliberative voting mechanisms receive...On what basis should we judge ourselves as morally responsible for our voting but deny that Karen is morally responsible for her voting?[23]

Long summarizes his critique by stating that although the Fischer-Ravizza account of guidance control wants and needs it to be the case that a certain fixed mechanism can operate on various different inputs, "the only way to make sense of Fischer's response to my examples is to think that Schmidt would have to be responsible for his input acquisition as well as for the mechanism itself. This amounts to building the inputs into the mechanism."[24] As Long notes, this would be fatal to the Fischer-Ravizza approach.

IV. Reply to Long

As I said, cases involving manipulation or (putative) artificial induction of mental states are complex and difficult to sort through. I also suggested there are importantly different kinds of manipulation, and these differences may make significant differences in how we analyze and evaluate the cases. These considerations apply

---

[23] "Moderate Reasons-Responsiveness, Moral Responsibility, and Manipulation," p. 165.
[24] "Moderate Reasons-Responsiveness, Moral Responsibility, and Manipulation," p. 166.

to the scenarios presented in sketchy form by Long. Consider again the way in which he describes scenario two:

> A minute before Schmidt casts his vote, Block becomes convinced that Schmidt is going to vote against Hitler. Block goes into action: he *adds* new inputs into the *very same mechanism* that is operant in the actual sequence. Suppose that these new inputs come in the form of *reasons* for voting for Hitler. Block directly feeds into Schmidt's deliberative voting mechanism enough reasons, or reasons powerful enough, to ensure that Schmidt will vote for Hitler.[25]

Note that Long begins by saying that Block swings into action "a minute before Schmidt casts his vote." This suggests something important—or perhaps subtly frames the description in such a way that it would naturally suggest that "something" to the reader. The suggestion in question is that the implantation or manipulative induction of "reasons" is done immediately prior to the choice and subsequent behavior, and that there is thus no reasonable or fair opportunity for Schmidt to reflect on or critically evaluate the new input in light of his standing dispositions, values, preferences, and so forth.[26]

I contend that when "inputs" are implanted in a way that does not allow for a reasonable or fair opportunity to subject those inputs to critical scrutiny in light of the agent's normative orientation, then such manipulation does indeed remove moral responsibility. Crucially, I claim that such manipulation typically "changes the mechanism." On the other hand, if an "input" is artificially implanted in such a way as to leave it open to the agent (in a reasonable and fair way) to critically scrutinize and reflect on the new input, then this sort of manipulative induction of inputs *may well be* compatible with moral responsibility for the choice and subsequent behavior. Such manipulation could leave the ordinary mechanism of practical reasoning intact.[27]

---

[25] "Moderate Reasons-Responsiveness, Moral Responsibility, and Manipulation," p. 159.

[26] I am indebted for this kind of point, and in what follows, to Kristin Demetriou, "The Soft-Line Solution to Pereboom's Four-Case Argument," *Australasian Journal of Philosophy* 88 (2010), pp. 595–617. As Demetriou points out, the analysis I apply to the manipulation cases in the text also is relevant to Pereboom's "four-case argument": Derk Pereboom, *Living Without Free Will* (Cambridge, UK: Cambridge University Press, 2001), pp. 110–126. Although in past work I have suggested that Professor Plum may be morally responsible in all four of Pereboom's cases, Demetriou suggests an alternative approach, which is congenial to my analysis in the text of the manipulation cases presented by Long and Judisch.

[27] I favor an "actual-sequence" account of moral responsibility, according to which moral responsibility does not require that the agent have genuine metaphysical access to alternative possibilities. Although I speak in the text in terms of (say) Schmidt's having a reasonable and fair opportunity to evaluate a new input, this is solely for simplicity's sake; I wish to interpret such statements in terms of the properties of the actual-sequence mechanism. So, slightly more carefully, I would contend that the actual-sequence mechanism must exhibit the general power or capacity to evaluate the new input in relevant ways.

Long's examples are underdescribed in precisely this way—he does not make it explicit whether Schmidt has a reasonable and fair opportunity to evaluate the mysteriously appearing inputs in light of his overall normative orientation—his other values, preferences, and so forth. As I pointed out earlier, his description *suggests* that Schmidt would not have such an opportunity, and thus it is plausible (in my view) that such manipulation would rule out moral responsibility.[28] Perhaps then it is not surprising that Long himself seems to exhibit a certain sort of ambivalence about the scenario—at first suggesting that it appears that Schmidt is not morally responsible, and then subsequently claiming that, upon reflection, Schmidt is responsible. The ambivalence may reflect the underdescription of the case; filled in one way, we are inclined to deny responsibility, but filled in another way, we are inclined to affirm responsibility. Either way, the Fischer-Ravizza approach yields exactly the correct results.

Recall Long's statement that I "infer" from my intuition that Schmidt is not morally responsible in scenario two (interpreted in the way I have explained) the conclusion that the alternative sequence would involve a *different* kind of mechanism (from the mechanism in the actual sequence). This of course would be an uncomfortably tight circle. One wants at least some sort of story by reference to which it is independently plausible that we have a different mechanism in the alternative sequence; I would like to sketch some elements of such a story.[29]

Ordinarily, when we have some new "input" to our practical reasoning, or we simply find ourselves with some new mental state—a new desire or a desire with a new intensity or urgency—or perhaps a new tendency to recognize or weigh reasons in a certain way, we can pause to reflect on this new element of our mental economy or normative orientation. We can then filter it through our practical reasoning in the sense that we can bring to bear *other* (presumably, non-manipulatively induced) elements of our character or standing dispositions; we can typically affect the new element in light of standing features. This may involve affecting the intensity or even "direction" of a desire, or affecting the way one identifies or gives weight to reasons. What is crucial is that we have a fair and reasonable opportunity to filter new elements of our mental economy through our character as a whole.

---

[28] I wish to emphasize that I am not contending that the timing in itself makes a difference. Rather, what is important is that the actual-sequence mechanism exhibits the appropriate capacity to evaluate the new input. One could in principle have this capacity even with very little time between the induction of the input and the decision point, and one could lack this capacity, even with plenty of time between the induction and the decision point. What ultimately matters is the capacity in question, not the timing; but certain ways of presenting hypothetical examples, especially where there is little or no time after the induction and prior to the need to make a decision, *suggest* the absence of the relevant capacity.

Note that presumably we sometimes have "go-permissions" (to employ a term suggested to me by Manuel Vargas) as part of our total normative orientation at a given point in time; thus, on the basis of these go-permissions (fixed antecedently), we can instantaneously (as it were) react to new inputs in circumstances that require this.

[29] See also John Martin Fischer, "Reply: The Free Will Revolution."

Typically, of course, we do not have control over what the world presents us in terms of factors that correspond to or generate reasons, or even evidence for certain judgments. I agree with Long that it would be implausible to demand that, in order to be morally responsible, I must somehow be responsible for or in control of all the inputs to my mechanism of practical reasoning. But what *is* plausible is to demand that I have a reasonable and fair opportunity to filter a new input through my character and practical reasoning. Given that I have certain information from newspapers and political candidates, and stipulating that I have little if any control over much of what comes to me through these media, I can critically scrutinize and evaluate it. Similarly, if a desire or other "input" suddenly and mysteriously presents itself to me, I can typically subject it to critical scrutiny and filter it through my practical reasoning (employing the other elements of my normative orientation). Even if the input is implanted via clandestine manipulation or induction, I could in certain instances then subject it to critical evaluation and filter it through my practical reasoning. In these instances I could be morally responsible for my choices and behavior. But if I do not have this sort of reasonable and fair opportunity, then my character as a whole and my practical reasoning has been "bypassed."[30]

This then suggests a natural way to respond to Long's basic critique presented in his summary. There he states that my way of responding to cases such as the second scenario force the input into the mechanism, as it were; Long is certainly correct that this would be a fatal result for the Fischer-Ravizza approach, which presupposes that one can give the same mechanism different inputs (and thus have in certain cases different outputs). My response should now be clear. In a case in which there is a reasonable and fair opportunity to filter the inputs through one's deliberative mechanism, there is no problem with changing the inputs while maintaining the same mechanism. In those cases where one's deliberations or practical reasoning or, more generally, normative orientation is bypassed, then such manipulation does indeed change the mechanism; we no longer would have the ordinary human mechanism of unimpaired practical reasoning.

As practical reasoners and normative agents, we identify and weigh (or "process") reasons in certain distinctive ways. This way of identifying and weighing reasons might be physically implemented in the brain in various different ways, and by different physical parts; even so, it would still be the same unimpaired human mechanism of practical reasoning. This mechanism of practical reasoning involves the reasonable and fair opportunity to subject to critical scrutiny any emergent or newly presenting desire, or any tendency to identify or weigh reasons in a certain way. Although the specific way in which the more abstract processing is physically implemented can change compatibly with having the same mecha-

---

[30] Alfred R. Mele, *Autonomous Agents: From Self-Control to Autonomy* (New York: Oxford University Press, 1995), pp. 144–176.

nism, one cannot change crucial features of the processing of reasons, such as the capacity for evaluating new inputs in light of one's standing normative orientation without thereby *changing the mechanism*. Thus, anything that disrupts the typical relationship between the agent's existing normative orientation and a new element—sequestering the new element and rendering it immune from the causal interaction with the preexisting elements—cannot be the ordinary mechanism of human practical reasoning.[31]

Mechanism-individuation is required for both components of the account of guidance control—mechanism-ownership and reasons-responsiveness. I fully admit that I do not have a reductive account of mechanism-individuation, and that, lacking such an account, the theory of guidance control is, at best, incomplete. But an incomplete theory is not thereby an inadequate or fundamentally misguided theory. And my approach to guidance control and moral responsibility is no different from most promising philosophical theories in being incomplete. Further, some important philosophical theories are incomplete in a similar respect; theories such as reliabilism in epistemology and generalization in ethics (of both the consequentialist and non-consequentialist sorts) rely implicitly on views about the individuation of the relevant kinds of belief-producing mechanisms or actions without developing explicit, reductive accounts of the sort of individuation at issue.

I have suggested a "holistic" methodology whereby one relies on certain "clear" intuitions about mechanism-individuation in provisionally applying the account of guidance control, and then sees where this leads. As the theory gets applied to various cases, one will see how mechanisms must be individuated, if the account is to be plausible (i.e., if the account is to match our considered judgments about moral responsibility). I do not think this is in itself disturbing or problematic. What *would* indisputably be problematic is if one individuated mechanisms in inconsistent ways—wiggling one way in one example and another way in another example, as Robert Nozick once put a similar point—simply to get the "right" results (results that match our considered judgments about moral responsibility). In this instance the theory would not be generating the intuitions, but quite the reverse.

V. Judisch's Example: A Related Challenge

Here is a challenging example presented by Neal Judisch (which raises similar worries to those raised by Long's example just discussed):

---

[31] This sort of sequestration gives one instance of what Mele must have in mind when he invokes his important notion of "bypassing" the agent's practical reasoning; see *Autonomous Agents, From Self-Control to Autonomy.*

Consider the case of Chum. Aside from the unfortunate name (what *were* his parents thinking?), Chum is a perfectly ordinary adult.[32] He was raised in a happy home, received a normal moral education, and took responsibility (when a young man) for his mechanisms of ordinary practical reasoning and the like. Never once was he subjected to the slightest form of manipulation, and his moral and social development has left him a well-adjusted and responsible man. Now suppose that one night, while Chum is soundly asleep, he spontaneously develops a debilitating brain lesion. The lesion is situated in his neural network in such a way that his capacity for practical reasoning is severely impaired—the relevant mechanism no longer even approximates the standards of moderate reasons-responsiveness. Imagine now that a benevolent neuroscientist, Dr. White, is somehow made aware of Chum's plight. Without rousing Chum, he springs into action. Unfortunately, there is no way he can remove the lesion without causing irreparable damage to Chum's brain, but White has a few handy electronic devices that enable him (literally) to get around that problem. Here is how the devices work. The first, placed just "upstream" of the lesion, takes as inputs the messages sent through the neural pathways headed right for the spot where the lesion is located, and it transmits the incoming data via radio signals to the other device located just "downstream" of the lesion, which device, in turn, relays the appropriate impulses to the neural pathways just downstream of it. The result is that the lesion is both successfully isolated and bypassed, its potentially deleterious effects completely cut off from the rest of Chum's brain; indeed, Chum's post-surgery cognitive architecture is *functionally equivalent* to his pre-surgery brain... When Chum awakens, he is of course completely unaware of the evening's events; as far as he is concerned, it is business as usual.[33]

Judisch's view is that Chum can legitimately be considered morally responsible for his subsequent behavior. He contends, however, that in the Fischer-Ravizza approach, Chum cannot be deemed morally responsible. After all, we contend that if scientists manipulate your brain in a clandestine fashion, you have not taken responsibility for the mechanism that actually issues in your behavior (the "manipulation-mechanism"), and it seems to Judisch that we should say the same thing about the case of Chum.[34]

---

[32] Amusingly, my father-in-law's (now deceased) former wife was nicknamed, "Chum"! She seemed to like this nickname.

[33] Neal Judisch, "Responsibility, Manipulation, and Ownership: Reflections on the Fischer/Ravizza Program," *Philosophical Explorations* 8 (2005), pp. 115–130.

[34] I understand that the United States Central Intelligence Agency (CIA) makes a distinction between "covert" and "clandestine" operations. In a covert operation, we are allowed to know that some intervention is taking place, but the source of the intervention is secret. In a clandestine operation, even the fact of the intervention is not supposed to be known. For me, "covert" and "clandestine" interventions are not phenomenologically detectable by the relevant agent, and he is otherwise unaware of the intervention.

This is a difficult challenge. I would seek to reply to Judisch's powerful critique in the holistic spirit adumbrated previously. And as in the discussion of Long's case, I am inclined to distinguish various kinds of intervention by neuroscientists. Neuroscientists can covertly implant desires (inputs) in such a way as to preclude critical evaluation of those desires (say, for a certain defined period of time); this sort of situation was discussed in my analysis of Long's critique. Alternatively, the neuroscientists can influence the ways inputs are processed and lead to outputs (where these ways are defined "functionally" or at a higher level of abstraction than the physical realizations of the relevant mental states); the ways inputs are processed here correspond to ways of weighing reasons in one's practical reasoning. In both of these cases I think the neuroscientists bring it about that a *different* mechanism operates—a mechanism different from Chum's "ordinary practical reasoning." After all, as I argued in my discussion of Long's critique, ordinary practical reasoning essentially involves the capacity to subject a given "input" to critical scrutiny—to pass it through one's "normative orientation"; additionally, if the way Chum tends to process inputs is fundamentally altered, this changes *Chum's* mechanism. For example, if Chum is (say) highly risk-averse prior to the manipulation and very adventuresome after, or if he is egoistic before and altruistic after, the intervention has changed Chum's mechanism—his signature way of weighing reasons.

In contrast, neuroscientists may replace a biological part of the brain with another part, a part of the same or slightly different biological materials, or perhaps even made of synthetic or artificial materials. As I understand Judisch's thought-experiment, this latter sort of intervention is roughly what he has in mind. His intriguing example involves the analogue of a heart "bypass" operation, but in the brain. An artificial mechanism is installed which allows the brain to function (considered abstractly) in the same way it has always functioned, but the electrical impulses bypass a problematic area. It functions in the same way both from the phenomenological perspective of Chum, and also in the sense that the "function" from inputs to outputs is the same (even if it is realized in a slightly different way). Thus, I am inclined to think that this sort of intervention (in contrast to the first two) does *not* install a different kind of mechanism. Thus, in the Fischer-Ravizza approach to moral responsibility, Chum could indeed be considered morally responsible for the relevant behavior (in accordance with Judisch's intuition about the case).

After all, if neuroscientists secretly installed a physically different part of my brain that functioned equivalently to the biological part, this would surely *not* create a different kind of mechanism. As far as I'm concerned, this would be like replacing one's carburetor with a functionally identical carburetor but made of slightly more durable material; it would still be the same kind of engine (for most conceivable purposes). Making the inputs inaccessible to reflective scrutiny or tinkering with the way the inputs are processed (in the sense of modifying the function from the inputs to outputs) would indeed change the mechanism; but merely changing the physical realization of the processing that goes on (without changing the inputs or the processing of those inputs) does *not*, it seems to me, change the mechanism-kind.

Of course, I am employing the holistic strategy previously sketched. It would perhaps be implausible to suppose that on some sort of independent grounds it is obvious that the first two sorts of intervention would install new or different mechanism-kinds, whereas the third sort of intervention would not. Rather, we can learn from a careful consideration of a range of examples, and also we can be guided by an attempt to secure a match with our considered judgments about moral responsibility. The question then becomes whether there is some intuitive plausibility to the emerging way of individuating mechanisms, and, perhaps more importantly, whether this way of individuating mechanisms can be *generalized* to a broader range of cases in a *consistent* way.

VI. Conclusion

Guidance control, I have argued, is the freedom-relevant condition on moral responsibility. I have analyzed guidance control in terms of two major elements: mechanism-ownership and moderate reasons-responsiveness. Here I have discussed some objections to both elements.

I began by considering cases presented by Al Mele that suggest that a certain subjective attitude is not required for mechanism-ownership and also that my account of moderate reasons-responsiveness should be revised modestly. My main point in reply to Mele is that if one makes the adjustments suggested by his examples, I can still maintain the central theses that causal determinism is compatible with moral responsibility, that moral responsibility does not require genuine metaphysical access to alternative possibilities, that moral responsibility is essentially a historical notion, and so forth.

I then turned to a family of objections based on "manipulation scenarios" presented by Long and Judisch. Manipulation scenarios are diverse and resistant to simple, one-size-fits-all analysis. I have argued that Long's scenario two is underdescribed. When the description is filled in suitably, we can see that he has not produced a counterexample to the Fischer-Ravizza account of guidance control and moral responsibility. I have also argued that Judisch's scenario does not constitute a counterexample. The discussion of these cases helps to clarify my views about mechanism-individuation. In some cases of manipulation, such as cases in which the input to the mechanism is implanted and rendered inaccessible to critical reflection or cases in which the ways the inputs are processed (the ways reasons are weighed) are changed, the manipulation issues in the operation of a *different mechanism*. In other cases of manipulation, such as cases in which a new physical part is implanted with preservation of the same functioning (the same capacities for critical reflection and ways of weighing reasons), the manipulation need not issue in a different kind of mechanism. I note that we have here explored cases that might be called "local manipulation," in which one input is manipulatively implanted but the other elements of one's character or normative orientation are not tampered with. A more comprehensive treatment would seek to address global manipulation cases of various sorts.[35]

It might be useful to have a taxonomy of my strategies of response to some of the salient kinds of local manipulation cases. An input (desire) might be manipulatively implanted but not be irresistible; here the agent may well be morally responsible, but his or her (say) blameworthiness might be diminished or expunged, given specific facts about the manipulation and the nature of the input. (If the manipulatively induced desire is indeed irresistible, then the agent is not, in my account, morally responsible; his actual-sequence mechanism is *not* appropriately reasons-responsive.) If the (resistible) desire is capable of being evaluated in terms of the agent's normative orientation, the agent can be morally responsible; the manipulation has in this instance not changed the mechanism from ordinary practical reasoning (for which the agent has presumably taken responsibility). But if the (resistible) desire has been manipulatively induced and also sequestered from the agent's normative orientation, then the manipulation *has* indeed changed the mechanism, and the agent is not morally responsible in this instance.

A final thought. Some philosophers (some of whom are compatibilists) have an easier time with manipulation scenarios: they simply banish them! That is, they assert that for conceptual or perhaps scientific reasons they are skeptical of even the possibility of the artificial implantation of mental states. Sometimes these philosophers invoke their considerable knowledge of neuroscience, and sometimes they invoke their impressive analytic skills; they like to make fun of "armchair philosophers" who believe in the coherence of thought-experiments involving "nefarious neurosurgeons" and their ilk.[36]

Oh, how easy it would be not to have to address the range of manipulation cases! If it turns out that the skeptics are correct (for whatever reason), then it will

---

[35] John Martin Fischer and Mark Ravizza, *Responsibility and Control: A Theory of Moral Responsibility*, pp. 230–236 and John Martin Fischer, "Responsibility and Manipulation."

[36] Daniel Dennett is an example of a compatibilist who is inclined to brush aside both the Consequence Argument and the range of manipulation scenarios. See Daniel Dennett, *Elbow Room: The Varieties of Free Will Worth Wanting* (Cambridge, MA: MIT Press, 1984), and *Freedom Evolves* (New York: Viking, 2003). For a critical discussion of some of these points, see John Martin Fischer, "Dennett on the Basic Argument," *Metaphilosophy* 36 (2005), pp. 427–435. Dennett seeks to respond in Daniel C. Dennett, "Natural Freedom," *Metaphilosophy* 36 (2005), pp. 449–459, esp. 451–454. One also finds considerable skepticism about thought-experiments involving putative manipulative induction of mental states in the work of such compatibilists as Gary Watson, Thomas Scanlon, Pamela Hieronymi, and Angela Smith.

Now I do not wish to suggest that there are no perfectly reasonable worries—both conceptual and scientific—about the possibility of artificial induction of mental states. These worries are deep and significant, and I do not in any way mean to dismiss their importance. I simply point out that if they are decisive, my form of compatibilism is that much easier to defend; for the sake of the argument, I am willing to put aside worries about induction and still attempt to defend my form of compatibilism. Despite what some philosophers appear to believe, I am in no way committed to the coherence of thought-experiments involving artificial induction of motivational states; if anything, they make my (philosophical) life more challenging!

be that much easier to defend compatibilism, as one would not have to work so hard to distinguish responsibility-conferring causally deterministic paths from those causally deterministic paths that rule out moral responsibility; that is, one would not have to worry about this subclass of causally deterministic paths (involving putative artificial induction of mental states via direct electronic stimulation of the brain).

But I have always thought that one can make the best case for the compatibility of causal determinism and moral responsibility only by being maximally charitable to the opponent—the incompatibilist. I have felt that it is only by taking incompatibilism seriously and fully engaging the incompatibilist that one can get the best argument for compatibilism. It has never seemed promising simply to dismiss the Consequence Argument (as so many compatibilists seem to do), nor has it seemed promising simply to dismiss the possibility of manipulation. It has always seemed better to take these worries seriously and to seek to address them head-on.[37]

---

[37] I am deeply grateful to the generous, gracious, and thoughtful comments by Todd Long delivered at the Inland Northwest Philosophy Conference, March 2006. I have also benefited from questions and comments by other participants in the conference, including Randolph Clarke and Manuel Vargas. Additionally, I am grateful for comments by Ish Haji.

12

The Triumph of Tracing
Coauthor: Neal A. Tognazzini

The Past! the dark, unfathfom'd retrospect!
The teeming gulf! the sleepers and the shadows!
The past! the infinite greatness of the past!
For what is the present, after all, but a growth out of the past?

—WALT WHITMAN, "PASSAGE TO INDIA"

History is a nightmare from which I'm trying to awake.

—STEPHEN DAEDALUS, IN JAMES JOYCE'S *ULYSSES*

I. The Trouble with Tracing

It is widely agreed among theorists of moral responsibility that the following two statements, if true and uttered sincerely, will excuse someone from apparent responsibility:

(1) I couldn't help it (interpreted as, "I was forced or compelled to do it").
(2) I didn't and couldn't have been expected to know that it would happen.

If Kevin's kleptomania is so severe that it produces in him a literally irresistible desire to steal, then there is a straightforward sense in which he couldn't help himself (at the time he steals). This sort of severe kleptomania is plausibly thought to excuse Kevin's behavior on the grounds that his behavior was not sufficiently under his control. So, it looks like some sort of "control condition" will be a necessary component of any plausible theory of moral responsibility.

Similarly, if Kevin's friends are planning a surprise party for him but they neglect to tell Dan that it's a surprise and Dan subsequently talks openly with Kevin about the party, Dan's ignorance plausibly excuses his behavior. Since he didn't know (and, we suppose, could not have been expected to know) that the party was a surprise, he didn't know that talking openly with Kevin about the party would amount to ruining the surprise. His ruining the surprise is excused because of his impoverished epistemic position. So, it looks like some sort of "epistemic condition" will be a necessary component of any plausible theory of moral responsibility, as well.

Arguably, one more component must be added to get a plausible theory of moral responsibility, and it may cause trouble when combined with the epistemic and control conditions. Suppose that Dan gets drunk at Kevin's surprise party and drives home, but his reflexes are so impaired that he runs over a pedestrian on the way. Whatever sort of control is required for moral responsibility, suppose that he didn't have that control at the time he ran over the pedestrian. In a straightforward sense, then, he couldn't help it. But is he therefore not responsible? Of course not, because in another straightforward sense, he *could* help it. After all, presumably he had control of whether to get drunk at the party in the first place. In this case, Dan is morally responsible for running over the pedestrian even though he didn't satisfy the control condition at the time of the accident. To account for this, our theory of moral responsibility should include some notion of *tracing*. In this sort of situation, Dan's moral responsibility can be *traced back* to an action of which he had control—namely, his getting drunk.

Of course, as we've seen, it wouldn't be enough merely to trace Dan's responsibility back to an action of which he had control. He would also need to be in an appropriate epistemic position with respect to the consequences of that action in order for tracing to be appropriate. That is, not only must Dan have had control of his getting drunk, he must have also known that getting drunk might well lead to his driving home drunk and to his running over a pedestrian. It seems that tracing only works if the situation to which we trace is one in which the agent both has sufficient control of some action *and* can be reasonably expected to know the likely results of that action. Drunk-driving cases are unproblematic precisely because everyone knows (or at least *should* know) that too much alcohol will impair the ability to drive a car.

In an influential and highly provocative recent article, Manuel Vargas has presented a number of cases that bring out an apparent tension between the idea of tracing and the epistemic condition on moral responsibility.[1] We will examine these cases in detail below, but the tension raised by each is this: in some situations in which it seems that we need to invoke tracing in order to explain our intuitions of moral responsibility, there is no prior time available at which the agent in question could have reasonably foreseen the consequences of her actions to serve as the terminus of the trace. Indeed, these cases appear to show that we are faced

---

[1] Vargas 2005. In a recent article, Michael McKenna said: "The point I will set out [developing some putative troubles with tracing] is fully and impressively developed with striking results in Manuel Vargas's recent, 'The Trouble with Tracing,' (2005)" McKenna 2005, p. 33.

with three, equally troublesome options: (i) The idea of tracing needs to be either abandoned or refined, (ii) the epistemic condition on moral responsibility needs to be either abandoned or significantly refined, or (iii) we should admit that we are morally responsible much less often than we are ordinarily inclined to think.

Now, it is certainly true that a fully adequate theory of moral responsibility will examine the nature of both tracing and the epistemic condition in detail. So we don't want to discourage anyone from conducting these important research projects. However, we are not convinced that the cases Vargas concocts are indeed as troublesome for extant theories as he alleges. In what follows, we will examine Vargas's cases in detail and we will argue that theorists who are attracted to tracing have nothing to fear from them.

The four cases that Vargas presents are quite different and, as we will see, no one response will take care of them all. But there is an abstract structure that they all putatively share. Each is intended to present a scenario according to which the following conditions hold:

(i) The agent is morally responsible for the relevant outcome
(ii) The agent does not satisfy the control condition on moral responsibility (at the time of his behavior) with respect to the relevant outcome, and
(iii) There is no suitable prior time at which the relevant outcome was reasonably foreseeable for the agent

To account for the apparent inconsistency in (i) and (ii), it looks like we need to invoke some sort of tracing. However, when we consider (iii) together with some plausible epistemic condition on moral responsibility, it looks like no attempt at tracing can be successfully completed. In order for Vargas's cases to make trouble for tracing, he needs them to satisfy all of the above conditions. We will argue, however, that each case fails to satisfy at least one of them. In none of Vargas's cases is it plausible to think that all of the conditions are satisfied. We shall then go on to apply a similar analysis to some intriguing examples presented by Angela Smith[2]; in the end, our contention will be that tracing emerges unscathed.

II. Jeff the Jerk

Consider first the case of Jeff the Jerk:

Jeff is a middle-aged middle manager in a midsize company located somewhere in the Midwest. To him has fallen the task of alerting "downsized" employees of their new status as job seekers in a gloomy economy. That Jeff

[2] Smith 2005.

has the task is unfortunate for those about to be laid off, not only because they are about to lose their jobs, but—to add insult to injury—because Jeff is a jerk. He is rude and inconsiderate about the feelings of others. And he is unreflective about it. When people react poorly to his behavior (something they avoid doing because he is large, imposing, generally unsympathetic, and even a little frightening) he always writes it off as a shortcoming on the part of others. One afternoon, his superiors tell him that he needs to give notice to a group of longtime employees that they will be laid off. He does tell them, but in an altogether rude and insensitive fashion. Is Jeff responsible for the way he laid off his employees?[3]

This is the initial story provided by Vargas, but he goes on to fill in some pertinent details about how Jeff came to be the jerk that he is. These details are important, as they supposedly provide us with reason to think that we won't be able to account for Jeff's moral responsibility in this case by invoking tracing.

When Jeff was 15, he realized that he was having much less success with members of the opposite sex than he wanted to have. Over time, and through the usual fallible mechanisms of belief acquisition, he came to believe that the only males who consistently had success at gaining the attention of female classmates were those at least *we* might describe as jerks. In Jeff's hormone-ridden 15-year-old mind, this putative insight, coupled with a somewhat enterprising disposition that later served him modestly well in the business world, led him to adopt a plan for self-improvement. To the extent to which he was able, he inculcated in himself all the behaviors and attitudes that we would perceive to be jerklike, and therefore, ultimately conducive to success with his female classmates. Now this initial decision to undertake the program of self-improvement was not an obvious choice for Jeff. He was worried about what his friends would think when he started attempting to behave differently. Would they make fun of him, noting that he was pretending to be something he wasn't? What if people found out why he was doing it? Could he overcome the shame and humiliation that would result from his female classmates learning of his subterfuge? These were the sorts of thoughts that Jeff had

---

[3] Vargas 2005, p. 271. Michael McKenna develops a case similar to that of Jeff the Jerk:

Consider the young boy who consciously chooses to cultivate his aggression and thick skin in order to survive in the locker room during his junior varsity football days. He will have very little reason to expect that it will someday be the source of his coolness and tragic distance from his own children. In general, so far as various aspects of our own character traits are concerned, we are often the hapless victims of our own unwitting earlier free choices. We do not possess the foresight of gods, and so who we will become, from the vantage point of who we are, is sometimes just a crap shoot. (McKenna 2008, p. 33.)

while he deliberated. After a period of uncertainty, however, Jeff decided to undertake the plan. And so he set about becoming, if not a jerk, at least jerk-like.

With surprisingly little effort, he succeeded. In fact he more than succeeded—it didn't even take the whole academic year for him to go from being jerklike to being a full-on jerk. Part of the reason was undoubtedly rooted in his social context. The context was such that there was little cost to behaving in jerklike ways when he would have been sensitive to those sorts of feedback. (He was a "latch key" kid, largely ignored by his permissive parents who chalked up his increasingly rude behavior to being a typical teenager. So, they tuned it out and treated him in a largely hands-off fashion.) Moreover, what feedback he did receive and did care about was overwhelmingly positive. For whatever reason (perhaps it was merely the growth spurt that struck around the same time), he came to have tremendous success at attracting the attention of the opposite sex. However, at no point during the process of becoming a jerk, and certainly at no point before he undertook the program of becoming jerklike, did Jeff even conceive that his plan for personal improvement would include in its outcomes that he would some day lay off employees in a despicable fashion. But it did, even though this was not at all reasonably foreseeable given his age and context.[4]

So goes the case of Jeff the Jerk. Vargas thinks that upon reading this case, we will have the following three reactions. First, we will judge that Jeff is morally responsible for the jerky way in which he laid off his employees. Second, we will judge that due to the specific nature of his jerky character, he doesn't satisfy the control condition on moral responsibility with respect to laying off his employees in the way in which he did. These two insights together should lead us to invoke tracing in order to account for Jeff's moral responsibility. However, our third reaction should be that when Jeff voluntarily undertook to acquire a jerky character, he could not have reasonably been expected to have foreseen that his acquiring a jerky character would lead to his firing the employees in the precise manner in which he did. Thus, the epistemic condition on moral responsibility will prevent us from tracing Jeff's moral responsibility back to his adolescent decision to acquire a jerky character.

Let's look closely at each of these expected reactions. We think it is quite plausible to suppose that Jeff is indeed morally responsible for the way in which he fired his employees. So we agree that this case satisfies (i). What about (ii)? Does Jeff satisfy some plausible control condition on moral responsibility when he fires his employees? To answer this question, we'll need to elaborate a little on what exactly is involved in the control condition.

---

[4] Vargas 2005, pp. 275–276.

There is, of course, much disagreement about just what capacities an agent needs to have in order to have the control necessary for moral responsibility. Fortunately, there is no need to take a stand on this issue in order to conduct a fruitful discussion of Vargas's cases. There is no need to take a stand here on whether the control condition should be interpreted in a compatibilist or an incompatibilist way.[5] Further, there is no need to decide between an "alternative-possibilities" interpretation and an "actual-sequence" interpretation. So, for example, one could interpret the control condition as requiring freedom to do otherwise (or freedom to bring about a different consequence, etc.); alternatively, one could interpret it as requiring "acting freely." In what follows, absolutely nothing will hinge on adopting one interpretation over another.

Just for simplicity, we will adopt the "acting freely" interpretation; we emphasize, however, that, if you prefer the "could have done otherwise" interpretation, you can make the substitution with full preservation of content. Nothing in our critique of Vargas's cases will depend on adopting a particular (plausible) interpretation, rather than another. According to one account of "acting freely," an agent acts freely and thus satisfies the control condition on moral responsibility with respect to some action insofar as the action in question issues from the agent's own, moderately reasons-responsive mechanism.[6] Roughly, the mechanism in question must be one for which the agent has taken responsibility and also one that displays a specific combination of receptivity and reactivity to reasons.[7] Details aside, is it plausible to suppose that Jeff does not satisfy this control condition when he fires his employees?

Vargas indicates that Jeff's action is done "unreflectively," and perhaps this is meant to give us reason to suppose that Jeff fails to satisfy the control condition. But it is not at all clear that unreflective actions are *ipso facto* not under our control. Indeed, it seems perfectly compatible with the situation as Vargas has described it that Jeff's firing the employees in fact issued from his own, moderately reasons-responsive mechanism. Insofar as it is plausible to suppose that there is a mechanism of *nondeliberative habit*, there seems to be no problem in supposing that this mechanism might be both moderately reasons-responsive and also one for which the agent has taken responsibility.[8] Thus, on a plausible interpretation of the control condition, the mere fact that Jeff's action is unreflective does not entail that the control condition is not satisfied.[9]

---

[5] Vargas agrees: Vargas 2005, p. 270.

[6] Fischer and Ravizza, 1998; Fischer and Ravizza call this sort of control "guidance control."

[7] In particular, the mechanism must display regular receptivity and at least weak reactivity with respect to a range of reasons that include moral reasons. For details, see Fischer and Ravizza 1998, chapter 3.

[8] For the details, see Fischer and Ravizza 1998, pp. 85–89.

[9] Note that, as we stated, nothing here depends on adoption of the "acting freely" interpretation of control, or this specific account of acting freely; we could simply note that there is nothing in the case, as described by Vargas, that should preclude Jeff's refraining from firing the employees. After all, the mere fact that behavior is unreflective does not entail that the agent could not have done otherwise.

Further, we would typically assume that even a very jerky jerk satisfies the control condition. That is, even someone whose jerkiness is ingrained and significant—issuing in strong urges to jerky behavior or a fixed disposition to ignore non-jerky options—is assumed to have the capacity to rise above his jerkiness. We typically hold jerks responsible for their jerky behavior precisely because we assume that their behavior does not result from literally irresistible urges—or anything close. So even as Vargas develops the story, one might be skeptical about whether Jeff really fails to satisfy the control condition, quite apart from issues about the relationship between unreflective behavior and the control condition.

We wish to emphasize the point. We believe that it is a framework assumption, or general presupposition, of our moral responsibility practices that almost all choices and even patterns of choice and behavior over time in adolescence do not render one literally out of control (in the sense relevant to moral responsibility). So, even adolescent males who undertake fitness regimens to become "studs," such as Jeff, are assumed *not* to thereby render themselves literally out of control subsequently. Again, we would typically assume that even someone with persistent and strong impulses toward insensitivity or just plain jerkiness can *rise above* these inclinations; we would typically assume that such individuals do indeed control their behavior, despite whatever inclinations they have. Perhaps the inclinations come from choices and behavior in their past, or perhaps they come from early upbringing or even genetics; but the situation would have to be highly unusual and "extreme" in order for it to be plausible that the jerk is literally not in control of his choices and behavior.

So it is quite unclear that we have here a case in which the control condition is not satisfied. But we are willing at this point simply to grant, for the sake of argument, that Jeff in fact does *not* satisfy the control condition when he fires his employees. Given that Jeff's case satisfies both (i) and (ii), it looks like we will need to invoke tracing for the sake of consistency. So the next question is whether there is any prior time to which we can successfully trace. Vargas maintains that there is no such time, since the most natural candidate—the time when Jeff decides to acquire a jerky character—is a time at which Jeff is in an inadequate epistemic position with respect to his much later action of firing his employees. To assess this claim, we should consider the formulation of the epistemic condition on moral responsibility that Vargas takes as a working hypothesis throughout his paper:

> (KC) For an agent to be responsible for some outcome (whether an action or consequence) the outcome must be reasonably foreseeable for that agent at some suitable prior time.[10]

What makes a prior time "suitable"? Well, we take it that it is a prior time at which the agent must have been able to foresee the outcome in question and also met the

---

[10] Vargas 2005, p. 274. Vargas labels this condition "KC" for "Knowledge Condition."

control condition with respect to the outcome.[11] So, more specifically, there must be a prior time at which Jeff's firing his employees is reasonably foreseeable and also at which he freely brings it about that this consequence will occur (later). Now, in Jeff's case, there is surely *some* prior time at which his firing his employees in a jerky way is reasonably foreseeable, if only just a few minutes before it happened. But we take it that this is not a *suitable* prior time, since at that point Jeff's jerky character has already been formed (and so he doesn't *at that point* freely act in such a way that he subsequently fires the employees).[12]

As Vargas points out, the most natural time to which to trace back is during Jeff's adolescence as he deliberates about whether to become a jerk in order to raise his chances of success with the opposite sex. Surely at that point, Jeff was in control of whether he would later fire those employees in a jerky fashion.[13] But, of course, it is unreasonable for us to think that 15-year-old Jeff should have taken into his deliberations the fact that if he were to become a jerk, he may well lay off future employees in a despicable manner. Since such an outcome is not reasonably foreseeable for Jeff at that point in his life, the most natural place to trace back to won't serve to ground his later moral responsibility, since (KC) would not be satisfied.[14]

We can now see why Vargas thinks the case of Jeff the Jerk satisfies (iii) and (i) and (ii), and hence should lead us to worry about tracing. But we're not convinced that there really is no suitable prior time to ground the tracing in question. We agree, of course, that it's unreasonable to expect a 15-year-old to be able to foresee what sorts of specific actions he will perform some ten years or more down the road while engaged in the daily routine of a career that he has no idea at this point he is even interested in pursuing. This would certainly set the epistemic bar too high. But we also see no reason to suppose that this is the only way to ground the tracing in question.

---

[11] Again, we have adopted the "acting freely" interpretation of the control condition, but one could just as well adopt the "could have done otherwise" interpretation.

[12] Perhaps another way of putting the point is that at the prior time in question, Jeff does not freely bring it about that he later fires the employees in a jerky manner; he does not freely bring about this consequence. For an account of the relevant sort of control of consequences (on which Jeff lacks control of bringing it about that he later fires the employees in a jerky manner) see Fischer and Ravizza 1998, chapter 4.

On the "could have done otherwise" interpretation of the control condition, we trace back to a prior time at which it is both true that the agent could reasonably foresee the outcome in question and also has it in his power to do something that would have prevented the outcome from occurring. In this sort of interpretation, we'll have to look for a time at which Jeff could both foresee the outcome in question and could have still done something to prevent it from occurring.

[13] For example, to put the point in terms of the "could have done otherwise" interpretation of the control condition, he was at that point able to do something—namely, decide against becoming a jerk—that would have prevented his much later action of firing his employees from occurring.

[14] Again, nothing hangs on the adoption of a particular interpretation of the control condition—so long as it is plausible. We could have just as easily pointed out above that at the prior time he freely did something that brought it about that later he fired the employees in a jerky fashion.

Now consider what "outcome" must be reasonably foreseeable at the prior time in question in order for tracing to succeed. (KC) itself does not tell us just how finely the outcome in question must be specified. If we specify the outcome narrowly (as in our discussion thus far), then it certainly won't have been reasonably foreseeable for Jeff's 15-year-old self.[15] However, if we specify the outcome more broadly, then it's not clear that the outcome won't have been reasonably foreseeable. Indeed, there will be a range of specifications, each more coarse-grained than the previous, and while some will not have been reasonably foreseeable, others will. For a few examples, consider the following ways of specifying the outcome in question:

(Outcome 1) Jeff fires *those* employees who work for *that* company on *that* precise day in *that* precise manner.

(Outcome 2) Jeff fires some of his employees at some company or other at some point in the future in a despicable manner as a result of his jerky character.

(Outcome 3) Jeff treats some people poorly at some point in the future as a result of his jerky character.

As the outcomes become more general, it becomes much more plausible to suppose that they are reasonably foreseeable to Jeff's younger self. While it's extremely implausible to expect Jeff's 15-year-old self to have been able to foresee Outcome 1, it doesn't seem at all implausible to suppose that Jeff's 15-year-old self could have foreseen Outcome 3. So our question now becomes: which outcome does Jeff's 15-year-old self need to have reasonably foreseen in order for us to successfully trace back to that time without violating the epistemic condition on moral responsibility?

We suggest that all tracing requires in this case is that Jeff could have reasonably foreseen Outcome 3 at the time he decides to acquire a jerky character. Why do we hold Jeff responsible for unreflectively firing his employees in such a despicable manner? We hold him responsible partly because he freely decided to become a jerk at some point in the past, and it is reasonable to expect Jeff's younger self to have known that becoming a jerk would in all probability lead him to perform jerky actions. Need Jeff have known that his becoming a jerk would specifically lead to the firing of *those particular employees* on *that particular day* in the future in order to be morally responsible for firing them in the way he did? Surely not. Need Jeff have known that he would fire *some employees* at *some point* in the future in order to be morally responsible for firing them when he did? Again, this would likely set the epistemic bar too high. (KC) leaves open just how the outcome in question should be specified, and it seems that there is a perfectly good way of

---

[15] For simplicity's sake, sometimes we will use locutions such as "Jeff's 15-year-old self." We are not seeking to make any special point about personal identity; rather, we use this term as shorthand for "Jeff when he is 15 years old."

specifying the outcome so that we can successfully trace Jeff's moral responsibility back to the time when he decided to become a jerk. Further, this would seem to be the natural way of understanding our responsibility-practices in general. When you choose to be a jerk, you can be held accountable for your subsequent specific acts of jerkiness—but you might not know in advance what they will be in all their particular glory! Similarly, when you choose to get drunk, you can be held accountable for your subsequent behavior, even though you presumably do not know what it will be in all its florid particularity.[16]

In fairness, Vargas is aware of this sort of response, and more or less concedes in a footnote that the case of Jeff the Jerk needs refinement for precisely this reason. He goes on to suggest a potential refinement.[17] To get around the problem, Vargas suggests that we amend the story so that Jeff acquires his jerky characteristics "while conceiving of them under a different guise (e.g., being "cool"), while blind to the negative aspects of the acquired trait or characteristic." So Jeff's 15-year-old self does not think he is becoming a jerk, and hence it is now unreasonable to expect him to have foreseen that he would treat others badly in the future as a result of his jerky character.

But we're not sure how this amendment is supposed to help. First, we simply note that we did not interpret the original case, as presented by Vargas, as requiring that Jeff was aware of the negative aspects of the newly acquired characteristics; we had already thought of Jeff as simply seeking to be "cool" and being fully oblivious to the dark side (even in the short term) of what he was doing. Further, whether Jeff conceives of the relevant characteristics as "cool" or "jerky" doesn't seem to change the fact that acquiring those characteristics will in fact lead to his treating others poorly and that Jeff should have expected that it might do so. When you are a jerk to someone, your behavior is not excused by pointing out that you thought you were just doing the cool thing. It may be cool to be a jerk, but that certainly doesn't excuse jerky behavior. At the very least, we would have to hear more about how this amendment to the case is meant to help.

Our reply to Vargas emphasized first that it is a presupposition of our moral responsibility practices that even rigorous regimens in adolescence (or in "delayed adolescence"[!]) do *not* leave agents (such as Jeff) literally unable to resist their jerky inclinations. In exploring the possibility that Jeff is indeed "out of control" in the relevant sense, we pointed out that nevertheless there is some coarse-grained

---

[16] One might be worried that if we are allowed to specify outcomes broadly for tracing purposes, then most people will turn out to be morally responsible for too much. After all, everyone ought to be able to foresee that they might inadvertently offend someone at some point in their lives! While we are inclined to think that our approach does allow for moral responsibility in such contexts, we do not think that this is a problem, since it may well be that you are morally responsible for inadvertently offending someone even though you are not *blameworthy* for doing so. What sort of epistemic requirement is a condition for blameworthiness is an important and interesting question that we do not take up here.

[17] Vargas 2005, p. 277, n. 12.

state of affairs (or consequence) he can reasonably be expected to foresee at age 15 with respect to the morally salient consequences of adopting a jerky character. (Alternatively, we could invoke the notion of coarser and finer-grained descriptions of future states of affairs.) Now consider the following objection to our view suggested independently by Samuel Newlands and David Braun.

Let C represent the coarse-grained state of affairs that Jeff can reasonably be expected to foresee, and let F represent the finer-grained state of affairs involving Jeff's rude interactions with (say) Diane and Sue fifteen years later when he informs them of their being laid off. We're supposed to conclude that Jeff is morally responsible for F, in our account, because Jeff stands in the relevant epistemic relationship to C at age fifteen and F is a more fine-grained instance of C. But this cannot be an adequate general account of tracing, because it will clearly allow for "too much" moral responsibility.

We can see this by noting that (for example) it is reasonable to expect me to know that my driving my car will have *some* consequences C*, for example, the motions of certain molecules in the air, exhaust being created, and so forth. Suppose that I drive my car safely, but a child suddenly darts in front of it, chasing a ball into the street, and I cannot avoid hitting the child. In virtue of my standing in the right epistemic relationship to C* and the fact that F* (my running into the child) is a finer-grained instance of C*, it would seem that our account would imply that I am morally responsible for running into the child. But this is implausible, and one could use this example as a template for constructing other cases with ever more implausible results. Indeed, if we were offering the account in question as a general account of the tracing component of moral responsibility, it would seem that we would be committed to attributing to agents moral responsibility for way too much.

We completely agree, but we wish to emphasize that we are not seeking to provide a general account of tracing of the sort under consideration. A full and fully adequate response to Vargas's examples—or related examples—would presumably provide a reductive account that specifies exactly what the relationship must be between the relevant C (coarse-grained state of affairs or description) and the relevant F (fine-grained state of affairs of description). What we are claiming is simply that there is a natural way of specifying a "morally relevant" coarse-grained state of affairs in any given context. For example, in the drunk-driving case, it is reasonable to expect an individual to foresee that drinking too much alcohol may well lead to losing control of the vehicle and harming someone. And in the case of Jeff, perhaps it is reasonable to expect even an adolescent to know that certain *extreme* regimens may well lead to behavior that is insensitive or hurtful to others.

We are willing to concede to Braun and Newlands that we do not have a complete account of the relevant sort of tracing. Rather, we should be understood as giving part of such an account, on the assumption that we are confident that, presented with any case, there will be "natural" ways of specifying the coarse-grained state of affairs (or description) on which there will be sufficient consensus. It would certainly be an interesting project to seek to give a reductive account of the level of coarseness appropriate to the account of tracing; the general problem is that there needs to be some sort of principled link between C and F that is neither too tight nor too loose. Finding just the right kind of link—and characterizing it reductively—would be part of a more comprehensive account of tracing.[18]

We think it is fair to take the case of Jeff the Jerk as the most plausible scenario in Vargas's arsenal; Jeff the Jerk is the "poster boy" in the campaign against tracing. Our analysis of the case has issued in the following skeptical conclusions. First, the mere fact that Jeff's relevant behavior is "unreflective" does nothing to show that it does not meet the control condition. Nor would we typically deem agents such as Jeff to be governed by literally irresistible urges to jerkiness (or anything close to irresistible urges). But even assuming that the control condition is really *not* met at the time of the relevant behavior, we have defended the possibility of tracing back to a "suitable" prior time by focusing on whether to define the outcome in question broadly or narrowly. We think that the broader sort of definition is more plausible, and it yields the result that Jeff is indeed morally responsible for his jerky firing of the employees; after all, he could at that "suitable" past time reasonably foresee that his behavior could lead to jerkiness, and he need not be required to envisage the particular details. Thus Jeff can be deemed responsible, and there is no insurmountable trouble for tracing here.[19]

III. Britney the Bride

At this point, let us leave the case of Jeff the Jerk behind and move on to Vargas's other three cases. The next in line is the (strangely familiar) case of Britney the Bride:

> Britney's first experience of true love was with a boy who could really dance. Although the relationship eventually ended, it left her with a special place in her heart for men who could dance. Sadly, Britney was not especially fortunate in love. A particularly low moment came during a period of deep loneliness and difficulty with her job. She invited a childhood friend to Las Vegas

---

[18] We are indebted to Newlands and Braun for pressing this challenge. Although we are not convinced that Vargas's examples establish decisive troubles for tracing, perhaps Vargas is onto something deeply challenging—to provide a reductive account of the link between the coarse-grained and fine-grained states of affairs (descriptions). This is an important and worthwhile challenge.

[19] Our analysis should apply also to McKenna's example of "the young boy who consciously chooses to cultivate his aggression and thick skin in order to survive in the locker room during his junior varsity football days" and to a whole class of similar examples.

for the weekend, and after lots of drinking and flirting they ended up getting a quickie marriage, followed by an annulment within a few days. Though she wasn't aware of it, the bad wedding experience (with a guy who couldn't dance, no less!) made her especially want to settle down and "do it right" as soon as possible. A few months later, she met a charming professional dancer named Kevin. When the relationship turned serious, and Kevin proposed marriage, she instantly said "yes!" Her love of him was so deep that she could not even conceive of having told him no. Is Britney responsible for agreeing to marry Kevin?[20]

Again, this is the initial description of the case, but Vargas goes on to fill in some necessary background information:

Though Britney does not realize it, her spontaneous and unreflective acceptance of Kevin's marriage proposal has roots in her past. In particular it was rooted in that night in Las Vegas when she first agreed to get married to that other man, her childhood friend. Unbeknownst to Britney, her booze-addled decision to walk down the aisle that night carried long-term ramifications for her. In particular, that decision and the unpleasant consequences that followed (together with facts about her personality and personal history) created in her a powerful disposition to accept marriage proposals from men (1) to whom she felt a certain attraction and (2) who were professional dancers. What the idea of a professional dancer did for her was to confirm an earlier, childhood commitment to a certain ideal of marriage and to a certain ideal of what a romantic partner should be like. This was nothing conscious, of course. Britney was unaware that her annulment would trigger a retreat to certain childhood images and ideals. And, it certainly was not forseeable to her the night she got married in Las Vegas that this would lead her to become the sort of person who instantly accepts a marriage proposal from a professional dancer named Kevin. But it did. When she met Kevin, the dancer, she was already predisposed to find him immensely appealing in light of her earlier disastrous decision to get married. When, after only a small period of dating, Kevin surprised her with a marriage proposal there was, for Britney, nothing left to deliberate. Her hope and fantasies for marriage, operating at subconscious levels, left her ready to accept marriage from anyone who was both a dancer and a source of physical attraction. And so she agreed.[21]

So goes the case of Britney the Bride. Vargas thinks that upon reading this case, we will have the following three reactions. First, we will judge that Britney is morally responsible for accepting Kevin's marriage proposal. Second, we will judge that

---

[20] Vargas 2005, p. 271–2.
[21] Vargas 2005, p. 279.

due to the dispositions she came to have on the basis of her earlier foray into marriage, she doesn't satisfy the control condition on moral responsibility with respect to accepting Kevin's marriage proposal. These two insights together should lead us to invoke tracing in order to account for Britney's moral responsibility. However, our third reaction should be that when Britney voluntarily agreed to marry her childhood friend, she could not have reasonably been expected to foresee that this action and its consequences would create in her a strong disposition to marry the next attractive professional dancer she came across. Thus, the epistemic condition on moral responsibility will prevent us from tracing Britney's moral responsibility back to her decision to marry her childhood friend.

As we did with Jeff, let's carefully consider each of these reactions. Is Britney morally responsible for accepting Kevin's proposal? Given the way Vargas has described this case, we think it is unclear whether Britney is in fact morally responsible. Of course, we typically think that when someone accepts a marriage proposal, they are morally responsible for having done so. But Britney's case is a bit odd, since it's unclear how large a role the dispositions in question played in influencing Britney's acceptance. Did they produce a literally irresistible desire to accept the proposal so that there was a clear sense in which she couldn't help herself? If so, then it is plausible to suppose that her decision to accept the proposal did not in fact issue from a moderately reasons-responsive mechanism and hence that she is not in fact responsible for it. On the other hand, if the dispositions she acquired from her earlier botched Vegas wedding did *not* produce in her any sort of irresistible desire to accept Kevin's proposal, then why not say that she is morally responsible for accepting, and also that there is no need to invoke tracing?

In order for this case to have any bite, Vargas first needs to secure both the judgment that she is morally responsible for accepting the proposal *and* the judgment that she didn't satisfy any plausible control condition on moral responsibility at the time of acceptance. But we don't see how Britney's case can be described to elicit both of these judgments. To the extent that the story of Britney emphasizes the irresistible influence of her dispositions, we will be inclined to excuse Britney from responsibility, and to the extent that the story emphasizes Britney's responsibility, we will start to think that she does satisfy the control condition, after all. Hence it looks like we need not even invoke tracing in this case at all.

It may help in this case to look at what Vargas actually says about Britney's dispositions and their influence on her subsequent action. First, Vargas points out that her accepting the proposal was "spontaneous and unreflective." This alone, however, should not lead us to think that Britney didn't satisfy the control condition when she accepted the proposal. As we pointed out in the case of Jeff the Jerk, there seems to be no reason to suppose that unreflective behavior cannot issue from the agent's own moderately reasons-responsive mechanism and thus meet the control condition. But Vargas also points out that when she accepts Kevin's proposal, "her love of him was so deep that she could not even conceive of having told him no." Marrying her childhood friend "created in her a powerful disposition" that "left her ready" to accept Kevin's proposal. These descriptions do not help us get a very clear picture of just what is going on when Britney accepts the proposal. She had a powerful disposition, but how powerful? It left her ready, but how ready? She supposedly could not even conceive of declining, but is this meant to be taken literally? Given the unclarity about Britney's precise motivational structure, we suggest that it's equally unclear whether she is morally responsible for accepting Kevin's proposal. Moreover, there does not appear to be an easy way of gaining clarity that will also succeed in sustaining the two intuitions Vargas needs to make his case against tracing.

IV. Paulina the Paralyzed

There are two more cases to consider before our response to Vargas is complete. Next is the case of Paulina the Paralyzed:

> Paulina is visiting Florida for the first time. She takes her 2-year-old son, Paul, on a walk in a park just outside of Tallahassee. They eventually find a small clearing and decide to sit down and eat lunch. After a while, Paul gets up and starts wandering around with half-eaten food in his hands, on his face, and on his clothes. Paulina, being a responsible mother, keeps an eye on Paul and warns him against straying too far. Near the edge of the clearing, about 20 feet away, Paul bends over to pick up a rock that catches his attention. Paulina watches him do this, but at that moment realizes that there is an alligator staring at Paul from about 30 feet away. Paulina is paralyzed by surprise and some degree of fear. She feels a rising sense of panic, but remains frozen as the alligator starts to move in the direction of Paul. Alas, the alligator moves surprisingly quickly, and snaps up poor Paul. Only then does Paulina finally unfreeze, and then she screams. Is Paulina responsible for not doing more to save Paul?[22]

Vargas fills in the background details as follows:

> Paulina has a standing habit of taking Paul for walks in a park in the afternoon. It was the first time she had been to Tallahassee, and because she just never bothered to think about it, she did not have any expectations about the native fauna. When she did see the alligator, she was paralyzed because of several interacting factors. First, she did not expect to see an alligator. She was simply surprised. Second, it was big—a lot bigger than she thought alligators were. Third, it brought forth a visceral fear she hadn't felt in years—a fear of live reptiles with lots of big teeth. The absence of any one of these

---

[22] Vargas 2005, p. 272.

conditions would have meant that she moved to attempt to save Paul, but the confluence of these conditions is what left her paralyzed, swamping her desire to try and save her son for just long enough. Here's the thing: she could have undergone therapy that would have reduced or mitigated her fear of reptiles with lots of teeth. After all, her father was a therapist and her mother a herpetologist—so, she grew up knowing that she was afraid of these creatures, and she knew that if she really wanted to she had available to her the means to overcome her fear. But, the last time she thought about this fear she had no reason to believe that it would affect her ability to save her son (indeed, at the time, she didn't even have plans to have children). So, she decided to let sleeping fears lie.[23]

This is the case of Paulina the Paralyzed. Vargas thinks that upon reading this case, we will have the following three reactions. First, we will judge that Paulina is morally responsible for not doing more to save her son. Second, we will judge that the complex interaction of her surprise with her phobia of large toothy reptiles makes it the case that she doesn't satisfy the control condition on moral responsibility with respect to not doing more to save her son. These two insights together should lead us to invoke tracing in order to account for Paulina's moral responsibility. However, our third reaction should be that there is no plausible prior time when Paulina could reasonably have been expected to foresee that these facts about her would interact in such a way as to leave her temporarily paralyzed. Thus, the epistemic condition on moral responsibility will prevent us from tracing Paulina's moral responsibility back to any point in her past.[24]

Once more, it is clear that in order for this case to work the way Vargas intends, *all three* of these reactions must be elicited and sustained. Let's go through them one at a time. First, is Paulina morally responsible for not doing more to save her son? The case breaks down even at this first stage. It seems clear that, given the way Vargas described the case, Paulina is *not* in fact morally responsible for not doing more to save her son. Would we not excuse her from responsibility upon learning that she was *literally frozen* by her fear and surprise? Indeed, the same problem that haunted the case of Britney the Bride seems to be present here as well. If the case is described with an emphasis on the paralyzing role played by her fear and surprise, we will be inclined to judge her not responsible, and if the case is described with an emphasis on her responsibility, we will be inclined to judge that her fear was not in fact overwhelming and perhaps her omission did issue from a moderately

---

[23] Vargas 2005, p. 281.

[24] Note that whereas the cases of Jeff and Britney involved responsibility for a particular *action*, the case of Paulina is supposed to involve responsibility for a particular *omission*. We are invited to have the intuition that Paulina is morally responsible for *not doing more to save her son*. Whereas this is indeed a difference between the cases, it's unclear whether it makes a difference, so we will just flag it for now and move on.

reasons-responsive mechanism after all.[25] Thus, either we will judge Paulina responsible and in control or else not in control and thus not responsible (in any plausible interpretation of control). Either way, the case does not prove troublesome for tracing, since tracing need not be invoked at all.

Let us suppose for the sake of argument, however, that it's true both that Paulina is morally responsible for the relevant omission and that Paulina fails to satisfy any plausible control condition with respect to that omission. Now, we will need to invoke tracing. Is there no plausible prior time to trace back to? Vargas seems to suppose that the most natural way to accomplish tracing in this case is to trace Paulina's responsibility back to a time when she could have undergone therapy to rid herself of her fear of toothy reptiles. He rightly points out, however, that the times when she could have undergone therapy are also times when she could not have been expected to foresee being in a situation where her fear would play a role in the death of her son. Thus, this sort of tracing would violate the epistemic condition on moral responsibility.

But we think that, insofar as we are willing to judge Paulina morally responsible at all, there is a much more plausible place to which to trace back. There was no doubt some point prior to her trip to Florida when Paulina could have educated herself about the potential dangers of Florida wildlife. Vargas points out that it was her first trip to Florida and "since she just never bothered to think about it, she did not have any expectations about the native fauna." But surely this was negligent of Paulina. Had Paulina and her son vacationed in Minnesota during the winter, would it be negligent of Paulina not to think about whether she wouldn't need a winter coat for her son? Had they gone camping in the California desert and her son got bit by a rattlesnake because she wasn't expecting to come across any rattlesnakes, wouldn't that count as some sort of negligence? Insofar as it does seem that Paulina should have known about the dangers of Florida's fauna, we think it is reasonable to suppose that Paulina is to some extent morally responsible for not doing more to save her son. Even if she failed to satisfy the control condition at the time, there was a line of inquiry that she could have (and should have) pursued prior to visiting Florida's parks in the first place.[26]

---

[25] On how omissions can issue from moderately reasons-responsive mechanisms, see Fischer and Ravizza 1998, chapter 5. Here again, nothing depends on accepting the "acting freely" interpretation of the control condition, or any specific account of acting freely. On the "could have done otherwise" interpretation, one would say that Paulina is morally responsible for not doing more to help her son insofar as she could have done more to help her son.

[26] Suppose the case were amended so that Paulina and her son happen upon an alligator while walking the streets of downtown Manhattan (perhaps it escaped from a zoo nearby). We would argue that it is even clearer in this case that Paulina is not responsible for not doing more to save her son. Insofar as this case is a clearer case of nonresponsibility, this seems to show that what may have been leading us to judge Paulina responsible in the first case was the fact that she and her son were in Florida, and it is reasonable to think that people who visit Florida should know something about the wildlife there.

Note that we think it's plausible to trace Paulina's moral responsibility back to her negligence in not learning more about Florida before visiting *only on the supposition* that she is indeed morally responsible for not doing more to save her son. As we pointed out, however, we don't think this latter supposition is plausible in the first place, given the nature of her paralysis.

V. Ruben the Unfortunate

Whereas the cases of Jeff and Britney involve responsibility for actions and the case of Paulina involves responsibility for an omission, Vargas's final case appears to involve (fundamentally) responsibility for a failed attempt. Here is his initial presentation of the case of Ruben the Unfortunate:

> It is the month of December. Ruben, a life-long fan of the Miami Dolphins football team, has just returned from seeing a real-life, in-the-stands Dolphins game for the first time. Even better, the Dolphins won the game, which in recent years is somewhat unusual, especially in December. As Ruben is wont to do, he enjoyed a few beers during the game. When he gets home from the game, his four-year-old niece is visiting. As is their customary ritual, he picks her up and throws her lightly in the air. Alas, because of his excitement about the football game and the lingering effects of an elevated blood alcohol level, he throws his niece up with more enthusiasm than usual and he fails to catch her on the way down—although she wiggled more than usual because of excitement about the throw. At any rate, sadly, she breaks her leg as a consequence of the fall. He views himself as responsible. But never mind that—do you think Ruben is responsible for dropping his niece?[27]

Vargas later expands on the story a bit:

> [Ruben] freely acquired his fandom of the Dolphins, and we can suppose that he actively took steps to maintain his enthusiasm as a fan. Similarly, he freely started the habit of lightly throwing his niece into the air, and when he has forgotten to do so on the rare occasion, he freely agrees to resume the practice when his niece begs her Uncle Ruben to greet her in the customary way. And, let us suppose that had any of the described elements been missing (the booze, the Dolphins win, the presence of his niece, the habit of greeting her in a particular way), no injury would have been done. What Ruben would have needed to know was that all of these things would interact precisely as they did, when they did. But that was not reasonably knowable. He had no reason to believe his niece would be

---

[27] Vargas 2005, p. 272.

home, and that he would unthinkingly lift her up as he habitually did. It simply is not plausible to insist that he should have reasonably known this when he was ordering a beer at the football game, or when he walked in the door, and so on. Even at the moment he is lifting her up, he cannot reasonably foresee what will happen, precisely because what is happening is a habitual, undeliberative action.[28]

Vargas thinks that upon reading the case of Ruben the Unfortunate, we will have the following three reactions. First, we will judge that Ruben is morally responsible for dropping his niece. Second, we will judge that the complex interaction of the booze, the Dolphin win, the presence of his niece, and the habit of throwing her lightly into the air makes it the case that he doesn't satisfy the control condition on moral responsibility with respect to dropping his niece. These two insights together should lead us to invoke tracing in order to account for Ruben's moral responsibility. However, our third reaction should be that there is no plausible prior time when Ruben could reasonably have been expected to foresee that these facts about him and the circumstance in which he found himself would interact in such a way as to lead to his dropping his niece. Thus, the epistemic condition on moral responsibility will prevent us from tracing Ruben's moral responsibility back to any point in his past.

Unlike the cases of Britney and Paulina, we think it is very plausible to suppose that Ruben is in fact responsible for dropping his niece. It's true that he didn't mean to drop her, but in many cases people are morally responsible for outcomes that are more or less accidental. We are inclined to grant that this scenario satisfies condition (i). What about (ii)? That is, does Ruben satisfy any plausible control condition on moral responsibility with respect to dropping his niece? To address this question, it may help first to ask exactly what Ruben is responsible for in this case. There are a few different candidates. First, there is his niece breaking her leg. Second, there is Ruben failing to catch her on the way down. And third, there is Ruben throwing her in the air in the first place. The way Vargas describes the case makes it seem as though he is focusing on Ruben's failure to catch her on the way down, so let us consider that possibility.

Now, does Ruben satisfy any plausible control condition with respect to failing to catch his niece on the way down? Given Vargas's setup, it is plausible to suppose that he doesn't. Although he doesn't come right out and say it, a charitable reading of Vargas's case would be to suppose that the mixture of alcohol, the Dolphin win, the presence of his niece, and the standing habit of throwing her in the air, maybe mixed with the extra wiggle she gives, all combine to make it the case that Ruben can't help but fail to catch her on the way down. Thus, we'll agree that condition (ii) is also satisfied by this case.

---

[28] Vargas 2005, pp. 281–2.

Now the question is whether there is any prior time that can serve as an appropriate terminus for tracing. The most natural place to trace back to is to Ruben throwing her in the air in the first place. Once she was in the air, he couldn't help but drop her, but surely he had control of whether he threw her in the air to begin with. But Vargas argues that this will not do, since at the time he threw her in the air, he could not have reasonably foreseen that he would fail to catch her on the way down. After all, he threw her up unreflectively and out of habit. One might next try to trace Ruben's responsibility back to the time when he chose to drink the beers at the game, but this move will encounter the same problem. If he couldn't have been expected to foresee dropping his niece at the very time when he threw her in the air, how much more unreasonable would it be to expect him to foresee dropping her when he is in the process of buying beers at the game? After all, he doesn't even think she'll be at home at that point. And the further away we get from Ruben dropping his niece, the more difficult it will be to make plausible that the terminus of tracing is an action for which Ruben satisfied the epistemic condition on moral responsibility.

But we think that there is no need to go back very far to find a suitable terminus for the tracing. We think it is plausible to trace Ruben's responsibility back to his throwing his niece in the air in the first place. Such behavior, habitual or not, is risky. Surely Ruben knew when he started to acquire this habit that it brought with it certain risks. And while it's not plausible to suppose that he could have foreseen that he *would* drop her in this case, it certainly is plausible to suppose that he could have foreseen that he *might* drop her, and this seems enough to satisfy the epistemic condition.[29] According to (KC), one need not know with certainty that an outcome will occur. The outcome in question must only be *reasonably foreseeable*. And it seems clear that when Ruben throws his niece in the air, his failing to catch her on the way down is reasonably foreseeable. Thus, we are inclined to trace Ruben's responsibility back to this prior action.

At this point, Vargas might respond in two ways. First, he may insist that the outcome in question isn't reasonably foreseeable when Ruben throws his niece in the air. Why not? Precisely because, as Vargas says in his description of the case, "what is happening is a habitual, undeliberative action." But it's unclear why this should rule out reasonable foreseeability. Although Ruben may not consciously consider it at the time, it's reasonable to suppose that he knows (or should know) that such behavior involves a certain degree of risk, and that there is no way he can *ensure* that his niece will never fall as a result of his throwing her in the air. It certainly doesn't seem a good excuse for Ruben to point out that he wasn't thinking about the possibility that he might not catch her on the way down. He quite

---

[29] Of course, bare possibility cannot be the relevant notion of "might," if tracing is to be plausible; this is a delicate matter, which we put aside here insofar as it is not the focus of Vargas's critique. A fully adequate and completely reductive account of tracing would have to address the issue of interpreting the "might" in question.

straightforwardly *should* have been thinking about that possibility. Or, at least, that possibility should always have been "in the back of his mind" ever since he started engaging in the risky behavior.

A second way Vargas might resist is by arguing that Ruben doesn't satisfy the control condition with respect to throwing his niece in the air, and thus such an action can't serve as an adequate terminus of tracing. But why think this? The only reason it seems Vargas could appeal to is, again, the fact that his throwing her in the air is "a habitual, undeliberative action." But, as we pointed out in our treatment of previous cases, we see no reason to think that habitual actions cannot meet the control condition.[30]

VI. Vargas's Cases: Summary of Our Critique

This completes our examination of Vargas's four cases that are supposed to spell trouble for tracing. To briefly rehearse our conclusions, we agreed that Jeff the Jerk is indeed responsible. The first point to note about Jeff is that mere unreflectivity does not entail that Jeff fails to meet the control condition. And we are skeptical whether the typical jerk—or even atypical jerks—really fails to meet the control condition. But assuming that Jeff is not really in control of his jerky behavior (at the time of the behavior), there is still a way of tracing his responsibility back to his decision to become a jerk. We need only to specify the relevant outcome broadly. A proper analysis of Jeff the Jerk—and related cases, such as McKenna's young football player—shows that they do not pose intractable troubles for an approach to moral responsibility that has a tracing component.

We argued that Britney the Bride either satisfies the control condition with respect to accepting Kevin's proposal and is therefore responsible, or else she does not satisfy the control condition and is therefore not responsible. We can't see any way of mending the case so that it will elicit both the intuition that she is responsible and that she fails to satisfy the control condition. Paulina the Paralyzed seems straightforwardly excused from responsibility, given the way Vargas described her case, but we argued that insofar as we hold Paulina responsible, this is because of her negligence in not familiarizing herself with the Florida wildlife. Finally, we argued that although Ruben is indeed responsible for dropping his niece despite his not satisfying the control condition, his responsibility can be naturally traced back to his throwing his niece in the air in the first place. We conclude that none

---

[30] For example, we do not see why they cannot issue from an agent's own, moderately reasons-responsive mechanism. (Alternatively, one might point out—as before—that because an action is habitual does not rule out that the agent could have done otherwise.) And if these contentions are right, then Ruben's throwing his niece in the air may well satisfy the control condition on moral responsibility after all.

of Vargas's cases requires us to use tracing in a way that runs afoul of the epistemic condition on moral responsibility. The truth about tracing is that its troubles are not as severe as Vargas has suggested, if they are even troubles at all.

VII. Smith's Cases

Before closing, we'd like to consider some relevant and very intriguing recent work by Angela Smith.[31] Although Smith does not present a critique of tracing per se, some of the examples she adduces in favor of her position seem to presuppose such a critique. It will be illuminating to see how a proponent of tracing might reply to Smith's cases.

Smith argues against accounts of moral responsibility that she dubs "volitional." According to volitional accounts,

> what ultimately makes an attitude attributable to a person for purposes of moral assessment is that it is connected in some way to her choices: she made choices in the past which led to the development of the attitude in question, she made a choice in the present to endorse or "identify with" it, or she has the ability to modify her attitudes through the choices she makes in the future.[32]

Smith suggests that most accounts of moral responsibility on the market are volitional, since they reserve a special role for the notion of *choice*. Smith maintains, however, that such views cannot do justice to our actual practices of holding each other morally responsible. In particular, Smith puts forward a number of ordinary examples in which we apparently are inclined to hold someone morally responsible for something that was neither directly the result of any choice nor traceable to any choice in the past or the future.

Rather than making moral responsibility primarily a matter of *choice*, as volitional accounts do, Smith instead argues in favor of a view that makes moral responsibility primarily a matter of *evaluative judgment*. She calls her view "the rational relations view" and according to this view, "a mental state is attributable to a person in the way that is required in order for it to be a basis for moral appraisal if that state is rationally connected in one of the relevant ways to her underlying evaluative judgment."[33] Smith maintains that her view can account for all the cases the volitional view can account for, *as well as* the cases that apparently cause trouble for a volitional view.

Part of the reason that Smith rejects a volitional view of moral responsibility, it seems, is precisely that the idea of tracing is seemingly impotent when it comes

---

[31] We will focus on Smith 2005, in particular.

[32] Smith 2005, pp. 238–239.

[33] Smith 2005, p. 262.

to explaining certain important cases. Since we are attracted to a view that invokes tracing, her cases provide a powerful challenge that is worth addressing. So, let's begin by considering one of her cases:

> I forgot a close friend's birthday last year. A few days after the fact, I realized that this important date had come and gone without my so much as sending a card or giving her a call. I was mortified. What kind of a friend could forget such a thing? Within minutes I was on the phone to her, acknowledging my fault and offering my apologies. But what, exactly, was the nature of my fault in this case? After all, I did not consciously *choose* to forget this special day or deliberately *decide* to ignore it. I did not *intend* to hurt my friend's feelings or even *foresee* that my conduct would have this effect. I just forgot. It didn't occur to me. I failed to notice. And yet, despite the apparent involuntariness of this failure, there was no doubt in either of our minds that I was, indeed, responsible for it. Although my friend was quick to pardon my thoughtlessness and to dismiss it as trivial and unimportant, the act of pardoning itself is simply a way of renouncing certain critical responses which it is acknowledged would, in principle, be justified.[34]

Smith is surely right to point out that we encounter cases like this all the time. To constitute an objection to volitional accounts of moral responsibility, though, the case needs to exhibit the following features:

> (i) Smith is morally responsible for forgetting her friend's birthday.
> (ii) Smith's forgetting was neither the direct result of a choice nor traceable to any past choice.

If some volitional view of moral responsibility is correct then (i) is true only if (ii) is false. So if the birthday case exhibits both (i) and (ii), then no volitional view of moral responsibility can be correct.

Smith contends that what explains her moral responsibility in the birthday case has nothing to do with any choice of hers, but rather with how her forgetting reflects her evaluative judgments. As she puts it:

> If we value something and judge it to be worth promoting, protecting, or honoring in some way, this should (rationally) have an influence on our unreflective patterns of thought and feeling. We commonly infer from these unreflective patterns, or from their absence, what a person really cares about and judges to be important.[35]

Since she forgot her friend's birthday, it is reasonable to infer that she doesn't care about her friend as much as a friend should, and it is this fact that best explains why we are inclined to hold her morally responsible for forgetting. Were her

---

[34] Smith 2005, p. 236.
[35] Smith 2005, p. 247.

forgetting the result of hypnosis, on the other hand, we would of course excuse her from moral responsibility, but again Smith maintains this has nothing to do with any lack of choice. Rather, what explains our willingness to excuse her in the hypnosis case is the fact that her forgetting does not plausibly reflect her evaluative judgments.

While we certainly agree with Smith that whether a bit of behavior or an attitude reflects one's evaluative judgments is an important part of explaining one's moral responsibility for the relevant behavior or attitude, we think that this insight can be incorporated into a certain sort of tracing-based account of moral responsibility. It is crucial here to distinguish a "volitional" approach to moral responsibility from a related but different approach: a "control" approach to moral responsibility. Whereas a volitional approach requires that we trace back (directly or indirectly) to a *choice* in order to justify attributions of moral responsibility, a control model requires that we trace back (directly or indirectly) to an exercise of control, where such an exercise of control might be a choice, and action, or an omission. In the birthday case, in particular, we think that it is plausible to suppose that Smith's moral responsibility for forgetting does in fact trace back to some previous free action or omission. If we are right about this, then the birthday case will not after all tell against control-based accounts of moral responsibility.

To see why we think some sort of tracing must be going on in the birthday case, consider the fact that Smith failed to choose to do various things which were such that, had she so chosen, she would have had a better chance of remembering her friend's birthday. So, for example, perhaps Smith omitted to choose to put her friend's birthday on her calendar, or perhaps Smith failed to choose to set up her "e-mail client" to alert her to her friend's birthday, and so forth. Part of what it is to be a good friend is to take these steps to minimize the likelihood that you will forget your friends' birthdays. If you don't take these steps, and then forget, you are legitimately morally assessable for your forgetting *precisely because* you failed to do something to make your forgetting much less likely (and you were in control of this failure). This is just to say that your moral responsibility for forgetting *traces back* to these past omissions. Indeed, we would argue that your forgetting reflects a poor evaluative judgment only insofar as you failed to take the necessary steps that any friend would take to remember friends' birthdays.

Now Smith might respond by adding details to the case so that she *did* in fact take all reasonable precautions with regard to remembering her friend's birthday, but then forgot anyway. Perhaps she did put her friend's birthday on her calendar, she did tell her e-mail client to remind her, and she even put a note on her bathroom mirror! We can suppose that, despite all her efforts, she still simply forgot. Surely in this case there is no plausible place to serve as terminus of any sort of tracing. However, in our view, these added details serve to etiolate (and, arguably, to eliminate) the intuition of moral responsibility that made the case so plausible in the first place. Surely if it's true that Smith did everything she could do to make forgetting her friend's birthday less likely, then she isn't responsible if she accidentally forgets anyway. If Smith were to explain to her friend how much care she put into trying to remember the birthday, and that despite her best efforts, she simply forgot, we maintain that her friend would no longer be justified in holding her responsible for forgetting. (Presumably the case is still underdescribed, and the friend is still likely to wonder why Smith was forgetful, despite all her efforts to make sure she would remember the birthday; here we assume that the example can be filled in so that it is clear that *all* reasonable efforts were made by Smith to ensure that her memory would be triggered, that she wouldn't have a tendency toward forgetfulness—maybe she has attended a special self-improvement seminar for memory—etc.) Perhaps it is only if her forgetting reflects her evaluative judgments that her friend can hold her responsible, but the best way to determine whether her forgetting reflects her evaluative judgments is to see whether it can be traced back to some past free action or omission. If we are right about this, then the birthday case does not tell against tracing-based control models of moral responsibility after all.

To be fair to Smith, we do not disagree with her rejection of volitional accounts of moral responsibility. It might seem that what is problematic about such accounts is their tracing component. But we have separated the volitional idea from the tracing idea; we have argued that if we replace volition with a broader notion of control, where the pertinent sort of control can be exercised via an omission as well as (say) a choice, one can give an adequate and, indeed, a natural account of Smith's case above. Thus it is not the tracing component, but the volitional element, that is problematic. So, whereas we agree with Smith's rejection of (ii), we would urge replacing (ii) with:

(ii*) Smith's forgetting was neither the direct result of an exercise of control nor traceable to any past exercise of control.

Note that not only can (ii*) give an appealing analysis of Smith's example above, but it can help to explain a range of difficult "manipulation cases"—cases in which an agent's evaluative judgment is induced in some manipulative manner (such as via clandestine advertising, hypnosis, or even direct stimulation of the brain). Smith does have something interesting to say about such cases, but it is not clear that her rational relations model can adequately handle all such cases.[36]

---

[36] Smith says:

> One might well ask what it is in these "implantation" cases that makes the judgments in question "not the agent's own." And one might also wonder how these cases differ from cases of irrationality, in which the judgments reflected in a person's attitudes run counter to some of the other judgments she claims sincerely to accept. What differentiates implanted attitudes from these others, in my view, is that such attitudes are not based upon the agent's own evaluative appraisal of her situation and surroundings but are induced in a way that bypasses her rational capacities altogether. They do not, therefore, reflect the agent's own evaluative judgments and commitments. Even in cases of irrationality, I would argue, the irrational attitude reflects a genuine tendency on the part of the agent to see certain considerations as counting in

Let's consider another example presented by Smith, just to make our strategy of response clearer. This example comes from a passage in George Eliot's *Scenes of Clerical Life*:

> When the sweets were on the table, there was a mould of jelly just opposite Captain Wybrow, and being inclined to take some himself, he first invited Miss Asscher, who coloured, and said, in rather a sharper key than usual, "Have you not learned by this time that I never take jelly?" "Don't you?" said Captain Wybrow, whose perceptions were not acute enough for him to notice the difference of a semitone. "I should have thought you were fond of it. There was always some on the table at Farleigh, I think." "You don't seem to take much interest in my likes and dislikes." "I'm too much possessed by the happy thought that you like me," was the *ex officio* reply, in silvery tones.[37]

Here it is plausible to suppose that Captain Wybrow is morally responsible for his failure to notice that Miss Asscher dislikes jelly. It is also plausible to suppose that his failure to notice this is not the direct result of any choice on his part—that is, he didn't *choose* to fail to notice. Smith then argues that the best way to account for this sort of an example is again in terms of Wybrow's evaluative judgments. The fact that Wybrow fails to notice Asscher's likes and dislikes is a good indication that he does not care about her as much as he should, and hence Asscher holds Wybrow morally responsible. Again, it seems at first as though a volitional account of moral responsibility will not be able to handle a case like this.

But as before, we think that the best analysis of this case will invoke tracing. To be sure, the fact that Wybrow fails to notice Asscher's likes and dislikes does indicate that he does not care about her as much as he should. But, we would argue, one would intuitively hold Wybrow responsible here only if there was something in the past that he did freely (or omitted freely) that led him to be the

---

favor of certain responses. Implanted attitudes, by contrast, tell us nothing about the agent's rational or evaluative dispositions. I see no other way of giving content to the expression "the agent's own" here, however, except in a way which makes reference to the very network of beliefs and attitudes which I am suggesting ground our attributions of responsibility. This may seem to make this account of responsibility objectionably circular and uninformative, but I think that it is what makes it specially plausible and attractive: the seeming circularity is itself a reflection of what many philosophers have referred to as the "holistic" character of the mental. (Smith 2005, p. 262)

This passage raises many difficult issues. We certainly do not have a decisive argument that Smith's way of handling manipulation cases cannot work for all such cases. We do, however, wish to raise the concern that there are such cases in which the relevant rational capacities are not bypassed in the way suggested by Smith, but in which the agent is nevertheless intuitively considered to be not morally responsible. This would involve thoroughgoing manipulation of the mind, including the comprehensive network of evaluative beliefs and attitudes. Of course, such examples are contentious, and it is perhaps difficult for *any* theory of moral responsibility to give a plausible account of them.

[37] As quoted in Smith 2005, p. 242.

sort of lover that fails to notice things that he should in fact notice. Perhaps he chose to engross himself in his own affairs rather than think about the needs and wants of Miss Asscher; perhaps he omitted asking her certain questions about her emotional life when the opportunity arose, and so on. If there is nothing in the past that he should have done that would have made him much more likely to notice Miss Asscher's likes and dislikes, then we would argue that he can't properly be held responsible. But what's more likely is that there were times at which his free actions (or omissions) more or less secured his emotional indifference to her. Again, although his failure to notice her likes and dislikes indicates a poor evaluative judgment, this evaluative judgment does not seem to be properly *his own* evaluative judgment unless we can complete a trace back to some free action (or omission).[38]

Smith puts forward a number of nuanced considerations for the conclusion that the rational relations view provides a better understanding of our practices of moral responsibility than does the volitional view. We agree with her critique of the volitional approach, but we do not agree that one should conclude that a control-based approach with a tracing component is to be rejected. Indeed, such a view gives a natural analysis of Smith's examples, and it also has something plausible to say about a range of manipulation cases. Presumably, a more refined and comprehensive analysis of Smith's cases will invoke the considerations we presented in discussing Jeff the Jerk (and related cases): the outcome may be defined broadly and tracing can apply simply because it is reasonable to think that the agent can foresee outcomes that are broadly specified. But perhaps it is interesting to note that, whereas it is plausible to trace back to certain *choices* in the case of Jeff the Jerk, it is more plausible to trace back to certain omissions—certain *failures to choose*—in the cases offered by Smith. Since choices (and, in general, actions) tend to be more salient than omissions, it is perhaps a bit more difficult to see how tracing can be applied to Smith's examples than to those of Vargas.[39] But the truth is that tracing can indeed be applied.

---

[38] An anonymous referee points out the following distinct interpretation of this case. Perhaps Miss Asscher is not holding Wybrow responsible for failing to take note of her likes and dislikes and is instead holding him responsible for *pretending* to care about her when he doesn't really. This interpretation would also support our contention that Wybrow is responsible only insofar as there is something he did freely onto which his responsibility can latch.

[39] Franklin forthcoming argues that the difference between tracing back to actions and tracing back to omissions helps to understand the initial appeal of "Buffer Zone" versions of the Frankfurt-type cases. See Christopher Evan Franklin, "Neo-Frankfurtians and Buffer Cases: The New Challenge to the Principle of Alternative Possibilities," *Philosophical Studies* (forthcoming). He contends that it is difficult at first to see that one should apply tracing to such examples because the relevant item—the item to which one traces back—is always an omission in such cases, rather than an action (as in the drunk-driving cases). For a buffer zone version of the Frankfurt-type cases, see Pereboom 2001, pp. 20–21.

VIII. Conclusion

Much is at stake in evaluating a critique of tracing. We do not see how a theory of moral responsibility could adequately handle the range of drunk-driving cases, "Martin Luther cases," and manipulation cases without some sort of tracing component; tracing just seems both highly plausible and theoretically indispensable. Indeed, theorists as diverse as the libertarian Robert Kane and the "semicompatibilists" John Martin Fischer and Mark Ravizza have embraced tracing as a component of their theories of moral responsibility.

If tracing cannot be vindicated, this would seem to be a devastating challenge to theories such as Kane's and Fischer's—and *any* control-based theory of responsibility. Here we have offered a template for a strategy of defense of tracing against the sorts of examples adduced by Vargas, McKenna, and Smith. A defense of the plausibility of tracing is part of a defense of a plausible control-based account of moral responsibility.[40] Such accounts will need to take seriously the spirit (if not the precise content) of Lady Chiltern's remark in Oscar Wilde's *An Ideal Husband*: "One's past is what one is. It is the only way by which people should be judged."

References

Adams, Robert. (1985) "Involuntary Sins," *Philosophical Review* 94: 3–31.

Fischer, John Martin, and Ravizza, Mark. (1998) *Responsibility and Control: A Theory of Moral Responsibility*. (Cambridge: Cambridge University Press).

Franklin, Christopher Evan. (forthcoming) "NeoFrankfurtians and Buffer Cases: The New Challenge to the Principle of Alternative Possibilities," *Philosophical Studies*.

Kane, Robert. (1996) *The Significance of Free Will*. (Oxford: Oxford University Press).

McKenna, Michael. (2008) "Putting the Lie on the Control Condition for Moral Responsibility," *Philosophical Studies* 139: 9–37.

Parfit, Derek. (1984) *Reasons and Persons*. (Oxford: Clarendon Press).

Pereboom, Derk. (2001) *Living Without Free Will*. (Cambridge: Cambridge University Press).

Smith, Angela. (2005) "Responsibility for Attitudes," *Ethics* 115: 236–271.

Vargas, Manuel. (2005) "The Trouble with Tracing," *Midwest Studies in Philosophy* 29: 269–291.

---

[40] Robert Adams presents an important critique of control-based models of moral responsibility (with tracing components) in Adams 1985. For critical reflections on Adams, see Fischer and Ravizza 1998, pp. 255–259.

We have read versions of parts of this paper to the philosophy departments at the University of Notre Dame; the University of Calgary; the University of California, Irvine; and the University of Washington. Also, the paper was delivered as one of the Hourani Lectures on Human Values at the State University of New York at Buffalo in fall, 2008. We are very grateful to the members of those audiences for their helpful comments. We are especially grateful to: Samuel Newlands, David Braun, Cass Weller, Laurence Bonjour, and Ann Baker. Also, thanks very much to the following for their comments on previous drafts of this paper: Manuel Vargas, Michael McKenna, and Angela Smith.

INDEX

actions. *See also* behavior
 contexts of assessment of, 134
 control of, 207
 as free, 185
 guidance control of, 11, 187
 habitual, 226
 as matter of change, 93
 moral responsibility as matter of history of, 10–11, 10n12, 186
 moral responsibility for, 69
 out of character, 193–94
Adams, Robert, 233n40
addiction, 188, 190
agency, 183
 contributions for, 184
 intuitions about, 172
 requirements of, 184–85
 responsibility for, 169
Agency Line, 183–84
agents
 as acting freely, 211–13, 213n11
 behavior of, 77
 as blameworthy, 81–82
 capacities of, 211
 children's development into autonomous, 165–66
 choices by, 184
 contrastive explanation of choices by, 100
 control condition on moral responsibility not satisfied by, 208
 control of, 177–78
 freedom of, 143
 judgments by, 146
 moral responsibility of, 40, 54, 58, 70, 75, 135, 137–38, 140
 normative competence of, 159–60, 199
 omniscient, 59–60
 outcomes as foreseeable for, 208
 prior time and, 212–13
 reason-recognition by, 11
 reason-responsiveness of, 11
 relevant outcome and, 208
 in Rollback Argument, 91
 status as, 3–4
 total control of, 171–72
 triggering events chosen by, 131

valuational system of, 135
aggression, 209n3
agnosticism
 causal determinism and assumption of, 42–47
 causal determinism assumption of, 47
 relaxation of assumption of, 47–49
alcohol, 207
Alternate Possibilities and Moral Responsibility (Frankfurt), 33–34, 33n1, 127, 143
alternative possibilities. *See also* Principle of Alternative Possibilities
 access to, 73, 156
 causal determinism ruling out, 48, 73
 elimination of, 73
 moral responsibilities as not requiring, 54–55, 61–62, 66, 73, 102, 114
appraisal, moral, 152–53
arguments. *See also* Dilemma Defense; direct arguments; Frankfurt-style arguments
 four-case, 117–18
 indirect, 115
 Otsuka's dilemma, 79–80
 Vihvelin's regiment of, 63
 zoom out strategy for, 178, 181
 Zygote, 118–19
assumptions
 of agnosticism, 42–49
 of causal determinism, 87
 of Consequence Argument, 115
Asymmetry Thesis, 136n33
attitudes
 alternative judgments connection with, 146
 evaluative judgments reflected in, 229
 judgment-sensitive, 145–46
authenticity, 164
 requirements of, 165
authority, 22
autonomy, 164. *See also* self-creation
 conception of, 165
avoidability
 blame and, 76–84
 moral responsibility as requiring, 115
 in PAP, 121

behavior. *See also* attitudes
 of agents, 77